## ABOUT THE AUTHOR

As a third-generation intellectual, Áron Arnold Hidvégi (b. 1981) was raised in a family with Jewish and Transylvanian Armenian roots. He is a lawyer-economist and personal trainer, entrepreneur, and business consultant—passionate about design, fitness, politics, and personal development. He lives in Budapest, Hungary.

CONTACT: hello@aronarnold.hu
HOMEPAGE: aronarnold.hu

# Viktor Orbán

## The Underground Narrative

ÁRON ARNOLD HIDVÉGI

First edition

Published in Budapest, by Aron Store Ltd.

ISBN 978-615-00-7278-4

Edited by: Zoltán Hortsin

Design by: Áron Arnold Hidvégi, dr.

Typesetting by: Péter Deák

Printed in Hungary.

*In Memory of the Hungarian victims of the Holocaust and Church persecution.*

# Contents

## PART THREE

### IDENTITY

## PART FOUR

### TRAINING

## PART FIVE
### STARTUP

## PART SIX
### ART

# Introduction

Why did I write this book? Let me start with reasons that didn't inspire me. It was not for a commission or money. It was much more of a conviction.

You know the feeling when you are watching a movie and are annoyed by the fact that the protagonist does not notice the danger in the background? This is exactly the feeling I get when I read about Hungary in the foreign press. How can we be misunderstood so badly? Let me admit it quickly; I do not think for a minute such misreporting is intentional. It's just that we're strangers.

Malcolm Gladwell's book, *Talking to Strangers*, draws our attention to how we misunderstand each other when we try to bias each other out of our own perspectives when we do not approach the other person with curiosity and empathy. I am convinced that the nature of the conflict between the European People's Party and Fidesz, or Viktor Orbán and the liberal press, is a communication problem—as are the roots of almost every human problem.

In the eyes of foreigners, we Hungarians are strangers. Everyone in the world calls our country Hungary, we call it the Land of Magyars—*Magyarország*. Although we live here in Europe, as Europeans, our language is still isolating us. Our greatest treasure is the language that only we speak. This book wants to change that. I want to teach you a little Hungarian.

For Hungarians, the "illiberal state" is the Diet Coke of democracy—same taste, no calories. In Hungarian, the literal meaning of "liberal arts" would mean 'a works of art created by a person with liberal political views.' Liberal arts is called *bölcsészettudomány*, literally 'the science of wisdom.' In Hungarian, "liberal democracy" means 'the country is ruled not by law, but by parties with liberal views.' If someone asks your political views and your answer is "liberal," they probably think you are a weed smoking hippie, or at least a wannabe. We translate the word "liberty" in Hungarian to *szabadság*, with the literal meaning of freedom with a positive upbeat. In short, for the majority of Hungarians, liberal is pejorative, freedom is positive.

Judge us with more empathy and less prejudice, and the man who represents me too, us Hungarians in the world—Viktor Orbán.

My book is not primarily based on Hungarian traditions. I hope that the text is understandable to a foreign reader, even if you have no background in Hungarian. I want you to understand a little bit more about what our Hungarianness means to us—our love of homeland and responsibility of ethnic Hungarians across the border. What makes for our nation, freedom, and self-esteem.

Why read this book? The most straightforward answer is to learn something new. Not just about Viktor Orbán, but maybe yourself.

If you approach the "Rubik's Cube" with curiosity and patience rather than with a closed-mind, you will recognize the opportunity. In the six parts of the book, I can explain why.

**My grandmother,[i] a central personality of Hungarian** intellectual life, always finds common ground with those who have different worldviews from her. A public intellectual, she

---

i Katalin Dávid, b. 1923, is an art-historian, and has been made an honorary citizen of Budapest and has received the highest awards of both Hungary and the Vatican.

endorsed Viktor Orbán for two reasons: he is neither anti-Semitic nor anti-clerical. Her Jesuit education, a century of wisdom and the experience of surviving Nazism and communism informed her simple argument in Orbán's favor. When my grandmother turned ninety, Péter Esterházy[ii] and his wife paid a visit to her home in Budapest. As they were to leave, I asked Péter when he hoped there would be peace in our divided country. "We shall not exist anymore. We are too old for this. Peace is a mission for your generation." These words were one of my main inspirations for writing this book.

*– Is it for love that you want to go to America?*

*– Yup.*

*– What's her name?*

*– Lady Liberty.*

Áron Tamási wrote the above quote. I consider myself his soul child. Áron Tamási was a Transylvanian-Hungarian writer. He became well known in his native region of Transylvania and Hungary for his novels written in his original Szekler[iii] style. One of Tamási's most famous works from this period is a novel trilogy of the adventures of a Szekler boy called Ábel, a young forest ranger living alone in the Harghita Mountains. In the third part of the trilogy, Ábel goes to New York in the 1930s, and after his adventures, he returns to his homeland.

Like Áron Tamási my namesake and his character Ábel, I am inspired by America. Hence the title of this book and the recurrent comparisons between Orbán and Uncle Sam.

---

ii Péter Esterházy was one of the best-known Hungarian and Central European writers of post-modern literature.

iii The Szeklers are Hungarians who reside in central Romania.

America inspired my book, hence the Americano title: *Viktor Orbán—The Underground Narrative*. The highlighted words on the book's cover—or/or and the und/und—reflect the philosophy of this book. The underground narrative drafts an explanation on Viktor Orbán in the perspective of "and/and" instead of the dividing story of "or/or."

WHY AND HOW DID VIKTOR ORBÁN BECOME THE DARLING OF Hungarians? This book is an underground narrative, an unofficial playbook. I wrote it by myself and self-published it. The writing and publishing took four years. Unlike fiction that invites readers to escape this world, this book has something to say about our reality. Its fifty-six chapters are jam-packed with plausible lessons, sometimes more and sometimes less convincing to discerning readers. They are sometimes ironic, sometimes severe. I don't aim to cater to anyone's taste, and I especially cannot guarantee you will like it. My only promise is that I do not intend to lie. Perhaps I'm naïve. Still, I'm convinced that if intellectuals had a better understanding of the self-made man of Hungarian politics, I could live in a better country.

This book isn't for everyone, but maybe it's for you. Had you been a Hungarian, you'd agree that Viktor Orbán is a once-in-a-blue-moon opportunity like Saint Stephen I, the statesman Count István Széchenyi, or Duke Gábor Bethlen. He is a man who has risked his all in politics and set Hungary on the world map.

BEFORE WE GET STARTED, SOME TECHNICAL NOTES. FOR methodological reasons, I have simplified a few things. A writer's curse is to forget this his background knowledge and that of his readers are not automatically the same. Generally, the reader knows more, but this knowledge is different. That this book raises issues that other books have not is a step forward. Most of books about Orbán subscribe to his enemies' point of view, which are largely built on urban legends, while other books are boring biographies. This book is neither.

I wrote this book as I understood the essence of Orbán's magic. I had many *aha* moments that I am passionate to pass on to as many people as possible. Therefore, the reader may find it strange to encounter the names of Steve Jobs, Bob Dylan, and Arnold Schwarzenegger in a book about the Hungarian Prime Minister. I grouped chapters around six parts: biases, self-made, identity, training, startup, and art. I've structured each section . around a single thought. As my high school Hungarian teacher, Mariann Schiller used to say, "Period. New paragraph." **THE LOWERCASE WRAPPING WITHIN CHAPTERS SEPARATES OR EMPHASIZES SUB-IDEAS.**

*When a quote is formatted like this, it always comes from Viktor Orbán, unless the context indicates otherwise.*

# PART ONE

## BIASES

---

*"Too often, I've seen the smartest*
*people make the biggest mistakes."*

(Edward Teller)

# 1

# Imagine

The upcoming chapter seems unrelated to Viktor Orbán. *It seems* may even be a motto of the book. With this book, I want to give you a novel way of thinking based on analogies. Not only to help you understand Viktor Orbán better, but also the world around you.

FOR SIMPLICITY'S SAKE, LET'S CALL THE GLASSES THROUGH WHICH we view the world a worldview. Various filters and lenses aid or limit our clear vision—to see far and near, in light and darkness. The two most essential filters are our beliefs and emotions. We perceive the outside world through them: we see, hear, feel, and touch. Our brain tries to establish a causal connection between the sensory inputs, turning the pictures and sounds into a film. We call the script of this film the narrative.

Stories based on people's worldview, their beliefs and emotions, can describe the world (Seth Godin). There is a narrative behind everything tangible and abstract, from liberal democracy to Hungarikums. (Traditional goods made in Hungary with a select quality.) Humans create stories and give meaning to the impulses of the world with narratives. This essential feature, enabled by humanity's other great distinguishing feature, differentiates us from other living creatures on this planet.

A narrative tells the story from the viewpoint of the narrator. Every person has a tale of him/herself, and there's a story about every person being told in other people's heads. These two stories are internal and external narratives. You will be the narrator of your own story, but the narrator of the story about you is another person. For you, the first story is about how you perceive yourself from the inside. The second one is how the outer world sees you.

Here are two films about you. What are you like, and perhaps what kind of person might you be? The first narrative defines the second. As we change our internal story, our external story transforms as well. Based on our worldviews, we build stories in our heads, and vice versa: our narratives in turn shape our worldviews.

Ideally, our inner and outer narrative is more or less the same. In this ideal state of harmony, you are who you present yourself as. In extreme cases of imbalance, people will perceive you as crazy or overlooked based on the screenplay of your internal narrative, whether it reminds them more of the world of Greek mythology or Greek tragedy. Most people try to balance the two stories. To live in balance.

DEPENDING ON OUR WORLDVIEWS, WE NOTICE A STRONGER OR LOOSER connection with those whose narratives sound closer to our own. Besides from our worldview, cognitive biases also alter the accuracy of our stories. When our brains are unable to reconcile two substantially different frames, it employs heuristics and biases to bridge the cognitive gap. The convenience of heuristics and biases is that they simplify our brain's decision-making. Their disadvantage is that they can distort reality.

A narrator's style and the various elements that they employ shape the substance and hue of the narrative. The narrator embeds the narrative in a context, frames it, and helps to interpret the story. Descriptions can be experiential, emotionally colored, diverse, and ranging from fiction to reality, from myth to nonfiction.

Two people will have two different perceptions of you. The other person's worldview, background knowledge, and various distortions affect the narrative. Based on this, the other party develops a belief that leads to a conviction about your story—he will either trust you or not. Perhaps he based his judgement on another person's story, such as the one that a journalist records in a newspaper article or on the opinions of friends. If the narrator assumes that you are telling the truth, he will present your narrative differently than if he supposes that you are a liar. Thus, news about you can be of two kinds: objective or biased journalism.

Of course, we all wish to earn other people's trust. We want others to accept our stories at face value. We want them to say yes to a date, to buy into our sales pitches, and to vote for us as political candidates.

**TO GET AHEAD IN LIFE, YOU MUST OVERCOME OBSTACLES. STRENGTH** makes this happen. The stronger is more likely to succeed than the weak. Now, let's study the two narratives from the perspective of power.

- **HOW STRONGLY DO YOU FEEL YOURSELF OR SEE YOURSELF?**
- **HOW STRONGLY DO OTHERS PERCEIVE YOU?**

The currency of a healthy self-image is self-confidence. The more confidence you have, the stronger your superhero character will be. The less you trust in yourself, the weaker you will become.

The other person will have a story about you, about how powerful or how helpless you are. Everybody wants to be persuasive because this is how society measures success. Power does not mean only physical strength, but also knowledge and financial success. The strong conquer the weak, the wise outperform the stupid, big fish eat the little. Among other things, people go to school, meditate, or hire a personal trainer to grow stronger in knowledge, in spirit, and body.

It is seldom possible to instantly ascertain another person's physical strength, knowledge, or financial influence, but a handful of clues make educated guesses possible. People take an athletic built type more seriously than a weakling. Whoever has an academic degree, such as a Ph.D. after his name on the business card, will be considered more intelligent than others. Those who wear fancy labels are more likely to be treated kindly than those who wear casual clothing. Based on looks and behavior, and on others' opinions, we can assume that another person is stronger than us. Here's where self-confidence comes into play because where the other person will place us on his scale is somewhat a matter of our self-esteem—it is based in part on our own internal narratives.

We judge others through the lens of our worldview, our beliefs, and our emotions. Our expectations help us decide if we should consider another person to be authentic. Our feelings guide us in deciding if he is stronger or weaker. As I have written, many factors influence our decisions, from the opinions of others, from our background knowledge to cognitive distortions. One of the best-known biases is prejudice. As the name suggests, we judge before we learn the truth.

In this simplified model, when the protagonist of your film in the other person gives the impression of a strongman, you can trigger two kinds of emotional reactions: trust or fear, depending on their assumption whether you are authentic or phony. If we assume that the person is charismatic and has good intentions, we trust him. If we sense ill-will, we fear him.

From the point of view of your strength, your challenge in life is not what other people speculate about you, but what conclusions they draw from their speculations. What kinds of emotional reactions do you provoke from others as a strongman and how do they affect the actions that others take. Do they trust you, or will they fear you? Maybe both?

Therefore, to succeed in life, all you need are two well-written narratives. You only need to believe in your personal story, and it will follow that others will trust you, concluding that you are so powerful that nobody can overcome your powers.

For a moment, let's accept the premise that everyone buys your story. How would your life change if no matter what you do, everyone in the world, regardless of their outlook, would conclude that you are so strong that you cannot be defeated? You would be the world's first individual superpower! This rarely happens, though an example may come to mind: Uncle Sam. If we imagine him as a self-made man, he is someone who believes in himself, while others realize they cannot overcome his powers.

The internal narrative of the United States is the American Dream, which most Americans believe. It's not your birthright that matters, but how hard you work for it. One symbol of this spirit is the city of New York and the ideal type of this ethos is the self-made man. In the words of Barack Obama: "But in the unlikely story that is America, there has never been anything false about hope."

The outer narrative is that the United States is the most powerful country in the world. Regardless of other nations' worldviews, they all believe this. It is what America's allies believe as well as everyone else who fears its power. The USA is the world's leading technology, economic, and military superpower. It has the know-how and money to run the world, and it's the global peacekeeper too. America's success endures on a rock-solid foundation, namely that the world's seven billion people admit that it's number one.

However, wait a minute. Double or nothing is not just Uncle Sam's formula for success. There's a story of another self-made man. He wasn't born on the 4<sup>th</sup> of July, 1776. But on the 31<sup>st</sup> of May, 1963.

**THIS BOOK IS ABOUT HIM.**

# 2

# Nineteensixtythree

The underground narrative is that Viktor Orbán is the most significant statesman in Hungarian history since the 19th century Hungarian Reform Era. He, a single person, has exerted a life-changing impact on the lives of all Hungarians, and the beginning of this hallmark of a quintessentially Hungarian success story is 1963.

In 1963, Bob Dylan wrote his album *The Times They Are A-Changin'*, and its protest cover-song:

*For the loser now*
*Will be later to win*
*For the times they are a-changin'*

Viktor Orbán's narrative—his life and politics—is the story of a loser becoming a winner. It is an emblem of the explosive power of change. From the poorhouse to college, from college to university, from Oxford to the limelight of history, to Parliament, and at 36, as the Hungarian Prime Minister, to Bill Clinton's White House. 2002 was a turning point for this winner who lost everything. 2010 was another turning point, when hope recovered from the pitfall of despair and he made his way from the scourge of losers to the panopticon of winners.

This is the story of how the anti-church young man becomes the most significant political ally of the church. How the smallest party in the Parliament wins an overwhelming majority, how the hopeless right-wing takes the lead over liberal hegemony. From a goldfish to a shark, from the Prime Minister of 10 million inhabitants to the leader of 15 million, a historical figure of Hungarian politics and an international political superstar. How to turn headwind to a tailwind? The curved line straight? And turn politics into an art?

Based on the democratic standards of America's "Americanness," the technology behind his power is the power of the double narrative: believe in yourself, and the world will believe in your strength.

Orbán's unique 'dualist' mindset and his problem-solving skills have written the narrative of the underdog to an outlier. His politics is inspired by European football (soccer) and the principles of physical conditioning, reinterpreting Hungarian cultural traditions and history, Christian values, and the tactics of disruption.

His character blends three self-made man archetypes: the self-inventing superstar, the visionary founder, and the hero role model.

As the Nobel-laureate Daniel Kahneman says:
*Success = talent + luck.*
*Great success = a little more talent + a lot of luck.*

After Daniel Kahneman, we can freely associate the following equation:

**ORBÁNIAN SUCCESS = ORBÁNIAN TALENT + ORBÁNIAN LUCK**

The protagonist of the story is Viktor Orbán, the Hungarian Prime Minister, who has become an inevitable international player, variously respected and hated as Europe's new strongman. Critics of the authoritarian press set him aside Trump and Putin, the two superpower presidents. Nowadays, because of Viktor Orbán, Budapest is no longer confused with Bucharest, and Hungary is an ascendant European nation whose power the world increasingly recognizes.

Viktor Orbán drew his identity on a blank slate, creating a strong political vision for Hungary. The thread of the external narrative is a strong Hungary modeled on the United States and enabled by wide-ranging security and a healthy economy.

Hungary protects its borders, and thus Europe's, from the threats of migration. The world views Hungary as Europe's frontier march, similarly to how it sees the role of the United States as the global policeman. Besides effectively addressing the migration crisis, the narrative fosters the feeling of safety in its citizens with a heightened police presence translating into a reduction of crime. Family-friendly policies and the subsidization of homeownership champion mental security as well.

The image of Hungary's economic power builds on the foundations of its ambitious foreign affairs and trade policy, along with international sports events. Confidence in the country's financial strength comes from its economic growth and record-low unemployment, and its daring investments: objective facts earn trust in the country's future prosperity.

Viktor Orbán rewrote the Hungarian narrative. Through his personal example, he convinced his compatriots that through the power of love and union there is hope for success.

The National Creed embodies the society's internal narrative, the essence of which is to "base the order of Hungary on the cooperation of the nation." National thinking and belonging, self-esteem, and pride—"more respect for the Hungarians"— and its symbolic manifestations such as dual citizenship for ethnic Hungarians living abroad, the Szekler flag flying atop the Parliament building besides the Hungarian flag, historical memorials, and the reinforcement of the core messages of national holidays. The stories built on the beliefs of Hungarians are emotionally nurtured by sports games, Christian celebrations, and traditions, and fostered by the cohesion of national events. The direction of education and cultural policies mark a profound change in the national narrative.

Viktor Orbán founded his system on disciplined principles, a fluid administration, and several hundred exceptionally skilled and talented personnel who manage their field with professional competence. Along with building up his enormous political power, Viktor Orbán laid the foundations of his political front's loyal media empire, a new wealthy elite, its intellectual ring, and a fully-fledged political establishment. It is a better organized apparatus than that of any of his competitors. In one word, he established his sovereignty.

On the political battleground, the frames of his film established a charismatic leader in some viewers' eyes and a charismatic dictator in others'. Followers and haters haved arrived at the same conclusion: his power is unsurmountable. His own political organization's bulletproof block structure and the disintegration of his opposition resulted in three legislative landslide victories, earning two-thirds of the Parliament seats in 2010, 2014, and 2018.

As the self-made man of Hungarian politics, Viktor Orbán established a new system that took control over the minds of its people with the American formula of awe-inspiring power and the fostering of national unity. *Americano á la Orbán*, seasoned with Hungarian traditions, the eternal laws of football and of Christian liberty.

Through control over the minds of common Hungarians, Orbán achieved the highest mastery of power in practice. Without resorting to physical violence or force, he brought about his own sainthood among, and inspired the hatred of tyranny among his opponents. The temple of Viktor Orbán's power stands on two rocks, not one: his supporters and opponents, all fifteen million Hungarians believe in his power.

From the compromised world of politics, Viktor Orbán created the art of the uncompromised.

THE TONE OF THIS BOOK IS RESPECT, APPRECIATION, AND CURIOUS observation. Its purpose is to point out the common themes behind the unmatched success of Viktor Orbán.

These findings are brainchildren of my intellectual associations. This underground interpretation is about how I understand Viktor Orbán's story and what I have learned from it. Whoever considers him a genius but didn't realize what that genius consists of now receives a new framework of interpretation and narrative. Anyone who hates, from now on will hate me too.

## 3

# I Know the Yellow Rose
# Will Bloom

My generation takes freedom for granted. In the age of my grandparents and my parents, there was no self-actualization. *You will never make it,* was the mantra. "Here, shall you live and die." There were a few things they could hold on to, though. Some like-minded intellectuals and relatives who occasionally visited from their lives abroad as émigrés would meet with them and inspire hope. A few artists also composed narratives of hope. The lyrics of *Why have we let it all happen this way* by János Bródy, and Lajos Illés from 1973 was one of the most iconic Hungarian protest songs of all time. The blooming yellow rose became a symbol of freedom for the Hungarians. In the next chapter, I will quote some lines of this famous song. Here is my translation of the original song:

> *Do you believe the yellow rose will bloom?*
> *Do you believe we obey your fake words?*
> *Do you believe we'll always forgive everything?*
> *Do you believe we'll give up our dreams forever?*
> *Our dreams forever.*

So, let me begin this book with the expression of my gratitude toward those who made it possible for me to write and publish this book today. I want to thank my friends, who encouraged and supported me in this venture. Special thanks to Márton Dávid, Péter Deák, Zoltán Hortsin, László Horváth and my father, Máté Hidvégi. I would like to thank Zachary Harrison Blinkinsop for proofreading and editing the English translation.

# 4

# Dreams, Lies, Forgiveness

This chapter will summarize the 30-year history of politics in Hungary, the fall of communism, and the rise of Viktor Orbán. A narrative of winners and losers describes Hungarian history after the change of regimes and storytelling based on people's worldviews shaped politics. Differences in worldviews shaped Hungarians' dreams, the forces of lies, and lack of forgiveness.

Intellectuals started to cut to the change of regime by asking, "Why have we let it happen this way?" Thirty years later, they think the same. The opposing tribes accuse each other of *lying words* and cannot forgive each other.

THE FIRST REGIME CHANGE IN THE HISTORY OF HUNGARY DEFINES the period between 1987 and 1990, during which a pluralist, democratic political system replaced the fabricated Communist dictatorship, which turned Hungary's constitutional form into a republican state. The intellectual caste orchestrated the first democratic change in a series of negotiations between the ruling Communist Party and the new democratic political parties and organizations. Between 1989 and 1990, protests and roundtable negotiations (Roundtable of the Opposition founded in 1989) mutually agreed to a schedule of peaceful transition. The first democratic parties formed during this period were the Hungarian Democratic Forum (MDF, 1987), the Federation of Young Democrats (Fidesz, 1988), the Alliance of Free

Democrats (SZDSZ, 1988), the Hungarian Socialist Party (MSZP, 1989). On October 23rd, 1989, Mátyás Szűrös (the provisional President of the Republic) proclaimed the Third Hungarian Republic. Hungarian Democratic Forum, representing national-conservative values, won the first free election, so József Antall became the first Prime Minister and formed a government. A few months later, the Parliament elected Árpád Göncz as President of the Republic. Hungary joined NATO in 1999, the European Union in 2004, and the Schengen Area in 2007.

The two poles of the political sphere were the traditional conservative Hungarian Democratic Forum and the more cosmopolitan, urbane Alliance of Liberal Democrats. Besides the two main political tribes, we must mention the minor political parties. The Farmer's Party and the Christian Democrats became less prominent. In 1993, István Csurka, a member of the Hungarian Democratic Forum, founded a far-right party Hungarian Right and Life (MIÉP) with insignificant political influence. Besides the SZDSZ, the Federation of Young Democrats (Fidesz) identified itself as a liberal political organization with a generation-only policy.

THE WORD LIBERAL HAS A DIFFERENT CONNOTATION IN THE HUNGARIAN language. Everyday language couples liberalism with the values of 18th-century Enlightenment, atheism, sexual freedom, globalism, and a free-market economy. In Hungarian, we do not use the word liberal or arts in the term liberal arts. Today, liberalism represents a tiny percentage of the population's political views. Many of the founding members of the Free Democrats had a (non-observant) Jewish identity, which became a source of anti-Semitic abuse. The party had an energetic intellectual upbeat, and despite its lower popularity wielded significant influence. Definitive opinion leaders in the media, the financial world, and the cultural scene were among their most loyal supporters.

When Orbán says "illiberal," 99.9% of the Hungarian people understand that the country and its democracy is not ruled by politicians of the former Socialist-Liberal coalition and its successors, who before Orbán's 2010 landslide victory, led the country almost to bankruptcy. I've graduated from one of the best ranked high schools in Hungary and hold a master's degree in Law, but during my education years, I have not ever heard anybody calling democracy a liberal democracy (not even in textbooks written by law professors with liberal views). Recently, the term liberal democracy is coupled with the 1989-1990 change of regime, when the first government lead by József Antall had to sign a deal with the liberal party SZDSZ (Alliance of Free Democrats), agreeing on the "terms and conditions" of the new system (The MDF-SZDSZ Pact). At that time SZDSZ had 20% of the votes in Parliament so they were able to influence the legal framework of the democracy, even though they were in opposition.

**FIDESZ (FEDERATION OF YOUNG DEMOCRATS) WAS FOUNDED ON MARCH** 30th, 1988, by thirty-seven young intellectuals at the István Bibó College in Budapest. Bibó István was the most important political thinker of 20th century Hungary. Because of his position in the 1956 Revolution, though not executed, he was forced into retirement for the rest of his life. The specialized college that bears his name provided a once-in-a-lifetime opportunity for law students interested in politics at the time of the change of regime, given that a significant number of professors were actively involved in preparing the new Republic's rule-of-law framework. The students of the college became the founders of Fidesz, among many others Viktor Orbán, who was elected president of Fidesz in 1993 and had led the party ever since (with the exception of a few years). (As a personal point, I mention that Professor Csaba Varga, a philosopher of law who was one of the defining mentors of Orbán at Bibó College, became one of my favorite teachers at Pázmány Péter Catholic University after many years. His seminar on the rule of law in our democratic transition was a defining intellectual experience of my university years.)

The Orbáns represented the young generation, giving an opportunity for a member of the party to speak at one of the symbolic events of the change of regime, the historic reburial of Imre Nagy and his associates. Imre Nagy became Prime Minister during the 1956 Revolution and War of Independence and was executed after the suppression of the revolution. On June 16th, 1989, at the reburial of Imre Nagy and other martyrs, Viktor Orbán spoke on behalf of the young generation, demanding the immediate withdrawal of Russian troops. His brave words blew up the news, and Viktor Orbán became an overnight success.

DURING THE FIRST DEMOCRATIC ELECTION IN 1990, EACH PARTY HAD a different story, although they shared the narrative we will not give up on *our dreams*. The National Forum aligned itself with more patriotic values and Free Democrats with liberalism, while Fidesz wanted to fulfill the desires of younger democrats. These three parties identified themselves as anti-communist parties, sharply opposed to the reestablished Hungarian Socialist Party, whose predecessor was the Communist Party. The liberal Free Democrats and Fidesz had a friendly relationship, and the public considered Orbán's party an offshoot of the liberals. Young Orbán soon became one of the opposition's boldest figures. Hence, his party made less profit from his national reputation and personal popularity. In 1990, Fidesz won 5% of the popular vote in the first free election.

The narrative that proponents of the first democratic change espoused was the dream of a better life; the external story told of the birth of a democracy that peacefully replaced a communist system. At the time of the first free election, the majority believed in the story of József Antall, a wise academic historian. In 1990, Antall took over the country in a debt crisis. His government quickly became unpopular, was unprepared to govern a market economy, and was under constant fire from the opposition and the left-wing liberal media. Antall was diagnosed with Non-Hodgkin's lymphoma and died in 1993. Until the 1994 elections, Péter Boross served as Prime Minister. The disillusioned people felt deceived and swung their votes to the Hungarian Socialist Party, which aspired to the predictability of the communist Kádár era, and which won the majority of the mandates. In exchange for the promise of their dream of *expertise*, the Hungarians forgave Gyula Horn the sins of communism.

The story in 1994 was how the national tribe became a loser, and the once-beaten communists returned victorious. The Socialist Party's narrative overwrote the Hungarian Democratic Forum's, and the voting majority trusted the Socialist's story. They entered a coalition with the liberal Alliance of Free Democrats, which overwrote its anti-communist narrative, and by 2010 provided an existential opportunity for the liberal intellectuals who gave up its principles. Between 1994 and 1998 the popularity of the Socialist-Liberal coalition continued to decline with the introduction of economic restrictions, known as the Bokros-package named after the minister of finance Lajos Bokros. Privatization became a breeding ground for corruption. Privatization in the socialist system involved the sale of state-owned assets primarily to the Socialist Party's insider-network at a fraction of the market value. Many people got wealthy by privatizing companies. Among these was Ferenc Gyurcsány, who became a billionaire by acquiring an aluminum factory in the Hungarian heavy industry with his mother-in-law's assistance and family connections, a senior member of the Communist Party.

The dream once again vanished, and voters lost their faith in the ruling party, this time in the Socialists.

BETWEEN 1992 AND 1994, FIDESZ CHANGED ITS IDEOLOGICAL STANCE in a conservative turn. On his deathbed, József Antall appointed Viktor Orbán as his political successor, who had by then broken up with the liberals. The Fidesz split, and those who left the party joined the Free Democrats, and the liberal intellectuals and press who had previously sympathized with Orbán turned against him. From 1994, Viktor Orbán gave the party a new vision, renaming the Federation of Young Democrats to Fidesz Hungarian Civic Party, where Fidesz is the equivalent of the Latin *fides* 'faith.' The central message of the new program was the aspirational citizen, a member of the middle-class who subscribed to conservative Christian values, and who took responsibility for themselves. Orbán's dream was to build a new country on the new Christian-conservative middle-class. The leftist-liberal media could not forgive Orbán his U-turn, so the war between Fidesz and the press decided the outcome of the elections.

In 1998, before the elections, a televised debate took place. Gyula Horn was the Goliath, and called Viktor Orbán was David. Voters considered Viktor Orbán's story more authentic and in 1998 Viktor Orbán could form a government.

Viktor Orbán's first term in office as Prime Minister is a story of how dreams are born and how these dreams die. Viktor Orbán, who grew up in the small town of Felcsút, was admitted to the county's best gymnasium, studied law at Oxford, and was a guest of the White House at age 36 as the Prime Minister of

Hungary. He personally handed a letter to Bill Clinton sent by Zbigniew Pełczyński, who was their joint tutor in Oxford—a life-memory the Clintons have tried not to remember. A George Soros scholarship covered Orbán's Oxford studies to support him as a liberal politician during the first change of regime.

Yet despite the success of his first government's social policy and momentum, Orbán could not keep power. Despite the successful economic policy, social policy, and impetus of the first Orbán government, it could not maintain its hold on power. In 1998, Orbán's story overrode Gyula Horn's. People were fed-up with the Forum and the Socialists, and they wanted the action-oriented Orbán, believing in his young and the aspirational vision of a prosperous future. In 2002, the Socialists' negative campaign, if only by the margin of a hair, overwrote Orbán's narrative of success. Orbán lost and the candidate for the Socialist-Liberal campaign was Péter Medgyessy, and the central message of the campaign was Orbán's character assassination. The negative bullying campaign framed Orbán's cult and corruption with a jibe on religion, and built alongside him a sympathetic image of Medgyessy with personal and untrained qualities. Péter Medgyessy's popularity collapsed in the middle of the cycle, despite a *100-day program* that distributed record-high social benefits mostly paid for by loans. In 2004, Gyurcsány became Prime Minister. In the upcoming election of 2006, the Socialists' narrative was made credible by credit-funded social benefits. In 2006, socialist storytelling won again.

VIKTOR ORBÁN WENT FROM BEING A LOSER IN 2002 TO EVENTUALLY regaining his power and position. In 2006, everything was lost. Do you think we will give up our dreams? Everybody had given up. Orbán didn't. From 2002, he started to rebuild the disintegrated right, building grassroots *civic circles* around the party, decentralized groups of people without a legal form. The

Hungarian Democratic Forum's blindness, the short-sighted Farmer's Party, and the hostile media's overwhelming power didn't make his job easy. A stable, united, and powerful tribe, just like Rome, wasn't built in a day. It was done step by step, at the cost of systemic changes at the level of government and of two lost elections. "One flag, one vision" was the new slogan. The united center-right-wing was the cumulative work of an entire decade. Lost battles in that decade only paved the way for an inevitable victory. To dream is not enough. Do.

In the autumn of 2006, an anonymous source leaked a recording of Ferenc Gyurcsány delivering a speech to his party comrades in the party's hotel at Balatonőszöd. In the so-called *Őszöd Speech* the Prime Minister used dirty words and admitted that he didn't tell the truth to the people before the previous elections. Despite the scandal, the leftwing tried to shore up its support. The media invited leading public intellectual opinion leaders to endorse the validity of the speech. Philosophers and intellectuals flooded the state television's morning show, where they argued that the lie was actually truth, just in the olden communist days. Gyurcsány's speech led to street riots and demonstrations. On the national day of the 50th anniversary of the 1956 Revolution, police also brutalized peaceful protesters, while Gyurcsány all the while remained unwilling to resign. Finally, he stepped down in 2009, and Gordon Bajnai took over the Prime Minister's office and tried to avoid the country's financial crash and state bankruptcy. This time voters didn't forgive the crimes.

In the 2010 elections, the Forum and the Liberals didn't receive enough votes to get into Parliament. A new party, Politics May Be Different (LMP), came in, but they could barely cross the 5% threshold.

After resigning, Ferenc Gyurcsány left the Socialist Party (MSZP) shortly afterward, taking with him some members and formed a new party called the Democratic Coalition (DK). Bajnai and his circle formed Together, another liberal, technocratic party. In 2018, Bajnai's party received 0.8% of the votes and ceased its activities.

In 2010, another new party could enter the Parliament besides Politics May Be Different. It was Jobbik 'more right,' a radical far-right party, openly anti-Semitic and racist. By 2018, it could have become the most dominant party in the opposition. Still, Fidesz defeated them too in the 2018 elections, and most of the leading figures of the party resigned from their elected positions.

From 2010, opposition parties started to look for a way out. Their narrative became the line from the famous ballad: "Ain't no flowers, you ain't no more, / Ain't no answers today."

Since then, the national tribe could not forgive Gyurcsány, not only for his ugly speech or for what came after, but also especially for what preceded it. In 2005, the nation held a referendum on the dual citizenship of ethnic Hungarians living abroad. Before the vote, Gyurcsány encouraged his supporters to vote *no*, which the right has since considered being an anti-national crime. Coincidentally, one of Orbán's first measures was to secure dual citizenship and limited voting rights for Hungarians living abroad. Since then, Hungarians living abroad have overwhelmingly supported Viktor Orbán.

IN THE 2010 PARLIAMENTARY ELECTIONS, THE FIDESZ-KDNP ALLIANCE won 263 parliamentary seats, a two-thirds majority, with 52.73% of the vote. The once generation-only party became the most trusted political brand of the new Hungarian democracy. Viktor Orbán, who lost the elections in 2002 and 2006, returned with a two-thirds landslide victory in 2010. In 2014 and 2018, he won two-thirds of the seats in Parliament. The two-thirds mandate allowed Viktor Orbán to realize all of his dreams.

The transition from dictatorship to democracy took place in a non-violent, negotiated way, led by intellectuals. We consider it the first change of regime. In 2010, Viktor Orbán earned a two-third mandate, and in the Easter of 2011, he adopted a new constitution. The Fundamental Law, taking effect from January 1st, 2012, transformed Hungary's legal structure and in Orbán's own words, it implemented the second change of regime. By restoring the country's sovereignty and ambitious foreign policy, he put Hungary on the global map and granted dual citizenship to ethnic Hungarians living abroad. The system is built on the fundamentals of a work-centric and business-friendly economy, along with family-friendly social policies and a user-friendly reorganized public administration. The government's cultural policies encourage independent Hungarian voices. In a parallel move, Orbán consolidated a new wealthy elite and his own media empire. In short, he created a new country.

*On a particular intellectual horizon, we can sum up our journey so far, by creating, through thirty years of work, a new and real model of state theory, which is, in reality, a tried-and-tested one. We have created a Christian Democratic state. A Central European and Hungarian Christian Democratic state. Today's Hungarian state is based on Christian democracy and not on liberal democracy. Yes to freedom, and no to liberalism. This is our program. In retrospect, we can see that we came here in two steps, through two transformations of the system. With the first regime change, we ended the Soviet world. Soviet flags out, communist flags down, flags of freedom up. It was the first, liberating, liberal regime change, the great and soaring first love. Then came the struggle between Fidesz and the rising or rather revivalist socialists to determine the future. Twenty years of confusion. Ultimately ending in a socialist nightmare and*

*economic collapse, rebellion, a drift towards physical violence,*
*and anarchy. I still do not understand why the socialists do not*
*get that after 1990 it was by the margin of a hair they could get*
*away with it for the second time without consequences. There*
*would have been a demand for it. That they did not understand*
*that it was up to us to choose the constitutional revolution*
*instead of a revolution on the streets. If they had understood*
*this, they would probably be more modest and more restrained.*
*Then, in 2010, we took the advice of József Antall: "had you*
*made a revolution." After the soaring first love, there was a*
*healthy marriage.*

While interpreting politics in the context of storytelling
based on people's worldviews, let's not forget one thing. The
consequences of the past thirty years are that the citizens only
keep a government if it keeps its word and people feel fulfilled.
In 2010, 2014, and 2018, Hungarians elected Orbán by an
overwhelming majority as Prime Minister. After three landslides,
triumphs of two-thirds majorities, he wasn't just lucky. It was
proof that he had to be authentic, too.

# 5

# Parallel Stories

M y world may not be yours. There are two ways you can relate to this odd fact: appreciate it or take it as an offense. This is where the challenge of writing a good book about Viktor Orbán lies, as there is not yet a book that examines him from every angle. The story is either about Orbán being an innocent lamb or a wolf in sheep's clothing. There are two stories in people's minds, and whoever wants to write a book must choose whether he will portray him as Europe's strongman or savior. Both contain grains of truth, but what is the real picture?

**I START WITH TWO CARICATURES:**

 # 1 Viktor Orbán is the modern Hungarian leader. He is divinely mandated to unite the Hungarian nation and reestablish the once great and glorious Hungarian state. He is a victorious freedom fighter for and the incarnation of Hungarian national values, a successor of the 1848 and 1956 revolutions, who liberated Hungary from communist slavery, protects Christian virtues, and leads his homeland to a seat at the table of winning nations. He's a genius strategist who derived a magic formula to achieve a mighty, independent, and prosperous country. The prayers of Hungarians were finally answered. Viktor Orbán is invincible.

#2 Viktor Orbán is a modern Hungarian populist tyrant. The once liberal politician quarreled with himself, dismantled democracy, has implemented a mafia-like system in public life. He controls the media and the courts which he packs with loyalists. His regime is a hybrid of authoritarianism, a mafia state, and feudalism, where fair elections no longer take place. His illiberal policies have isolated Hungary on the international stage and he is conspiring to lead Hungary out of the European Union. His devotees follow chant their mantra in unison: "Viktor Orbán is invincible."

In people's minds, there are two stories about Viktor Orbán. The first narrative is the official version of those who trust Orbán. Those who don't believe the first story find the second more plausible. Illusion of either devotion or dread guide them to the same conclusion: nobody can overcome Viktor Orbán.

This is his magic. One author wrote both stories—Viktor Orbán.

# 6

# In God We Trust

For Viktor Orbán, leaning into his Christian faith outlined the direction of his political course, transforming the Fidesz from a liberal to an authentic Christian-democratic people's party of the middle-class. Orbán built his policy on the rock of monotheism, uniting people under the dome of the *fides*. Nothing is unusual in the Hungarian world of beliefs and symbols, from the ancient Hungarian shaman drum to the Virgin Mary of Csíksomlyó. Those who consider Orbán's conversion sincere find it easier to connect with him. Hence, not all Christians support Orbán's politics, but an overwhelming majority of voters say they are Christian. They do not necessarily attend services every Sunday, but their worldview is rooted in their shared understanding of the transcendent. A believer believes in the discovery of God's will in all things, so the fact that Viktor Orbán, a believer and family man, rules the country cannot be a coincidence. In the minds of the population, this correlation gains meaning through their Christian faith.

The turning point in Viktor Orbán's life was meeting God and experiencing the transcendent world. Because their worldview denies God's existence, atheists have interpreted Orbán's conversion not as divine will, but as a scam. Therefore their narrative maintains that Orbán is lying. According to them, Orbán ruthlessly took advantage of religious people's conviction—whom they otherwise disparage—and sold them his fairy tale in order to gain more power. They embedded their narratives within this framework, starting from the point that Orbán invented the story of his conversion for the sake of profiteering. Digging deeper into this, these sceptics somewhere recognize Orbán's political talent, as he was once an anti-Church, anti-clerical person that belonged to their tribe. This dislike for Orbán stems from a worldview that cannot believe that anyone will authentically convert. It is logical because had they believed this fact about Orbán, their God-denying worldview would have collapsed.

Pariahs excluded from public life have never had a universally accepted common denominator, but there are many similarities in their attitudes towards religiosity. New age atheism, the so-called cult of reason, the worship of the natural sciences, the witchcraft of alternative medicine, and to mention something of my profession: Philippe Starck's iconic lemon squeezer, the Juicy Salif, all derive from the same source. "Inside a temple is where one believes."[iv] Orbán knows this so-called 'enlightened' intellectual worldview well, as he was inculcated into it so at a young age. Those who do not believe in God find religion to be superstition, theology a pseudo-science, and celibate priests potential child abusers.

Liberal intellectuals could not step out of their worldview's box and made it a matter of saving face to persevere with an atheist worldview that excludes the transcendent. The mistake was made by imagining bad intentions behind Orbán's conversion. They could also have said, 'we cannot imagine someone converting, but you know what, good luck to you.' Furthermore, without emotions, they judge the action but cannot imagine the intentions behind it. It is understandable why Orbán's atheist former peers

---

iv This is a famous idiom, mostly popular in the era of communism. Many of my atheist teachers in school used to say this because it was a Marxist dogma that influenced their worldview.

were wary of religiousness. What is unacceptable on their part is cynical jesting, prejudice, and religion-phobia.

Nobody likes it when another person thinks you are not telling the truth. Especially when you have not said a word. At the root of the political conflict between the two tribes in Hungary is their divergent worldviews.

The first narrative builds on the belief that Orbán is honest. His devotees interpret everything through this lens. For them, the story is about how Orbán gave hope to the *conservative-Christian* middle-class for victory.

On the left, the second narrative's starting point is that Orbán is a liar. For the latter tribe, the story is about how Orbán took away the hope of the tribe of the *socialist-liberals*. I put the two attributes in *italics* because, in today's Hungary, it is not the right-republican or leftist-democratic values that divide people's affiliation toward politics, but who believes in which story.

# 7

# Fear and Fear of God

In his book *Blink*, Malcolm Gladwell tries to prove that people make decisions at lightning speed and stick with them, regardless if later facts contradict their original intuition. Another person will decide in a blink whether they like you, and will correspondingly perceive everything through the lens that they took on in that split second.

> *I am talking about those who used to write things that people under the Kádár regime were not afraid, and life went well, they have fit in. Now they come up with a tale you have to fear this 31-year-old kid from Felcsút. Isn't that ridiculous?*

Ridiculous or not, some fear him. Viktor Orbán's personality evokes similar emotions in both camps. The two tribes began to interpret the narrative through a filter of trust or fear, believing the story to be either authentic or fake. Those who believed the story recognized the charismatic leader in Orbán with the same level of confidence as they professed fear of God. Those who considered the story a lie constructed the narrative of a dictator. Just like in *Blink*, in eight seconds.

Fear was the main guiding force that distorted the judgements of the liberal tribe. Orbán climbed the social ladder from poverty to the racing-stable of the Budapest intellectuals. Most of his peers came from intellectual families and enjoyed the contingent privileges during their childhoods in the 1970s. Orbán was a tough country kid, tough as a nail and sharp as a tack. His toughness, fortitude, and intelligence raised fears in those who grew up in softer environments of the liberal arts. Orbán soon assumed the lead. So, when the Fidesz changed its political narrative, those who disagreed found it better to flee the fight and depart the party. From this point on, leftist-liberal intellectuals and the media that amplified their voices did everything they could to oust Orbán from public life: he could never be allowed to get close to power. Because the driving force was fear, they produced a narrative that was in sync with it: the image of the dictator. At the same time, they tried to cut down the popularity of Orbán's personality cut with character assassination, with more or less success.

This is the power of narrative. Depending on your worldview, you can interpret the same frames negatively or positively.

If I interpret Orbán's desire to go for the gold, I affectionately look upon character who works hard to overcome his disadvantages, who built a sturdy physique, whose quick reactiveness and razor-sharp intelligence augur the bright future of a charismatic statesman. If I interpret him through the lenses of artifice and fear, I descry a populist dictator on the horizon. Whether one related to him with confidence and or with fear is grounded primarily on one's assumption, about the authenticity of Fidesz's transition from liberalism to conservatism.

It is harder to hate a dictator than others because the fact of a dictatorship provides an excuse for opponents' lack of success. This is how I can explain to myself that 'I am not weak, but I'm fighting against heavy odds.' His opponents may explain to themselves that Orbán owes his success to his "lack of sportsmanship" and not because he worked harder than they did. This way, everyone can shirk their responsibilities. The image

of a dictator is useful not only because it takes the burden off
the less talented opposition politicians, but it also because tends
to make opposition voters inactive. The sentiment "It's all the
same, why give it a try" is an old Hungarian tradition. That is
why personal trainers direct people to set realistic goals because
if your goals are too hard to achieve, perhaps, in the end, you will
achieve none of them and lose motivation. In Fidesz, they apply
this principle against their opponents. By winning a landslide
election, they will prevent the opposition from even being able
to imagine a comeback.

> *You don't have to like us. Let's not get things confused. Fear and*
> *affection are different issues. People who dislike me: fair enough.*
> *[…] Affection is not essential in this regard, but appreciation.*
> *The real question is, do you recognize, appreciate the work,*
> *one's life's journey that a person leaves behind.*

The starting point of the underground narrative is that
Orbán was born a fair player, and one can safely assume that
his intentions are good for our country. The author's view is
that Orbán is an exceptional opportunity, one that occurs in a
nation's history once in a lifetime. This book intends to give a
new framework of interpretation to Orbán's politics without
having to believe in any of the two extreme narratives.

# 8

# Judgement

Viktor Orbán based his political power on the worldview of the people through storytelling that radiates energy and evokes extreme emotional reactions. The division between trust and fear provides power. That is why the narrative had to be constructed willy-nilly that the frames of the Orbán movie would lead Hungarians to the same conclusion as the world regarding Uncle Sam: nobody can defeat his power. In both camps, worldview triggers a reaction—their attitude towards faith and a chain-reaction of biases.

We are wired differently, as we say. We all wear mental glasses and hearing aids, through which we perceive the world, blurry or sharp, focused on details or from a bird eye's perspective, muted or amplified. We rely on our interpreting device—our beliefs and emotions—when we navigate the world. We judge others by our worldview, which is greatly influenced by cognitive biases. Where we do not know the answer, our brains try to fill in the gaps.

In the seventies, many questioned the rationale of classical economic theory about the reasonable man, including two psychologists from the Hebrew University of Jerusalem. Daniel Kahneman and Amos Tversky conducted experiments, distributed questionnaires, organized situational games, and published their findings in the journal Science. Their 1974 paper, *Judgment under Uncertainty: Heuristics and Biases*, revolutionized economics and

laid the foundations for a new discipline, behavioral economics.[v]
In his book *Thinking, Fast and Slow*, Kahneman wrote about these
heuristics and biases, rules of thumb that the human mind invents
to make it easier to make decisions. Scientists have identified
almost two hundred different cognitive biases since the 1970s.
One of the most well-known biases is the prejudice of rendering
judgement based on external features.

IF SOMEBODY DRESSES PREDICTABLY, HAS A STOCKY BODY TYPE, IS
popular, and aims for full employment, who else could he be
alike, then János Kádár?

During the Kádár era,[vi] Hungary was not sovereign. It was a
Soviet dependency and the Comecon limited the country's ability
to set its own path. We cannot talk about human rights in the
modern sense existing in those days. Fundamental constitutional
rights, the right to freedom of opinion and thought, to freedom
of religion and freedom of assembly were minimal. There was no
freedom of the press. Nor can we talk about the sanctity of private
property, with the state owning a vast majority of real estate and
companies. Private companies operated only in limited contexts.
There was no pluralist multi-party system, no separation of
powers, no free and democratic elections. The death penalty was

v Psychologist Daniel Kahneman was awarded the Nobel Prize in Economics
in 2001, which he shared with Vernon L. Smith for his pioneering work in
behavioral economics. The citation praised them "for having integrated insights
from psychological research into economic science, especially concerning human
judgment and decision-making under uncertainty." Tversky passed away in 1996.
Thinking, Fast and Slow greatly influenced my own thinking.
vi   Hungary's historic period from 1957 until 1989, from the end of the 1956
Revolution until the first change of regime, named after the communist leader
János Kádár. "Life was better in the Kádár era" was a populist mantra after the
first change of regime, as the communist system granted everyone a basic living
with the compromise of a dictatorship and a poor quality of life.

legal and regularly administered. People were not allowed to travel freely to the West—if they were lucky, maybe once every three years—and there were strict passport controls, visa applications, and minimal access to foreign currency. Living standards in the *good old days* meant that everyone could consume the same inferior quality goods. In Hungary there was no choice of goods, there were hardly any western products, and everything was in short supply. Recreational and entertainment facilities were under state control, and electronics, cars, and services were far below Western European standards. At one time, Malév Hungarian Airlines' planes crashed regularly, and people died on poor-quality roads in unsafe cars. To succeed in life, you had to be a member of the Communist Party. The secret service enlisted people who then had to report on their family, friends, and coworkers. Those who did not cooperate with state security services were blackmailed and they and their relatives were denied medical treatment and university enrollment, or even threatened with imprisonment.

Compared to this, Hungary is today a member of NATO and the European Union. Hungarian citizens are citizens of the European Union, and they can move around and work freely. EU-membership ensures the free movement of capital and goods. The state is a republic with democratic institutions and a freely elected government. Hungary's Fundamental Law guarantees human rights, the independence of the courts, freedom of the press, and other protections offered by any liberal state. Internet is part of our life, with social media, email, online commerce encompassing all aspects of society. Knowledge is accessible to everyone. Almost everyone in the Kádár era had a job and the situation is similar now with the Orbán government cutting unemployment to record-low levels. But the fact is that the country today does not resemble the Kádár system. The two have nothing in common.

SOCIAL PSYCHOLOGY HAS UNVEILED FURTHER LAWS THAT AFFECT OUR
decisions. Our behavior is different when we are alone compared
to when we are in the presence of others. In one of the most
famous series of experiments, participants sat in a room, and
researchers projected three long lines. First, subjects had to answer
which of the three lines had the same length as the control. Several
people were sitting in the room at the same time and all but one
of them answered one after another because the experimenters
were curious about the last participant, who was unaware that the
study was about him and that the researchers had set a trap for his
mind. Despite the apparent differences between the lines, when
the participants unanimously said the wrong answer out loud, the
participant usually parroted the wrong answer as well. He did not
want to stick out from the crowd. The effect of peer pressure is
called the Asch paradigm, named after the scientist Solomon Asch,
who investigated the study.

The underground narrative behind Orbán's turn from liberal
to conservative is not that he became "enlightened" but that
he just woke up. The "gifted young man" who spoke at the
reinternment of Imre Nagy and the eye-catching campaign of
Fidesz was enough for a disappointingly low 5% of the vote.
Liberal dogmas, which academics thought were a part of
mainstream society's ideology, turned out to be a worldview
propagated by of a fraction of the intellectual class. The peer
pressure exerted by liberal intellectuals made them believe that
Hungarians would buy into rebel politics. The founders of Fidesz
were probably not atheists in the first place, they only wanted to
live up to the expectations of the liberal intellectuals, and when
they realized that track was a dead-end, they rebelled. Common
sense likely dictated Orbán's change of direction.

Folks at the Free Democrats came to a similar conclusion in
1994. They too had a good grip on the situation. They could

never get into the office with their liberal dogma. Like Orbán, they overwrote their worldview, but they did not give in to anti-clericalism but rather to anti-communism. The Socialists remained as the only option for leftists. Orbán turned right, the liberals left, but both for the same reason: you cannot change the worldview of the people, so it is better just to align with it.

The relationship between *the person and the situation* is the study of social psychologists to see how little things matter when we judge the world. In an experiment with *The Washington Post*, a talented violinist, Joshua Bell, was asked to play a few pieces at a subway station during the morning rush hour. As expected, passengers rushed by without stopping, except for a small child whose mother forced him to continue. Researchers were curious about how people's judgements come into play when one of the world's greatest musicians performs not in a concert hall, but anonymously in a subway station and plays one of the world's most challenging violin concerts. Bell performed later that night in a traditional venue, and by then all tickets were sold out.

The narrative can build upon the knowledge we already gained or, on the contrary, on the recipient's ignorance or distorted worldview. Thus, an unfavorably photographed elderly gentleman, George Soros, will become a political target, which some perceive as the vilification of a Holocaust survivor, whereas others see an officer of the Illuminati and a leader of the world ruling class. Both narratives build on the background knowledge concerning the anti-Semitism of the viewer and create a causal connection between their beliefs and reality. From a polarized point of view, all good and evil come from the same source. In the right-wing mythology, George Soros is the Darth Vader of the dark forces which rule the world, while in the left-liberal mythology, he is the spiritual father of the open society and a curator of world peace. Both tribes believe in Soros, just like in

Viktor Orbán, but with one principal difference. Anti-Semites honestly believe that George Soros rules the world, while leftists only hope that he could.

The way the outside world sees us does not necessarily correspond to the story we tell about ourselves. The other party's worldview can distort our objective and accurate image of us, which is further altered by group pressure and the framing effects of situational factors.

So, some may say Áron's worldview is one-sided, while others say his book is worth reading. Either he's a wannabe muscle head or simply has pretension toward looking athletic, and that is that.

# 9

# Philosophers and Film Critics

Two institutions in the world force everyone to believe in their invincibility: the totalitarian dictatorship and the mafia. Regarding totalitarian dictatorships, the masses believe in or are rightly afraid of them, so overall, a single narrative prevails. The mafia's inside story is the acknowledgment of the Godfather, while the external description is intimidation of people who encounter the organization. Liberal intellectuals started to interpret the Orbán regime through a framework that set it parallel with dictatorships and the mafia. Because of their distorted assumptions, liberal intellectuals could not resolve the contradictions stemming from their biases, namely that Orbán does not use violence. Therefore, they focused on traits that are outside the scope of abuse but are nevertheless indicative of dictatorship or of a mafia. Philosophers that survived the Holocaust conceived of the concept of tyranny, while liberal film critics brainstormed the Godfather.

"I suppose it is tempting, if the only tool you have is a hammer, to treat everything as if it were a nail," said Abraham Maslow. Maslow's gavel is also known as the law of the instrument. The essence of the syllogism articulated by Orbán-phobes implies that "Orbán is a tyrant," that he is *il Duce* of today. They glaze over facts in order to link Orbán with the dictatorships of the 20th century, thus unintentionally diminishing the Holocaust.

Ágnes Heller was a woman of words, sometimes taking what

she heard too seriously. Not only did she have a loud voice, but she also used it to speak up. She made the world believe that Orbán deserved a place next to Putin, Erdoğan, and Duterte on the cover of *Time*, and to depict the Hungarian Prime Minister next to Le Pen and Trump on the cover of the authoritative *The Economist*. Only a single article in her life appeared in *The New York Times*, the one she wrote about Viktor Orbán. In her column *What Happened to Hungary*, she wrote about extreme right-wing populism, the Prime Minister-cum-tyrant—"But, in fact, he is"—and the unfairness of the elections. Obituaries remember her for being a die-hard critic of the Orbán regime. Instead, I respect her as one of the shapers of the Orbán-cult. Heller made a world star out of her fierce enemy and paved his way to a two-thirds victory.

The Hungarian-born Austrian journalist Paul Lendvai implies that the Orbán regime is a masked dictatorship, and his book, therefore, seeks to blow the lid off and reveal the truth. His book *Orbán* is predictable. It is a defining feature of genre books and columns to cater to the tastes of the frustrated masses. The book's take-home message is that Orbán is talented but dangerous. Lendvai, in his supposed objectivity, doesn't even consider a scenario in which the mask hides nothing malevolent.

A popular argument of such columns is that Orbán's rhetoric appeals to emotions. Orbán-phobes forget that sports competitions and indeed all advertising affect emotions, but we do not consider them marks of fascism.

Beyond the public architecture of Orbán's government, they hope to discover a fascist style. Still, if you look it in a certain light, an Apple Store also resembles the the fascist-style: a grandiose stone facade, steel, glass, minimalist furnishings, and a logo that is not the swastika, but an apple. There could be much to fear here.

Some say that Steve Jobs led Apple as a dictator. Still, nobody associates him with dictators because of his round glasses and great sense of humor, and the free spirit of Apple's products set suspicious minds at rest. Apple has in the meanwhile become the world's largest enterprise, with access to personal data from hundreds of millions of users. Apple, Microsoft, Google, and Facebook all act as dictatorships that do not resort to physical violence. We cannot imagine life without them. We all believe in their invincible power, and we all hold it to be self-evident that Mark Zuckerberg could decide the next President of the United States if he wanted to.

Would the mafia be a mafia if no one obeyed the boss? Adult liberals who grew up with the *Godfather* trilogy and the 1980s Italian TV miniseries *The Octopus* discovered Don Vito Corleone in Orbán's leadership.

As a byproduct phenomenon of Orbán's ostensible dictatorship, a smaller publishing ecosystem has emerged around scapegoating and Orbán-phobia. The biggest victims of the disruption of the status quo are the former members of the Alliance of Free Democrats and their intellectual circle. The product of their belief-based substitute is to smuggle the term *mafia state* in public debate, appealing to the marginalized generation with the imagery of the Hungarian Octopus trilogy and the Godfather cult. Only one ingredient is missing from the smorgasbord: *factfulness*. Swedish physician Hans Rosling, best known for his TED talks, coined the term factfulness, drawing attention to the fact that people were willing to live with the convictions they had formed many years ago at university. He brought the world's attention to a bias that we judge the world by our belief based on knowledge that is twenty- or thirty-years old thinking that reality is much worse than it actually is.

The bibliography of the Hungarian essay trilogy is self-explanatory: one can hardly find any peer-reviewed foreign-language references; a circle of close friends often refers to each other's Hungarian-language articles; third-party foreign publications are rare, drawn principally from the last decade. It is a pity that they did not invent the term mafia state. The title of the original work, *Mafia State*, written by Luke Harding and published in 2011, is about Putin's presidency. Neither Orbán nor Hungary even appear in the index.

Many accuse Orbán of anti-intellectualism. Yet, there is a crucial difference between Yuval Noah Harari and his Hungarian colleagues. Hungarian philosophers are experts on the French Revolution, Harari, also on the digital revolution. Steven Pinker's books contain hundreds of state-of-the-art references, whereas Bálint Magyar's colleagues are satisfied with a dozen.

Making everyone believe you are invincible, either because they like you or because they fear you, is not an American invention. Kingdoms, empires, and dictatorships are all built on this foundation. America is exceptional because it became the world's leading power through democratic means, not through physical force.

The liberal intellectual unconscious has correctly signaled that the masses trust Orbán, and that scares them to death. They realized that there was something peculiar in the Orbán system that made it different from any ordinary democratic system. In a democracy, one tribe only believes in their leader, and the other does not have to fear that leader, which gives balance to the rotation between the two political groups' time in power. The problem is that the liberals got it wrong; they fabricated their narrative on false premises.

Moreover, their limiting biased beliefs excluded faith in a positive outcome. Because of their atheist worldview, they did not realize that Orbán's rule works in the same way as the American model. Orbán realized Americanism in Hungary because he built his power through appeals to people's worldview. Because of their fear, his opposition caught a glimpse of abuse, abuse that was in reality a byproduct of Orbán's effective storytelling, just a hallucination in their minds. This phobia solidified into a conviction via peer-pressure and the liberal tribe leaders' appeals to authority. Orbán had no other choice than to tailor his politics for this worldview.

# 10

## "Fascism"

Madeleine Albright's book *Fascism* gives the impression of meticulous, objective, and honest work. Until you start reading, that is, when you discover after the first few pages that you are scrolling through an emotionally rich opinion-book.

Chapter 13 of *Fascism* deals with Poland and Viktor Orbán's Hungary. It contains eighteen references: three articles from *The New York Times*, two from *The Washington Post* and the *Financial Times*, two from the *AP* news agency, a Juncker quote, a Polish television quote, and three references to Orbán's speeches. The remaining four, i.e., four pieces of *evidence*, are other sources.

The tale presented by the former Democratic Secretary of State is humiliating to Hungarians. She stereotypes Hungarians as goulash-eaters as if the country's national economy consisted of sausage makers and paprika cultivators.

With all due respect to the former secretary, she could have honored the reader by not sculpting the chapter from one-sided newspaper articles. Before accusing Orbán of fascism, she might have bothered to gather information from other sources. Her references mostly present the reader with a one-sided, biased view that invariably lays the blame on Orbán team, a distorted opinion that dominates the foreign press.

The moral authority of speakers of fascism, including the former US Secretary of State, derives from the fact that they are descendants of Holocaust survivors. If Ms. Albright had not played this card in the beginning, I would not have played it in my own book. It was my grandfather's luck to escape the Nazis and, with an unknown person's documents, survive the Shoah. Grateful to his unknown savior, my grandfather kept the name and changed his name from George Hoffmann to George Hidvégi. One of my given names, Arnold, commemorates my great-grandfather who, along with my great-grandmother, was a victim of martyrdom in the last months of 1944, during a death march from the Újlaki brick factory in Óbuda, Budapest. My parents gave me my other given name, Áron, after the legendary Archbishop of Transylvania, Áron Márton, not to mention that my great-grandfather's Hebrew name was also Aharon.

Ms. Albright's book, also a memoir, describes her feelings about Vladimir Putin and Kim Jong Un whom she met as US Secretary of State. With the high standards of prudence and diplomatic courtesy, she pastes Orbán and Trump next to Mussolini, Hitler, Duterte, and Chavez. The title of the chapter is *We are who we were*, a quote that the author mistakenly attributes to Orbán. In a blink, Ms. Albright derives the doctrines of fascism from this quote, ignorant that the Transylvanian-Hungarian writer Kelemen Mikes said this line ("We are who we were, and we shall be what we are."). As such, she probably does not understand who the Szeklers or the Hungarians even are.

From Madeleine Albright's storybook, we learn that il Duce led Italy to bankruptcy, fought a disastrous war with Greece, and used brutal terror. Oh, and what if Orbán hasn't done any of these things? No problem, someone can still be a fascist. After all, he rewrote the country's constitution and suppressed other opinions. Meanwhile, the author polishes herself and trumps Trump. It is America's job to promote democracy throughout the world because it is the pinnacle of justice when America tells the people of another country, without their consent, how they should live.

Ms. Albright's memory is also selective because she forgets that the United States was the place where blacks lived segregated for a century. Today the US does not welcome migrants from the Middle East, and it was the United States that let down Hungary and democratic values in 1956. When the US' help was need, they did not render any aid. When, on the other hand, we do not accept their altruism, we are stigmatized as being anti-democratic.

The significance of the worldview is that with whom we share the worldview, we will believe the story. The Hungarian left-liberal intellectuals have hummed the accusations to their foreign counterparts. As Péter Esterházy wrote "It is deucedly difficult to tell a lie when you don't know the truth." Nothing could be further from me to assume deliberate deceit; It was the distorted worldview that made the biased headlines at *The New York Times*, which Ms. Albright handled as fact.

# 11

# Reflexivity

The cemented attitude of liberal intellectuals stems from a lengthy process that can be described quite precisely with the theory of reflexivity—it explains the development of market bubbles, the phenomenon where market players believe in a shared narrative that has no underlying reality.

Science assumes that the researcher, as an external observer, can objectively evaluate processes. The scientist is merely an external observer, not a subject of or active variable in scientific experiments. Classical economic theory also builds on this approach, trying to describe the laws of supply and demand as an external observer, focusing on the homo oeconomicus, the reasonable man who always prioritizes his optimal preferences. Behavioral economists have debated this latter thesis, as research has shown that people, as irrational beings, make decisions under the influence of cognitive biases and heuristics.

It was not only behavioral economist psychologists who questioned the dogma of classic economics. The author of *The Alchemy of Finance* argues that as market players themselves shape market processes and as prices reflect their expectations, new expectations arise that further influence prices. Reflections between expectations and estimates distort the accuracy of the value of the assets. Processes cannot be viewed objectively from the outside, because market players by themselves influence prices through their expectations and purchasing decisions, establishing a causal relationship between the fiction reflected by their expectations and the behavior of other market participants. Therefore, a vacuum, also called a bubble, is created between expectations and reality. Reflexivity, then, says that the distorting effect of expectations creates a narrative outside reality, that is, not a documentary but fiction.

Every investor begins with an initial assumption that he aims to verify through different expectations. The expectation is the pricing of the future, the present value of the future value of a business. Investors try to estimate the future value of listed companies at today's prices so that, based on the data that the company provides and the general economic environment, the value of the company is more or less than the current stock price. If the market values a stock more, the investor sells, if less, he buys. Each investor chooses its investment policy, while some investors are smart, others have less luck. When a circumstance confirms an investor's expectation, it verifies its initial assumption, so it seeks further evidence that reinforces its expectation. You pursue a justification of each expectation with as much evidence as possible because that is how you feel safe, in trying to lower your risk.

Both sides constructed their expectations about Orbán from a biased worldview. Depending on whether they consider Orbán's story true or false, they justify their expectations by divine providence or autocratic takeover. Several factors distort their relationships to Orbán in the series of reflexivity. Instruments misinterpreted him. His attitudes towards sports, discipline, religiosity, and national sentiment set off alarm bells that fascism had creeped back into Hungary.

The concept of a dictatorship and mafia state are bubbles, just as is the image of the chosen ruler. Orbán does nothing but try to win with an elite athlete's mindset. His drive for victory is a vestige of his time in the world of professional sports—thus he is interpreted by the opposition as a charismatic autocrat, and by believers as an enlightened leader on a mission.

The policy on Hungarians living abroad, namely responsibility for the Hungarians living in the diaspora, is based on the same principle as Tivadar Herzl's *Zionism* and modeled on Israel's responsibility for the Jews in the diaspora. Orbán has a good relationship with Israel, which also serves as an inspiration for him as a small nation that has gained a great deal of influence in the world by caring for its citizens outside the motherland. Yet, many of my left-liberal intellectual Facebook-acquaintances interpret care for Hungarians across the borders as nationalism, an interpretation that resonates with liberal opinion leaders, who see in Orbán nationalist and fascist aspirations. One of the best examples of an utterly distorted value judgement is that in 2018, the left-liberal political side wanted to collaborate with the far-right's openly anti-Semitic party. All of this because their starting point, that Orbán is lying, leads to the natural conclusion that one should fear him.

The right sees divine providence from the turning point of Gyurcsány's speech to the government's efforts to clear obstacles to advancement. This bias formed a similar conviction in the hardcore of Fidesz. Orbán does not emphasize the superhuman work of fighting evil every day, but the media strives to embed every result in the context of war and reassures citizens it needs them to be on standby every day. They keep the blaze under control, and as a result, Orbán's support has not weakened but has remained stable. While Orbán was interested in making the bubble as giant as possible, he worked hard to fill the gap between the bubble and reality. Warren Buffett, one of the wealthiest people in the world and a stock investment oracle, used to say that business is good if it's a castle surrounded by a thick wall and a moat. As a shareholder, he usually asks management two things every year: to reinforce the castle's wall and thicken the moat.

The new constitution and reforms reorganized the country's legal architecture which enabled more freedom. It gives Orbán greater room for maneuvering, regaining sovereignty, and achieving financial stability. Renewing national politics, writing new foreign and economic policy, occupying key positions, recapitalizing on entrepreneurial circles, fighting migration, fostering a sense of security, struggling against Brussels on the behalf of national freedom, and the programming an ascendant ideology strengthen the castle and expand its already thick moat. And we didn't even mention the marketing value of sports successes.

# 12

# The Real Enemy

Let's return to the stock market. After a while, the market realizes that it has deceived itself. With everyone wanting to escape the crumbling fiction, the bubble bursts and panic breaks out. Prices fall in what is commonly known as a stock market crash. In such cases, the winners are those who recognize the bubble before others, sell their investments at artificially overvalued prices, and speculate that the bubble will burst. It was a Hungarian-born man who burst the world's most famous bubble, predicting a fall in the British pound, which gave him the nickname "the man who broke the Bank of England." He also conceived of the theory of reflexivity and wrote the aforementioned book on that topic. This person is George Soros.

George Soros did not become Viktor Orbán's enemy because he was Jewish, rich, or liberal. Instead, it is because he is a rival expert on bubbles. He is an enemy instead of an ally because while Orbán was interested in making the bubble bigger, Soros would rather burst it—to make even more profit from the panic.

Interestingly, one would assume that Orbán and Soros are different. Let me provide some examples of how similar they are. For instance, Soros's investment tactics are akin to Orbán's. He develops a theory and tests it in limited circumstances at first. If it works, he establishes a strong position and then 'goes for the jugular.' The controversial anti-Soros campaign started with a tiny Manhattan cookie-shop, and when the cookies sold like hotcakes, the campaign switched to a large-scale cookie-factory.

George Soros' father, the lawyer Tivadar Soros, gave three pieces of advice to his two sons, *Gyuri* and *Pali*, which Viktor Orbán found worth considering:

- IT IS OKAY TO TAKE RISKS.
- WHEN TAKING A RISK, NEVER BET THE RANCH.
- ALWAYS BE PREPARED TO BEAT A HASTY RETREAT.

In the political world, changing people's worldview is a substantial risk. Closing shops on Sundays, internet tax, or Olympic candidacy is the practical application of this principle. The government wanted shopping malls and retailers to close on Sundays, to implement an internet-tax, and to obtain for Budapest the 2024 summer Olympic games. In all three cases, the government withdrew its proposals as soon as possible when people protested them.

Contrary to popular belief, George Soros is one of the most risk-averse people in the world. His success result from the confidence and skill of a French high-wire artist, Petit Philippe, who, in 1974, struck a steel wire stretched between two towers of the World Trade Center and walked it without a safety harness. (He prepared for his show for years.)

In the same way, Orbán had ten years of political experience before defeating Gyula Horn and the two-thirds left-liberal mammoth in 1998. In 2010, two-thirds did not pass by random chance. From the beginning, Orbán speculated that the Socialists would fail with Ferenc Gyurcsány. He had the professional skills to expect that Gyurcsány's personality traits would lead to failure. Later, analysts have tried to make the 2010 two-thirds parliamentary victory a coincidence, but I prefer an interpretation that Orbán always knew he would win. Without confidence, he could not have been able to wage his campaign. The bubble is dangerous not only because it can burst, but also because it makes one confident, either positively or negatively so. Orbán never trusts himself, and before every election, he goes all in for victory. On the other hand, the opposition blew such a vast bubble that they would instead have to yield to their rival.

There is a watch that is often seen on George Soros, one of the refined models from one of the most coveted Swiss brands. The watchmaker's famous slogan is: "You never actually own a Patek Philippe. You merely look after it for the next generation." George Soros wants to preserve his wealth for the next generation. Viktor Orbán wants to take care of the Hungarian nation here and now. This is the crux of the difference between the two Hungarian geniuses.

# 13

## Two Gyurcsánys

Mrs. Donoghue arrived on a sunny Sunday afternoon, August 28, 1928, with her female friend at the Wellmeadow Café in Paisley, Scotland. Mrs. Donoghue ordered a Scotsman ice cream float, an ice cream with ginger beer. The waiter brought out the ice cream in the tumbler and poured ginger beer on it. The opaque beer bottle had the following label: D. Stevenson, Glen Lane, Paisley. When Mrs. Donoghue's friend poured out the remaining beer, a decomposed snail also floated out of the bottle. Mrs. Donoghue got sick and later sued the manufacturer. Mrs. Donoghue stated in court that she became unwell from this sight, had experienced abdominal pain, had been referred to a doctor the next day, who transferred her to an emergency hospital in Glasgow two weeks later, where she was diagnosed with gastroenteritis and shock. Donoghue v. Stevenson is a landmark precedent of the common-law legal system, which laid the foundation of the modern law of negligence, establishing general principles of the duty of care. In prior cases, liability for personal injury in tort usually depended upon showing that physical damage was directly or indirectly inflicted. In the case of Mrs. Donoghue, being made ill was also recognized as damage, which created a new type of liability.

In 2006, another decomposed snail slipped out of the bottle, this time not from Mr. Stevenson's bottle, but through the keyhole of the Socialist Party's closed doors. However, the speech in autumn, which caused abdominal illness in half of Hungary, did not come with the same consequences as the case in Scotland. The ruling left did not convict Ferenc Gyurcsány, nor did his liberal coalition partner, or the lunar court of left-liberal intellectuals. The author of *Parallel Stories*, whose words none would dare to question, said: "The speech given by the Prime Minister at the May party meeting is, in my opinion, a great speech, a pinnacle of rhetoric, including all non-salutary expressions, that are neither obscene nor profane because they are in their place."

Finally, in the 2010 elections, voters challenged the judgement of writer Péter Nádas. Since then, the left still has not been able to decide whether to get rid of Gyurcsány. If so, how, if not, what comes next?

Adam Grant has written a remarkable book on Viktor Orbán and Ferenc Gyurcsány. *Give and Take* is about two types of people, the Orbán team-player, and the Gyurcsány profit-maximizer. A taker wants to get out of every situation (*trade*) with a profit, and he wants to cash in the immediate gains. They are generally very successful and engaging in their work. It is the character of Gyurcsány, who is claiming credit from the very first moment, everything results from his success, and nothing is without him. Yet, he always steals opportunities from others or pulls others out of his chair when it comes to it. He came to the forefront of politics by leading Péter Medgyessy's campaign, whence he came to power by cleverly colluding with the liberals who helped dump the unpopular Medgyessy so that Gyurcsány could replace him in the Prime Minister's office. After his shameless speech, his revenge and ego tore apart the Socialist Party. Occasionally, he pops up in the media with some loud statement that turns out to be fake. He proclaimed that he had seen Viktor Orbán's Swiss bank account but could not muster any evidence to show to the public. He will say that he will protest forever and then blow it off two days later as if nothing had happened. Each time—three times since 2010, when the left lost its election—Gyurcsány disappeared for a short time and then returned. In what other role than as a savior of the left can he serve the country? Most Hungarians cannot stand him, but there is a devoted subculture where he is still liked. Some still believe in him.

The core message of Grant's book is that givers will become truly successful people who are not seeking glory for themselves but rather are devoted to helping their community, creating value, and not worrying about what reward they can expect in return. Viktor Orbán used to say that success belongs to the team, while he himself takes sole responsibility for failure. Gyurcsány turns this on its head.

*The result of the European Parliamentary election was that in the opposition there was one Gyurcsány and there now has appeared a pair of Gyurcsánys.*

Gyurcsány's wife, a leader of the Democratic Coalition's European Parliament list of 2019, has also become a politician. Klára Dobrev provokes sympathy with her stock-character of the smart housewife well-known from soap operas and commercials. She is the superficially knowledgeable presenter of the women's talk show, a kitchen fairy that respects her lord as befits Hungarian tradition. Caring and fashionable, who rubs her daughter's chest with menthol balm when she is sick, stocks the fridge with treats for her loved ones, uses only hypoallergenic fabric softeners, she finds time to pamper herself, too. A teacher's pet who nails the lesson. And what? If I compare her to the first ladies of the American Democratic Party, the question remains poetic. Where is Hillary's elegant thirst for blood, Michelle Obama's captivating kindness, or Eleanor Roosevelt's majestic sense of style? Moreover, talking about their husbands, where is Bill Clinton's versatility, the sound patriotism of Franklin D. Roosevelt, or the human-loving intellect of Barack Obama?

Philosopher and public intellectual Gáspár Miklós Tamás wrote in his column: "Gyurcsány once told the truth: he sincerely admitted that he was lying, and that statement was true. Everyone knew he was lying, but that was not a problem. It became a problem only because he was telling the truth about his lies. Now he pretends to tell the truth. It is much worse, but no scandal."

# 14

# I Never Read The Economist

Why did the victorious powers take over two-thirds of Hungary's territory after the First World War? Because force allowed them to. They did not have to consider minority opinion. At the heart of this history is cynicism. This political theatre was a distraction from its real purpose, the artful manipulation of obscure rules and institutions to guarantee the status quo to hold on power – to divide and conquer.

"At the heart of the degradation of Hungarian democracy is cynicism. [...] This political theatre is a distraction from his real purpose, the artful manipulation of obscure rules and institutions to guarantee his hold on power." "The achievement is bad for Hungarian liberty and its long-term prospects..." "In form, Hungary is a thriving democracy; in spirit, it is a one-party state."

These quotes sum up *The Economist*'s editorial. On August 31, 2019, the authoritative London weekly published an analysis of Hungary, drawing on the following persons and sources: Gábor Fodor, former rival of Orbán; an ex-judge lawyer who is one of the most daring critics of the justice system under Orbán; the head of the Hungarian Academy of Sciences' social-science institute; senior research fellow at the MTA KRTK KTI; the Chairman of GKI Economic Research Co.; Bálint Magyar, former Minister of Education, sociologist, lecturer at CEU; political science expert at Princeton University; Bernadett Szél, LMP Prime Ministerial candidate in 2018; Judith Sargentini, former Member of the European Parliament, author of the 'Sargentini Report;' and a political scientist at Rutgers University. Besides these professionals, the "man on the street" also asks for his name to be silenced: Lili, a student; Zsike, a graphic artist from Debrecen; Mary and her husband who emigrated to Austria; Mónika, an English teacher who read *1984* by George Orwell.

Therefore, I would like to summarize the content of the article in this way: in form, *The Economist* is a thriving democracy; in spirit, it is a one-party state—one perspective, one opinion, one prejudice.

I read *1984* too, and even Fukuyama, Tocqueville, Al Gore, I speak English well, I'm a polite driver, I eat with a knife and a fork, I am a quiet small-talker, a lawyer and economist, but I don't pour milk into my tea. However, *The Economist*'s informed press workers did not ask me what I see in the Orbán regime. Why would I come to their minds? One would expect that the Anglo-Saxon editorial team, proud of its democratic traditions, would pay heed to the ten plus four witnesses on the plaintiff's left in addition to hearing out the ten plus four on the defendant's right. "I Never Read The Economist." This witty campaign slogan laid the foundation for the brand's prestige. Once upon a time, it was meant as a joke. Today it is worth taking into serious consideration. The magazine's summary of the Orbán government would not meet the criterion of objectivity, not only in the United Kingdom but also in Eurasia. Unless they read Orwell? "Ignorance is Strength."

I quote from the Code of Ethics of the British Association of Journalists: "Newspapers and periodicals should take care not to publish inaccurate, misleading or distorted material." Through its biased glasses, *The Economist* misinterprets the Orbán system as a one-party system, even though Hungary clearly does not have a one-party system. At most, power is dominated by a worldview based on fundamental truths such as in the United Kingdom or the United States: the country has an interest in sovereignty, unity, and responsibility. The underground interpretation maintains that people vote for Viktor Orbán because the opposition disputes these trivial issues. That's all: voters didn't buy the opposition's narrative, but Orbán's.

If I qualify the speakers as impartial, the objective criterion is that they are unsuccessful in life. They credit Gábor Fodor with being the former founder of Fidesz, who then left the party after his conflict with Viktor Orbán, became a member of Free Democrats, and minister of the Socialist-Liberal government. In 2013, he left the sinking ship and founded the Hungarian Liberal Party, and by the generosity of the Socialists, he became a member of Parliament for another four years. Magyar and Fodor were the strongmen of the party that far surpassed their rivals in terms of intellectual capacity—*The Best and the Brightest*—yet in 2009 (under Fodor's presidency), it only gained 2.16% during the European Parliamentary elections. In 2010 they could not enter Hungarian Parliament either. András Vértes criticizes the government's economic policy with real or presumed authority as head of his co-owned private company, the GKI Economic Reseach Co. The only problem is that when he and the Socialists ruled, they were incompetent (from 1990 to 12 years, not counting the forty years before the first democratic change of regime, because then half a century would be the sum). The black and white facts are that the country almost went bankrupt. How shall such people provide expert advice to readers of *The Economist*? Had the Economist made a better choice, taken a more critical approach, they would have also interviewed economists and social science professionals. On Fidesz, Péter Tölgyessy, László Lengyel, or Gábor Török could have been consulted, in economic policy issues Attila Chikán or György Surányi, and if they wanted to strengthen the husband-wife story, they might have spoken with László Kéri and Mária Zita Petschnig. The writing qualifies *The Economist* as a professional who is once defenseless. But that's a problem for the shareholders of *The Economist*.

"Newspapers, whilst free to be partisan, should distinguish clearly between comment, conjecture and fact." Sounds good that Viktor Orbán 'shuttered' the daily newspaper *Népszabadság* (literal meaning: People's Freedom). However, in reality, Népszabadság wasn't closed by Viktor Orbán, instead it was its readership that refused to maintain their subscriptions to the newspaper. Instead, they flocked to *Index.hu*, which became a market leader because the gifted founding editor-in-chief Péter Uj translated his expertise from his time at Népszabadság. Then, after feeling limited in his independence, he resigned from Index, brought along his most talented associates, and founded the online worldview news blog *444*. The second-largest online newspaper, *Origo* is not based on print media either. Print publishing and online publishing in Hungary split because young and talented journalists have been overthrown by a sort of gentry that fears for the status quo. The Hungarian Socialist Party once owned the Népszabadság. They voluntarily sold the asset to a third-party investor, who later sold it to Mediaworks, who became the new owner, and which eventually decided to close. The Marxist innervation of 'everything should be free' has incentivized leftists not to subscribe to the newspaper. If Népszabadság was unimportant for them, why should Viktor Orbán keep his unfair enemy alive?

From the vantage point of the West, the research institute network of the Hungarian Academy of Sciences appears to be world-class. Still, these institutions have expelled many talented scientists. The Academy's research network was created or attached to the Academy under communism, so *The Economist*'s formulation of the significant role that the Academy played in language renewal and of its independence from Habsburg rule is a journalistic slip. Naturally, the leaders of the institutions of the Hungarian Academy of Sciences are anti-Orbán when their status quo is in danger. Nobody enjoys being held accountable and questioned about the usefulness of their work, especially if it even has a basis in reality. Hungarian taxpayers fund the institutions, why shouldn't the government elected by the Hungarian taxpayers be involved in them? The law does not restrict academic freedom; for instance, nobody restricted me from writing this book.

Sophisticated but insulting, *The Economist* stereotypes Hungarians and ethnic Hungarians living beyond the country's borders. They say, "Fewer citizens can read and write in a foreign language than in any other EU country, except Britain." Behind the domineering attitude is malicious ignorance, *The Economist* is unaware that thanks to Hungarian literary translators—such as Babits, Tandori, Weöres—and the zeal of Hungarian publishing, all books that matter in the world are available in Hungarian. They mention the citizenship of ethnic Hungarians living across the border who *plump* with Fidesz (used here as a word of pejorative meaning). Besides the fact that *The Economist* does not consider Transylvanian Hungarians independent human beings, they know little about the Hungarian electoral system either. Dual-citizen ethnic Hungarians living abroad do not play a significant role. One-representative districts elect 106 of the 199 seats, and 93 are distributed by multi-member votes (party-list vote), one or two of them being elected by Hungarians living abroad.

Twenty years ago, no one would have expected *The Economist* to publish an editorial that took into account only opposition views. In his thought-provoking bestselling book *How to be an Alien*, however, George Mikes did. "How to report this event? It depends which newspaper you work for."

*The Economist* and *The New York Times* are behaving just as unfairly as the Hungarian liberal intellectuals twenty years ago. Out of fear, they become the worst version of themselves. Their concerns are not groundless.

They are realizing that the world does not need them. Donald Trump tweets, no news report is required because the value of news coverage has sunk to zero. News used to be what the president said. Today, editors are fabricating news from comments packaged with the story. And that's how it becomes biased journalism. News and opinion are smudged. It's becoming increasingly difficult to sell newspapers. The reader wants to be informed; he hasn't subscribed to *The Economist* to be taken for stupid or to read about grouchy Hungarian politicians' whining. Dread is the rational explanation for this desperate manipulation.

Of course, *The Economist* is not afraid of Viktor Orbán, only of the mindset beginning to redefine democracy in the West which was first formulated by Viktor Orbán. What builds power is that the influence of the intellectuals is minimized, and the patriotism of a solid worldview is maximized. "America first." "Hungary first." The world doesn't need *The Economist*, only the economy. *The Times They Are A-Changin'*.

So, why did the two-thirds that Fidesz won reshape Hungary's constitutional system? Because they had a right to. They did not need to consider minority opinion. At the time of the first regime change, the parties agreed on the terms and shook hands.

Viktor Orbán has a vision, and he wants to realize that vision. However strange it may be that a politician has a vision, not a *campaign program*. He worked for twenty years to build himself and Fidesz from scratch, avoiding compromise with a two-thirds majority of voters and drawing a visionary structure on a blank slate. This structure is not about what the editors of a

London weekly decide is good or bad for Hungarian freedom, but what the Hungarian voter thinks. Dear *The Economist*, please look forward into the future, as István Örkény stated in his one-minute ironic short story (*A bright and distant future*):

*And should someone in London say, "I am going to magyar," it will mean: You see that gorgeous creature over there? Well, I'm going to go up to her straight away, put my arm through hers, take her home, and…." (Here a four-letter word follows.)*

# 15

# Opinion

Suppose I guess you are lying. (Because I read your mind.) Let's also assume that you haven't lied, although I believe otherwise. (Because I misread your thoughts.)

If I think you are lying, and I am convinced of that fact, even if I hold it true, the result, the story about you will be a lie. You say that because I assume you are lying is a lie because what you think truth is to be real. It is, in fact, the truth, because you didn't lie. It's only I who thinks that you did. Because I'm convinced of my truth, no matter what you say about me, I will consider what you say to be a lie. We are both convinced we are right. And we are both convinced the other is lying.

There are two types of press in Hungary. One defaults to falsehood—tells the story from the point of view that Orbán is lying. Beyond their point of view, they do not have to lie, because the result will become distorted, that is, a lie. The other side defaults to truth—tells the story from the point of view that Orbán is telling the truth. Beyond their point of view, they don't have to lie. However, those who think Orbán is lying will consider this version a lie. Although neither party intends to lie, both will be convinced the other party has told untruths.

All because the so-called rational intellectuals consider themselves mind-readers. They consider Vedic astrology a pseudoscience, but not the ability to read the thoughts and intentions of other people.

Can they seriously read Viktor Orbán's mind and know that he is lying?

How do they know for sure? One should not look through the filter of prejudice but without prejudice. Do not try to figure out another's intentions but abstract them from their acts. Or try to look at it from the standpoint of the other side. What conclusions would you draw from stepping into the other's shoes?

How much easier life would be if news chyrons provided context to a reporter's spoken words: "we assume Orbán was lying" because then everyone would know what their point of view was. And then what they say wouldn't be a lie. This is what they take, while others take the opposite.

*The New York Times* or *The Economist* defaults to lying—looks at the world from the point of view that Trump is a liar and Orbán is a liar, so their worldview distorts their insights and corrupts what their reporting. They expect they are informing us because they hold a belief in a worldview they no longer recognize as a distortion. That's one reason Hillary Rodham Clinton lost to Donald J. Trump.

The President of The Federation of Hungarian Jewish Communities (MAZSIHISZ) regularly meets with the Hungarian Prime Minister, and the Jewish Community receives all financial support. The Unified Hungarian Jewish Congregation (EMIH) also. Benjamin Netanyahu, Prime Minister of Israel, has a good relationship with Orbán, who is the most pro-Israeli politician in the EU. Hungarian Jews have not suffered any atrocity under Orbán's government. In light of these facts, when *The New York Times* describes Orbán as 'anti-Semitic' or 'far-right,' they report biased news. (In the form of an opinion, not as a statement of fact, they may say that although all Jewish organizations in Hungary and the Israeli Prime Minister maintain that Orbán isn't anti-Semitic, that the editorial board is nevertheless concerned.)

Of course, *The Economist* writes what they wish, so long as readers subscribe to the paper. However, if you pour Grand Cru news into a wine glass, it is not a good idea to dilute it with water. Such a prestigious journal should strive not only to be considered "fair" by Orbán-phobes. Regardless of worldview: objectivity begins here.

Why did Dale Carnegie, one of America's most famous communication trainers, advise against arguing? Because he recognized that people don't want to admit their mistakes. They feel that they are supposed to be wrong. Therefore, Orbán will not give an interview to the opposition media because it's pointless. If you are presupposed to be wrong, there can be no objectivity. The only thing you can do is move on and strengthen those who trust in you.

Opposition media and intellectuals today assume they are critical. They confuse prejudice with unbiased impartiality. That's how it becomes "real fake news." The conflict between the left and the right seems insoluble because the worldviews of the two sides are based on two axioms that exclude each other. The axiom of honesty and falsehood is toxic not only to politics but also to relationships. We call it jealousy when one party assumes the other is lying. This is my opinion.

# PART TWO

## SELF-MADE

---

*"The fact that I have come this far must be played by God,*
*luck and Viktor Orbán,*
*but I never privatized, did not nick anything,*
*I achieved everything through my work and wit."*

(Lőrinc Mészáros[vii])

vii Hungary's richest man in 2019, according to Forbes

# 16

# A Square Peg in a Round Hole

Not a historian, political scientist, psychologist, or mind-reader. But a lawyer-economist, a personal trainer, and a design expert. I first shook hands with Viktor Orbán over twenty-five years ago. Politics has always interested me. I read at least three hundred nonfiction books—mostly in English—to unravel the mystery of the "Orphan Victor," while also listening to him speak several times in private and standing among hundreds of thousands in the crowd.

I want to promise one thing first. This book is honest. I'm aware that my point of view is distorted. Every point of view is. I did not write this book on request or on behalf of anyone, and no one censored it before I published it. Because of this, it is "underground," and, in this sense, different from the rest.

Four years ago, it occurred to me that it would be worth writing a book about Viktor Orbán. Not a biography but something else. By then, I already read quite a few self-help books, and after each one, I concluded that the rules of life rules are descriptive of Orbán and not the opposition. What if not fascism, but professionalism?

Steven Covey's fifteen-million-copies-sold bestseller, *The 7 Habits of Highly Effective People*, enumerates seven habits that characterize productive and successful people.

First, strive to be proactive by widening your circle of influence and begin with an end in mind. You put first things first, visualizing the end of the process. As Warren Bennis said, "Management is doing things right; leadership is doing the right things." You prioritize, seek first to understand, and then to be understood. Finally sharpen your saw as a step-in continuous improvement. One of Orbán's greatest resources is that he is a life-long learner. An anonymous source of the journalist András Kósa mentioned that Orbán devotes one day each week to reading books and studying. "I have to admit how surprised I was, to learn Viktor Orbán reads a lot of contemporary literature. Much more than the average Hungarian reader. He knows contemporary authors, not only reads one title, and can place them in today's Hungarian literary space, too."

Covey's laws are valid for Orbán without exception, so I began to reinforce that view of Orbán may not only thank his success for luck. And the reason for the opposition's bad luck isn't because of some voodoo either. It's just that Orbán structures his life professionally, along with adopting habits and mindsets like self-made American men, while the opposition does not. One of the lines of logic in this book is to point out the structural differences that distinguish Orbán from his rivals. Most of the skills Orbán has mastered are learned and practiced with persistent diligence.

Time has passed by intellectuals—one of the essential reasons they have misdiagnosed Orbán. Politics, once a world of academics and theory, has changed. In the world of mass communication, a politician must be able to sell himself. For this, he needs skills that most liberal arts faculties do not teach.

The last fifty years have also revolutionized applied sciences, transforming knowledge for everyday use. Because this knowledge lies beneath high culture, one can understand why senior practitioners of culture look down their noses at it with contempt and prejudice. Populism is a target of this attitude. A politician must produce a mass product because in a democracy the masses decide. You need to make your message understandable, regardless of whether the recipient is a high school graduate or hold a doctorate. The fact is that Viktor Orbán has lined up almost three million people behind him, and other opposition politicians have not. This does not mean that he is a populist, but he does have pop.

One of my favorite marketing books is Simon Sinek's *Start With Why* which tells how the world's most successful leaders and historical figures gained the sympathy of the masses with inspirational creeds. These leaders did not promote what they offered, but rather why they did what they did. They preached their belief, their inner conviction, not the tangible. The fundamental difference between Viktor Orbán and his opposition is that Orbán primes the message for Hungary's vision. In this book, I call Orbán's 'why' a vision, this political product is not a specific program, but a worldview. On the surface, we witness a reduction in living costs, solution to a migration issue, or the granting of dual citizenship for ethnic Hungarians living abroad, but behind such political actions are a new worldview and narrative.

Canadian writer Malcolm Gladwell (b. 1963) became a favorite of mine among the so-called New York Times bestselling authors. Having read all of his books, I found that each is a crystal clear confirmation of Viktor Orbán's genius. I have already quoted his books *Blink* and *Talking to Strangers*. Now I'd like to talk about three others.

How did the idea of middle-class Hungary become hope for a change of government; how would a spring breeze turn into an overwhelming tornado? It is the question Gladwell raises in *The Tipping Point*, which has since become one of the world's most famous nonfiction books and which made Gladwell one of the world's most influential writers. The popularity of ideas, social changes, fashion articles, or television shows reaches a turning point under specific conditions before breaking out into a public epidemic. Besides the three key players, the memorability of the message and the strength of the context play a crucial role in reaching the tipping point. Gladwell's first law stipulates three key social roles embrace the new: connectors, mavens, and salespeople—the law of small numbers. The second law is to make the idea or product as sticky, memorable, imaginative, inspiring as possible. Third, each tipping point requires an appropriate evolution of the circumstances, described by contextual relevance.

Fidesz has always consciously built a network of key figures, and for their lack of resources, these roles intertwined. Consider the churches during the first Orbán government, the civic circles during the opposition years, or the celebrities who campaigned for Viktor Orbán. A sticky affair in the background helped to foster the right mood. The Tocsik affair, a corruption scandal involving Gyula Horn's government, the Őszöd Speech by Gyurcsány, or the anti-Soros theme. The vision of a middle-class Hungary or a strong Hungary set the long-term goals.

From Gladwell's *David and Goliath*, we learn about the critical elements of the Old Testament duel. Goliath had vision problems and was dressed in thick armor, unlike David, who was nimble and agile with a more explosive body type. Well-practiced slingers were able to hit targets accurately, swinging the sling with such power that a rock, such as the one that hit Goliath on his forehead and forcing him to fall back an die, would accumulate the power of a bullet. This effortless and sly fighting technique only works if the slinger gets close enough to the target. Goliath prepared to fight from afar, so David was out of his mind. Every Hungarian knows the television debate before the 1998 elections and its defining outcome: Goliath was called Gyula Horn and

David was called Viktor Orbán. It is clear why the Socialist Party failed. Because it was too big.

In *Outliers*, Gladwell analyzed the secret of success—a combination of hard work and opportunity. I realized, at the time of the democratic change of regime, the young age of the Fidesz politicians, and their poor background, that they had no other option than politics, later became their most enormous resources. As Microsoft's, Google's, and Apple's founders were living in the same geographic location, and of nearly the same age, who were *too old* to work for a big computer company like IBM, but they weren't too young not to dare to start a new business. Besides the parallel between Silicon Valley and the Opposition Round Table, it is also worth noting that in Hungary, the political generation changes every thirty years. The Orbán generation replaced the Antall-Horn-generation, while the 1990s-borne would replace the Orbán-generation—the gen of Ráhel and Gáspár Orbán's.

Gladwell's book helped me understand why journalists and political scientists born in the seventies became the biggest winners and losers of the Orbán system, depending on their affiliation. It's because, depending on their affiliation, they are either in their generation's greatest up and down. Orbán's tenure covers the most productive period of their lives. It is understandable why they constituted Orbán's most furious opposition in the press and political science faculties because it forces them to spend the most productive period of their lives in existential insecurity. Before 2010 they were too young and in 2030[viii] they will be perhaps too old. The 1990s generation of politicians will strengthen their peers. The angry ones well recognize that the Gyurcsány-led opposition is not interested in a change of government, as most senior politicians would like to secure a stable second place in their downstream

viii Orbán, in his 2018 Tusnádfürdő speech, outlined his plans until 2030.

careers. Free Democrat politicians fell out of politics ten years before retirement. Given the 2030 target date, LMP (Politics May Be Different) and right-wing politicians—also a generation of the seventies—may first breath fresh air five to ten years before retirement. Besides, most Hungarians who emigrated to other EU Member States were born in the seventies and eighties, too. LMP and right-wing politicians representing this generation have a much more difficult task than parties that target later or earlier generations. For example, the socialists, the new-wave parties, or even Fidesz, which reached 80% support among the youth in the 1990s and took this generation with them, broadening it with their parents and children. Generational structures also cement the fate of the Hungarian opposition.

In Hungary, culture often means copying Western patterns. Perhaps this is why Hungary has few significant artists because although they are gifted, they lack originality. For example, the rooms of the Ludwig Contemporary Museum in Budapest are wallpapered with such high-quality works that they fit into the mainstream. The generation that grew up on the supremacy of liberal aesthetics has not even guessed about America inspired Orbán's art, because the product in appearance does not resemble America at all. With the Free Democrats, one always felt the influence of liberalism and the worship of the French Enlightenment, and with Ferenc Gyurcsány, the flow of Tony Blair and the British Labour Party. Let's admit that Viktor Orbán first learned politics by copying, Fidesz initially tried to implement the heritage of the beat generation's lifestyle into Hungarian politics. After the conservative turn, Helmut Kohl and the legacy of German Christian Democrats inspired Orbán's politics, which he tried to emulate in the Hungarian context.

Orbán's policy has been original since 2010 and has since found its voice. Why don't his opponents consider this voice democratic? Because in their rage, they couldn't figure out anything better. Most of the books on Orbán are hostile. Even friendlier biographies only show events in a chronological order without considering one key question: why Viktor Orbán differs from other politicians. This book changes the framework in which intellectuals so far interpreted Viktor Orbán. Through American-centric applied sciences, I seek to present the secret of Viktor Orbán's success.

# 17

# The Self-Made Workout 2.0

Why 2.0? Because this book is the second one inspired by Viktor Orbán. My book, *The Self-Made Workout*, promotes fitness. The book is entirely free of politics, though Orbán (and his opposition) inspired me. How to spoil your workout? And how not to mess it up.

The mission of *The Self-Made Workout* is to make muscular physics more accessible to my generation of male peers. I wanted to give like-minded intellectuals a friendly user's guide to help them to be able to change their lives. I wrote the book to encourage my generation to take action, provide a non-athletic intellectual a handbook, and convince them of the importance of training. So far, I haven't been able to break down the wall between intellectuals and gyms. Maybe after reading this book, they will be inspired to get more exercise.

Like all other men, I have always wanted to be more muscular throughout my life. Growing up, I settled on the fact sports were not for me. In the words of Susan Cain, as a *quiet* introvert, I bought into misconceptions about people like me and I did not believe in exercise. When I realized a different approach to training, my life changed. As a Doctor of Law, I became a personal trainer and, with this qualification, wrote a book with an intellectual tone. *The Self-Made Workout* is about raising fitness training to a higher level, beyond merely 'pumping iron.' The secret made me realize that you can't understand Orbán's politics from the type of books that claims to know the essence of politics but from the type of publication that offers a training guide or manual. As you experience the magic, you'll discover the secret during kettlebell sets and street workout drills.

I understood Orbán, and the intellectuals' attitude toward him, from strength conditioning and self-made man role models. For me, Viktor Orbán's life is a self-made workout. The personal experience of the training led to many realizations. Why and how does a disadvantage become an advantage? How does overcoming a difficulty become a source of strength? There is only one way to win: to take no shortcuts.

"Practically, not just theoretically, the *self-made* way is the only right way. Building strength comes primarily from our *own sources,*" as József Szájer, the leading thinker of Fidesz, said.[ix]

"If we stop the decline in population, foster our families, we will do our job wisely and diligently. By making our economy competitive, reindustrializing our country, making it fair to bear the burden formerly on the rich, putting an end to stifling debt, defending our borders and people's security with a strong army, re-uniting the lifeblood of our great nation, standing up for ourselves, working together with our friends and partners so joint action contributes to our success. That is if we trust ourselves. Self-power, success comes from within."

ix Highlights are my own.

# 18

# Sports Democracy

" *The popular caricature of me is an authoritarian tyrant with a lust for power. Not surprisingly, I beg to differ. I'll plead guilty to having a thirst for winning and being fixated on maintaining complete control, but […] those are requisites for effective leadership. The skipper of any ship incapable of controlling its course, or altering its speed is not going to arrive safely in port. The same goes for a football club. A leader who seeks to take control is very different from one who craves power.* "

In his book *Leading*, Sir Alex Ferguson, Britain's most successful football club manager of all time, writes. The Master retired in 2013, and in 2015, with the contribution of Sir Michael Moritz, published his autobiographical book summarizing his managerial experiences. Thirty-eight cup trophies (five FA Cups, thirteen Premier League, and two Champions League) are credited to his leadership at Manchester United.

Viktor Orbán built his power on the model of football (soccer). His government resembles a football club, of which he is the manager: Fidesz is the club team's support camp; Hungary is the field; opposition is the rival team; Hungary's constitution—The Fundamental Law—set the rules of the game. This novel system rewards different qualities and personality traits in which Orbán outperforms his rivals.

Anyone who wants to understand Orbán must first change his perspective. For Viktor Orbán, football is not a "royal fad."

Football is not a hobby. It is not for fun, and it is not about spending time either, but about learning. For him, something like a hobby doesn't exist. "Everyone gets up in the morning for something different: for Viktor Orbán it's politics." He lives for power, not for football, but football inspires his power. Football works like an operating system that controls computers, an algorithm to define your thinking. As simple as it sounds, it's as effective. Just as artificial intelligence needs learning to give its algorithm more and more accurate answers, in Orbán's world, football games play this role. The world simplifies into two sides. Two teams face each other, and two stories must be set up. He implements the movement pattern of the sport to a speculative level and forms his policy by the logic of "relevant, non-relevant," "or-or," "and."

Orbán's patriotism, encouragement, and national union builds on sports. The stadium symbolizes the Carpathian Basin. The fans are the Hungarian people, and the national team is the government. Here is where Orbán's motto comes from: "Go, Hungary! Go, Hungarians!" The work-based economy, one of the main principles of Orbán's politics, also stems from sports. Sport teaches the lesson of hard work and diligence guarantee results.

### DISCIPLINE. WORK-ETHIC. CONVICTION. FOUNDATION. TEAMWORK.

"I was to help everyone else believe things they didn't think they were capable of. [...] It was to make everyone understand that the impossible was possible. That's the difference between leadership and management."

If we look at Ferguson's principles for leading Manchester, we will return without exception to Orbán. With Orbán's opposition, however, we find the opposite. It is not the case that Orbán established a dictatorship. In fact, Orbán may not even need a dictatorship to rule by two-thirds. For the opposition, this situation is much more overwhelming—one could at least expect a dictatorship to collapse eventually.

Two of Manchester's world-class players, David Beckham and Cristiano Ronaldo, owe their worldwide success to talent and untold dedication. For the socialist Prime Ministers, this was not the case. Neither Horn, Medgyessy, Gyurcsány, nor Bajnai gained power by building a social base. Instead, a circle of the socialist-liberal elites chose them. People followed Orbán for his talent, but socialist candidates earned the following because a small group of people decided so and confronted the voters with their pre-ordained decision.

Post-regime arrangements favored the election in which the left-liberal media constructed the candidate, not the candidate himself. Orbán has built a system that spells out democracy different. The winning team takes it all in, so the laws of gaining power are those of winning the football match. Players' diligence is more important than their *talent*. The importance of training, the planned construction of the elections, is increased— coordinated team play matters, not individual play. Orbán's sports democracy has two main features that make the difference: the performance of athletes as a team and the will of the people.

THOSE WHO CRY FASCISM DO NOT BELIEVE THAT A POLITICIAN CAN MAINTAIN power by himself. Indeed, they themselves would be unable to do so. The American concept of democracy sets up a system of checks and balances as restricting power while limiting freedom. The people's right to free choice—the so-called main tradition of liberal democracy is that the system of checks and balances is itself anti-democratic. Because of various gatekeepers and controlling mechanisms, the system will filter out putatively dangerous candidates, meaning that it may not be possible for anyone popular among the people to come close to power.

Instead, one can only become a presidential candidate who is approved by the gatekeepers and party supervisors first. The same worldview of the gatekeepers, irrespective of party affiliation, may be the reason the entire American electorate lines up behind the American presidents.

Donald J. Trump was the first to break this tradition. The book *How Democracies Die* admits that the American presidential system has prevented anyone from gaining the presidential nomination. Some people don't like the Trump presidency because his life story is a primer in attaining social class, a billionaire reality-show celebrity, that they consider inappropriate for the president's office. Trump's rise to power is a failure of American democracy, arguing he has played the gatekeepers of the Republican Party. For his reputation and the power of social media, he hypnotized people with his charisma and demagogic lies. They blame the democratized internet for not having the checking mechanisms that the founding fathers built into the system. President Trump's link to Viktor Orbán is they both owe their power to the core ideology of democracy-warfare: they broke the rule of the kingmakers and connected with the people.

# 19

# Brains and Sports

Philosophers and film critics do not consider the Ferguson regime a dictatorship, though Manchester United has dominated the world of football for twenty-seven years. Why would bibliophiles and cinephiles, who grew up on Immanuel Kant and Jack Kerouac, invent such insanity?

Perhaps because sports play a secondary role in the life of masterminds, who are people of the brain. It is not physical exercise that determines their mindset. Working out means something else for them, a hobby rather than a lifestyle. The intellectual attitude is introverted—one reason strength training repels many intellectuals and not just because of its implied extroversion. The fitness industry is harsh, often aggressive, and it lacks sophistication—from the design of gyms to the music on offer and the clientele. An introverted or intellectual person is more sensitive to the smallest details, which sometimes evoke fascism, on either an assumed or on a sound basis. It is a challenge for an introvert to treasure and even enjoy this world.

Bodybuilding is like America: others shall admire or fear you and you believe in yourself.

"Whether a sign of virility, the manifest reward of hard work, or a badge of self-confidence, a buff-body delivered untold benefits," writes Jonathan Black in his book *Making The American Body* that was evangelized by Joe Weider, the father of bodybuilding, who made bodybuilding the most popular form of workout in the twentieth century. Bodybuilding is the rise of "modern fascism" that has transformed into fitness since the 1970s and has become the world's leading recreational movement. Through the case study of iron-pumping, I would like to reveal the distortion.

In Umberto Eco's essay, *Ur-Fascism*, the cultural theorist lists fourteen general properties of fascist ideology, almost all of which echoed in the gym. Bodybuilding is characterized by the cult of tradition, a glorious past, the worship of strongmen, or bodybuilding legends. Pagan mythological symbols or military tunes often define the visual theme of functional or Spartan training. The cult of action, 'Just do it,' is the cult of heroism: "no struggle for life, but life is lived for struggle." In locker room talk, often out of ignorance, one hears conspiracy theories, sexism, stories about boozing, and even anti-Semitism or racist remarks. Elitism is a typical aspect of fascism: fitness clubs' business model thrives on 'popular elitism,' and group exercises thrive on 'qualitative populism.'

What usually scares the man of brains is the cult of the strong. In physical training, everything revolves around strength—training which in particular subordinates all types of conditioning, and values everything in its own currency. The Italian word *fascismo* comes from the Latin fasces, which was a symbol of the ancient Roman magistrate, a bound bundle of wooden rods, sometimes including an ax with its blade emerging, symbolizing the power of unity. The foundation of strength conditioning is the synchronization of muscle fibers, and from this perspective, the developing strength is building a "fascist dictatorship" over your muscles.

Viktor Orbán's *"fascism"* is strength conditioning. He did indeed adopt the technique of building power, but he did not copy the fascists but athletes. And did not build a dictatorship, but America. They interpret it as a dictatorship because it does not copy America aesthetic but drew from Hungarian traditions. In the following chapters, I would like to prove that Viktor Orbán rose to the top because he was better than his rivals. And he stayed on top for the same reason. Because, as Viktor Orbán quoted Mark Twain: "It is not the size of the dog in the fight, it's the size of the fight in the dog."

# 20

# Intellects and Fair Play

Viktor Orbán was a young man in the Kádár era and two big ideas influenced his thinking at that time: football and America. Both are legacies of a working man's dreams under communism. Sports had an overvalued prestige in the socialist world. Living under a communist dictatorship, a worker saw the land of promise as the United States, the dream world of America.

The underground narrative interprets Viktor Orbán with the help of two keywords: self-power and strength training. It was Orbán's innovation to introduce a new way of thinking into the rule of politics by which he outperformed all rivalry. By taking inspiration from a world beyond the dogma of political science and state philosophy, therefore, his rule can only be described to a limited extent with orthodox concepts.

*We listened to the radio with my grandfather [Mihály Orbán] since I was five or six. I knew the precise results of the national football league. Not only did I know who was first and who was last, but also who was in sixth and seventh place.*

The socialist dictatorship privileged top athletes and many people have found it an attractive career. The Golden Team, also known as the Mighty Magyars, marks the golden age of Hungarian football. Viktor Orbán had a childhood dream of becoming a professional footballer. Ferenc Puskás was his number one role model, a superhero in Hungarian football, the legendary striker of the Golden Team who became a world-famous star with Real Madrid. Today, the former People's Stadium bears his name, while the Pancho Arena in Orbán's birth town, Felcsút, bears his Real Madrid nickname.

Puskás stands in as a role model for a politician because he was a master of skill, feat, aplomb, and strategy. Many interpret Orbán's political talent as his understanding of these connections, of being three-four steps ahead of others and the world. His life's thesis is football; its antithesis is law; the synthesis is politics.

Ferenc Puskás: "All football depends on deception. I must fool my opponent: if he goes right when I pull to the left, I win. [...] The winner is the one who tricks his opponent more times. Or if that doesn't work, he'll mislead the judge. There's one ball for twenty-two people. If you don't trick the other player, how do you get the ball? Go beyond your opponent's mind, play him out, mislead him, else he does it, and he becomes the winner."

For the generations growing up under the communist dictatorship, it was not only football that had prestige, but America too. The legacy of communism is anti-communism, the turn towards America. Ronald Reagan's politics and the struggle to overthrow communism also became part of young Orbán's program. During his university years, he was educated in a left-wing liberal environment, his teachers, his fellow college students, and later the founders of Fidesz were rebellious young folks of the beat generation.

"We believed in liberalism. We saw no other way out. For us, liberalism meant America, freedom, and independence. Our favorite movie was Easy Rider and we read Salinger, Kerouac, and Updike. We loved freedom. We went to concerts every weekend. [...] I wanted to go to America. That was my big dream. But then

Fidesz came in the picture. For me, it was a whole new thing. A revolution. A burst. Kövér and Orbán, they knew where they were going. I haven't come this far. We just wanted a rebellion." (Zsolt Bayer)

From the outset, the Orbáns preached freedom, the message of freedom of education and sexual liberation wraps the rebellion of young democratic intellectuals in the metaphor of the kiss: "Make a choice!" reads the gag poster that defines Fidesz's identity to this day. One the upper half is a photo of Brezhnev and Honecker kissing on the lips, while the bottom picture shows the same act by a young couple. Accompanying the witty poster was Roxette's *Listen to Your Heart* hit, which has been Fidesz's anthem ever since. This line inspired the memorable slogan of Fidesz: "Listen to your heart, vote for Fidesz!" It is the influence of America that made Fidesz into the fresh brand of freedom and love.

**THERE ARE NO RULES OF THE GAME IN A DICTATORSHIP. WHERE THERE** are no rules of the game, there is no fair play. Therefore, from the outset, Orbán fought to get the parties to agree on the laws of the game first, knowing that this was the only way he could have a chance. He trusted his inner ability to deal with the handicap, provided the game was democratic. Free competition, market competition results from America's influence. Orbán wanted nothing more than to compete, and in this, he proved to be stronger than his rivals.

> So for us Hungarians it is also good that we have now unless they don't want to change the rules of the game. Because, if the current rules of the game remain unchanged, then we, Hungarians are gifted enough to find our calculations alongside these rules of the game. Just don't change the rules of the game during the match.

Dictators design the rules book so that others cannot compete. Orbán is just the opposite. The system rewards work and diligence more than following the dominant status quo. Another issue is that with practice and persistence, you can gain a dominant position.

In Orbán's system, the entry threshold for democracy is shallow, in contrast to the extreme or nonexistent lower limits of dictatorships. Within the Orbánian electoral system, a group of youngsters in their twenties can get together and get into Parliament. The system favors Orbán not because he is the most potent political force, but because he will work harder. His desire for victory is always stronger, ready to work harder, and takes his opponents dead serious. Unlike his opponents, who are not interested in winning and who void hard work, underestimate him time and again.

IT IS THE MOST HUMILIATING INSULT TO ACCUSE A TOP-PERFORMING athlete of unsportsmanlike behavior. The socialists-liberals defeated Orbán in two elections by character assassination, by attributing to him a personality cult, and depicting him demonically as a corrupt tyrant. The first reaction of the Orbáns was what everyone would do in a similar situation, to try convincing people that this was not the case. After two failed elections, Orbán switched tactics. Rather than trying to change people's worldviews, he turned a headwind to a backwind. 'If the people think of you as having divine power and your enemies think of you as being a dictator, the more you act like that, the more you strengthen them in their worldview.' And the more they will trust in you.

Football has few rules; everything that is not forbidden is legitimate. Whoever scores more goals in the match will win. A final game can only have one winner. Orbán took advantage of his opponents' lack of skill. Why not, as everyone may choose his fighting style. The stronger defeated the weak. His opponents entered the ring and were knocked out in the first minute. What is not is okay to push away the responsibility and to blame others for the loss. There may only be one winner of a game, and anyone who enters the ring must evaluate the risk of a knock-out. Folks like to forget that it wasn't Orbán who hit first. Sportsmanship does not mean I cannot take advantage of my opponent's weakness. That would be losership.

Breaking the rules of the game is not unfair. In football, one can trespass the rules. At most, the player gets one yellow card, in case of a severe violation or after two yellow cards, a red card, and the judge awards a free-kick or penalties ad absurdum. Technical skill is not unfair either. Anyone who has been misled, injured, lost a position, or needs the status quo will have a conflict of interest. It is a natural human reaction to shift responsibility, as is blaming others. However, Viktor Orbán was never looking for excuses, but for a solution. In 2002 he began to reorganize the right, and in 2006 he recovered, even though he felt deceived, and determined that the way out was not self-pity and complaint, but the drive that is burned into the minds of top athletes: I will not give up.

Viktor Orbán plays fair. Whoever assumes the opposite, reveals himself.

Viktor Orbán did not demolish democracy, only its entry threshold. He created the rivalry between parties on the model of free-market competition, which I call political capitalism. As the American free market favors giant corporations, so too does Hungarian electoral laws favor larger parties. So, let's rephrase the latter: electoral law rewards the greatest prevailing worldview. Where there is a shared worldview, cooperation can thrive.

# 21

# The Underground Narrative

If one were to sum up the secret of Viktor Orbán's success in one word, would be America. That's why it works. The idea behind the whole system is America's spirit. It is an internal narrative of the desire to win based on teamwork and an external story of power-driven action. Orbán did not copy America but adopted its way of thinking through the art of deconstruction and reconstruction of Hungarian traditions and history. Studying and training in his childhood inspired him to overcome his opponents' cultural supremacy and even outperform them. He built politics on the paradigm of football as a team sport. Its strategy follows the pattern of strength conditioning along sports training principles. He designed the government's layout in the style of a football club's and interpreted political feuds as a football match. The strategy is the training program of national cooperation and its tactics are disruption of the status quo.

Politics becomes storytelling based on people's worldview. Orbán reinterpreted Hungarians' vision, aiming for a strong Hungary and a united Hungarian nation so that Hungary plays a more prominent role in the world relative to its size. This vision is to raise Hungary to the forefront of Europe and the world. Glowing power and shining confidence support the belief that everything is possible—if you want it enough. He outlined what Hungary needed to become a country of success: national unity, sovereignty, and Christianity. America has become the exemplar:

the mightiest Christian (Protestant) and free country in the world.

He understands the changes taking place in the world and plans a vision for the future that allows people to express their worldviews. He is a handshaker politician, not a theoretical philosopher. He is a master at his craft. Orbán's unique trait, which distinguishes him from other politicians, is versatility to operate at all levels of society. No one handles the masses, and no one builds a team like him. He is an exceptional decisionmaker, even in a crisis.

He embodies his politics in archetypes—the renaissance man, visionary, ruler, leader, coach, superstar, minister, and father.

You need a vision, a story, and a protagonist with an identity that compels the character. Action makes the character, who builds a worldview and outlines the story. The protagonist tells the story through a variety of role models: the self-inventing superstar, the visionary founder, or the mythological hero. Strength ties vision and character together—by the power of the protagonist, we believe in the power of Hungary.

You need to begin by building strength so that more people will trust in your invincibility, friends and foes alike. The source of power is the people, so you must first create the story within. At first comes a shared worldview and trust builds upon it. Empowerment stands on trust, creates action, and action becomes power. Power will reinforce belief, forcing the system into a self-reinforcing cycle. The voter is a member of a political community and a piece of the nation. The cohesive power of citizens is a shared vision of the Hungarian nation's future, faith in patriotism, personified by its trusted leader, and all in the form of a shared worldview.

Talk is not enough. You must also make strength tangible. Government is competence, action, and agility. The economy is performing well. The security of the country is guaranteed.

Conviction is beyond facts: the brotherly love of a national union, the emotional world of sports, and Christian symbolism. Hungarian history and Hungarian traditions provide the framework for the story.

Orbán has introduced humanity's brilliant inventions to the world of politics, systems that have been running for centuries and even millenia. Through these systems, the protagonist tells his own story: the story of Hungary. He touched the beliefs, fears, and innermost desires of the Hungarians—delivered by images and symbols. Viktor Orbán created a worldview. He forged a political union and all of it was self-made. So, let's begin our story here: **VIKTOR ORBÁN IS THE SELF-MADE MAN OF HUNGARIAN POLITICS.**

# 22

# The Self-Made Man

What is the secret of Viktor Orbán's success? We don't know, and that's why it's a secret. It's a personal spiritual experience, everyone experiences it themselves. However, as external observers, we can ask how and what made him successful. What qualities, abilities, patterns of action, and lifestyle habits made him invincible?

At first, the method is to seek answers, not just in the political sphere. Success is an abstract concept, independent of a specific profession. Second, let's not start with our emotions, but with the position of an outside observer, instead of blind hatred or worship. Third, the world in which we live has changed. The past thirty years should be our framework of interpretation, anything beyond leads us astray.

Control over internal and external narratives is a feature of a *mensch*, a self-made man.

The obsession with pulling oneself up by the bootstraps is one of the most significant marks of the second half of the twentieth century, and it cannot be ignored if one wants to understand Viktor Orbán. Writing your own story makes a self-made man a self-made man. 'I'm here now, and I want to be there.' He decides what kind of person he will be, not others. So too does he decide what his life is about, what he believes in, and what ideas determine his understanding of the world. He writes his own narrative on a blank slate.

The self-made man originally referred to a person from a poor or other disadvantaged background who broke the peak in financial, political, or other fields because of traits such as perseverance and hard work, as opposed to those who inherited their wealth, family relationships, or other privileges. In another approach, the self-made man is the player who takes advantage of the disadvantaged. This is the phenomenon of the second half of the twentieth century, the self-inventing superstar, the founder prophet, or the archetype of the sports role model: Bob Dylan, Steve Jobs, Arnold Schwarzenegger. A common thread connects each of their narratives: they discover resources for overcoming their disadvantages. Would Orbán be the archetype of the myth-creating superstar, a defier of the status quo, and the motivational guru?

I also wrote this book from an American perspective. Accordingly, it does not interpret Viktor Orbán's politics through political examples, but in a different context that goes beyond the dogma of political science. Entertainment, technology, and the business world have produced self-made mannequins like Orbán, but politics has not. Orbán, like Bob Dylan, Arnold Schwarzenegger, and Steve Jobs, is beyond jealousy and distortion but has not been treated as such so far because he is alone.

*Fidesz is a true self-made story. The Fidesz story is about ten to twenty or thirty guys coming from somewhere. Fed up with the world that surrounds them, rebel, flip their collars, and make it happen.*

Politics has been slow to catch up with the deluge of self-made men. The constitutional arrangements of individual countries and international treaties holds back progress. It is challenging to jump over the threshold of democracy when burdened with concrete structures and held back by lack of a network of relationships which makes it almost impossible to break through the rigors of interest. By the time a gifted politician becomes head of government, he has grown older in politics. Checks and balances, lobbying interests, internal enemies, pressure from the public, and the opposition limits his mobility. Orbán was at least twenty years more mature than his age, the first real self-made politician of the twentieth century to break the glass ceiling and change the status quo on his own merits. He was fortunate to become a member of Parliament at twenty, and at fifty-six he is only at the end of his first half.

*Character is something you can't learn. And there, in Fidesz, strong characters came into the community. People who count on themselves and each other. That's why Fidesz is more modern than any of its current rivals. When we get stuck in some things, we can shake ourselves, look around at the world, read, study, show interest in the new things of the world. It maintains a certain amount of mental excitement for us, but it comes more from character than from education.*

# 23

# Superstar

" The young man has no biography. Not that hundreds of journalists were not following him, not as if he had turned down interviews—at least for the six months of the year when he feels strong and willing to talk. As he explains, he was born under the constellation of Gemini [...], and the Gemini-borns have a versatile and fluid spirit, living half of a year with an open mind and revealing to the world, while the other six months are for introversion, submersion, disappearance. Born in the month of Gemini, he otherwise held a remarkable prose name. [...] The first [...] peoples' leader, superstar who invented his name, fame, character, biography from childhood to the present. Constantly rewriting it, adapting it to the fans' and youth's imagination [...], so he has two biographies: a real one that we hardly know anything about, and an imaginary one [...] of his imagination [...] that has woven into a myth."

This quote by writer-historian Tamás Ungvári sheds light on the essence of Viktor Orbán's identity: he flips the collar and makes things happen. The original quote is not about Viktor Orbán, but about a literary Nobel laureate who "... held to a remarkable prose name: Robert Allen Zimmerman. [...] Starting on August 9, 1962, officially Bob Dylan—the first solo singer artist, guitarist, peoples' leader, superstar who invented his name, fame, character from childhood to the present. Constantly rewriting it, adapting it to the fans' and youth's imagination. So Bob Dylan has two biographies: a real one that we hardly know anything about, and an imaginary one of Bob Dylan's fantasy (or the tough tactics of his manager's), that has woven into a myth."

Borne of the Gemini, Orbán's nymph is lauded with adoration and fame. His statements burst into public awareness. It is attributed to his charisma for being able to influence the masses, who trust him as their leader by conviction, and persists no matter what. Finding his own voice, his inner narrative is what I call identity. The mature character of today's Viktor Orbán results from four or five decades of evolution, namely as a political superstar who routinely triumphs with two-thirds of the political majority.

In the second half of the twentieth century, the music industry produced the first constructed characters, the first icons of self-realization. With a little exaggeration, Orbán's character is that of such a constructed superstar.

He improvises like Keith Jarrett and conducts like John Williams. A freebird, like Lenny Kravitz or Jimi Hendrix. A freedom fighter like Bono. Not as theatrical as Freddie Mercury. Not a prodigy like Michael Jackson. Skilled but not as eloquent as Elton John, nor as divisive as Prince. Hungarian like Paul Simon. His younger version is more Bruno Mars than Justin Bieber. He's not the archetype of John Lennon's or Mick Jagger's atheist worldview, though he belongs in the same weight category. His talent is not drawn from organic rawness like Eminem's, nor is he just a remixer like Moby or a distinct singer like Rod Stewart. He's not as schmoozing as Frank Sinatra, nor as theatrical as Leonard Cohen. He has a great sense of rhythm, a cult, and in the eyes of many he is a king like Elvis Aron Presley.

His body type is Fatboy Slim. He does not flatter with his smile as Robbie Williams nor with his charm as Julio Iglesias, nor is he as charismatic as Joe Cocker. Multi-faceted like David Bowie. Intellectual like Eric Clapton: they both *want to change the world.*

More extroverted than Sting, but less so than George Michael. Not flat like Phil Collins and not as predictable as Paul McCartney either. More disciplined than Kurt Cobain and a rocker in the tradition AC/DC's Bon Scott, only less wild. He's into hymns, without becoming Axl Rose. Folk, yet country like Johnny Cash, cinematic, yet kitschy like Vangelis, yet very far from Marilyn Manson, too. Not a one-song entertainer like the Muslim Cat Stevens or the Catholic Don McLean. Doesn't tittle-tattle like a rapper, but more talkative than blues. He plays the difference, like the world-class Stevie Wonder. Almost Bruce Springsteen.

**THE TWO ELEMENTS OF STORYTELLING BASED ON PEOPLE'S WORLDVIEW ARE** a worldview and storytelling. Two of the essential storytelling genres of the twentieth century are Billboard hit singles and Hollywood blockbusters. Pop music performers are often songwriters and lyricists themselves, with a unique and mature style. The first connection, however, is not this feature, but Viktor Orbán's explosive entry into the public. Like most musical talents, Viktor Orbán became an overnight success. József Debreczeni described the superstar's narrative as "a combination of extraordinary fortune and extraordinary talent."

My father used to say that the difference between talent and genius is that talent recognizes new truths, and genius re-tells old truths. On June 16, 1989, at the reburial of Imre Nagy and his associates as a young democrat, the self-made statesman made history with these words:

> *If we believe in our own power, we will put an end to the*
> *communist dictatorship. If we are determined enough, we*
> *can force the ruling party to submit to free elections. If we do*
> *not lose sight of the ideas of '56, we can choose a government*
> *that will immediately begin negotiations for the immediate*

*withdrawal of the Russian troops. If we dare to want all of*
*this, but only then, can we fulfill the will of our revolution. No*
*one can expect that the party-state will change by itself.*

Twenty-six-year-old Viktor Orbán's speech was also motivating
because he was re-telling eternal truths. "If we believe in our
own power, we will end ..."; "If we are determined enough, we
can force ..."; we can choose a life for ourselves ...; "If we dare to
want it all, then we can only fulfill it ..." No one can expect that
our life will change by itself.

I COULD UNDERSTAND THE UNIQUENESS OF VIKTOR ORBÁN'S
performance starting from Bob Dylan's. A legend built on the
Gemini-duality links Dylan's life with Viktor Orbán's identity.
Two trendsetters. The duality of folk and protest, the rebellion
expressed in a ballad made with folk motifs, the story of a man
standing alone in the world. Either of Hungarians or Hungarians
across the border. The parallel between folk and protest is also
the genesis of Fidesz, the rebellion of country boys against the
communist system.

Dylan's art is storytelling weaved in ballads. In 1963, he wrote
his album *The Times They Are A-Changin'* and its eponymous
protest song. The ballad is the story of Viktor Orbán, including
Hungary's vision, the ascendance of a winner:

*For the loser now*
*Will be later to win*
*For the times they are a-changin'*
The ballad also delivers a warning to the opposition:

*And admit that the waters*
*Around you have grown*

*[...]*
*The line it is drawn*
*The curse it is cast*

Will Bob Dylan reflect Viktor Orbán? Is the impression of a large-format statesman and a simple countryman, just like the superstar standing in front of tens of thousands and the harmonicist in jeans? Performing arts and high culture, a charismatic leader stirring up the masses and a re-thinker of the Hungarian state philosophy?

Dylan and Orbán are both playing for their audience. They are each benchmarks of a new era. Visionary *Tambourine Men*. Lyrical beyond words, *Knockin 'On Heaven's Door* embodies the symbolism of European culture: Christian morals, Greek philosophy, and the sense of justice in Roman law, and yet Dylan's rebellion is characteristically American, just as Orbán's rebellion is typically Hungarian. The song *Blowin' in The Wind* contains visual perception of hearing, words, metaphors, allegories, frame-by-frame, the evolution of becoming. The universality of their art includes everything that the second half of the twentieth century is about: *Things Have Changed*.

"Transylvania's peculiar genre is the ballad, this complex form that is part drama, part story, part verse, and the whole inkling, obscure and shocking," writes Béla Hamvas. In response, a quote from one of the world's most famous ballads:

*How does it feel, how does it feel?*
*To be without a home*
*Like a complete unknown, like a rolling stone*

After the Trianon, the Transylvanian Hungarians became orphans, just as the Hungarians stand alone among the mainstream of the European nations. Of the seven billion inhabitants of the planet Earth, every five-hundredth is Hungarian-born. Viktor Orbán is the cure for their traumatic fate. *Like a Rolling Stone* is our verse.

# 24

# Drawbacks Make Assets

If the self-made man is a player who overcomes hindrances, then the starting point of the next story is Steve Jobs, who launches Apple from a garage and becomes a prophet of the digital revolution. The self-made man of the digital revolution imagines the future. He challenges the status quo with the personal computer, the digital music player, and the magic smartphone and rethinks humanity's future on the Internet. He envisions how we might live our future and gives us the tools to live it. He drops the entry barrier for technology and thus democratizes the world. While Steve Jobs was free to create his products, customers were likewise free to decide to adopt them. A politician could not revolutionize the world so thoroughly.

Both Steve Jobs and Viktor Orbán had limited resources to achieve their breakouts. Their charisma, diligence, and imagination compensated for their rivals' dominance. Their cultural background, or as Orbán put it, "lack of culture," i.e., lack of traditions and roots, allowed them to choose their own identities. Steve Jobs reinterpreted Kriya Yoga, the Enlightenment, and American mass culture. Orbán reinterpreted what makes for a Hungarian, European, and Transylvanian and everything in between. The syncretism of the two is different, yet similar in the regard that they both built their identities on blank slates.

IT MAY SEEM CLEAR THAT ORBÁN'S CHILDHOOD WAS TOUGH.
The malicious say that childhood traumas caused Orbán's
domineering personality; they say that because he grew up in
poverty, he developed a sense of inferiority that he, as Prime
Minister, compensated for with megalomaniacal tendencies.

> *For example, while I was living in the village, I never had jeans.*
> *Country fashion differs from urban. It was a difficult transition.*
> *I felt like I was a villager. The photographs at the time show me*
> *wearing all the signs of rural life. It could also have collided*
> *with my speech. But I got into an excellent class and made a lot*
> *of friends. Coming from a village is not only a disadvantage; it*
> *can also give you strength, self-confidence, determination, and*
> *empowerment. And if you have the right self-awareness and*
> *take pride in where you come from, you will earn esteem.*

What are the circumstances that influence a child's
development? Authors Steven D. Levitt and Stephen J. Dubner
of the bestseller *Freakonomics* sought answers to this question.
They referred to a research paper on parenting. The study paired
questions and investigated the factors that correlate with the test
scores. I'd rather say the results.

It does not correlate if the child's family is intact (parents have
not divorced), the child's parents recently moved into a better
neighborhood, the child's mother didn't work between birth and
kindergarten, or the child has attended Head Start. It matters if
the child has highly educated parents, the child's parents have high
socioeconomic status, the child's mother was thirty or older at the
time of her first child's birth, or the child had low birth weight.

A child's development is unaffected if he is regularly spanked
or if the child frequently watches television. What matters is if
the child is adopted or if his parents are involved in a PTA (Parent-

Teacher Association). And what's surprising is that, according to research, there's no correlation if a child's parents read to him every day or if his parents regularly take him to museums. There is a correlation between a child's development and how many books are in his home, or the child's parents speak their native language in the house.

*– Did you have many books?*
*– A lot. […] Although the family had to count every penny, they always bought books.*

In Orbán's case, he met the all eight pairs of questions because, despite growing up in poverty and sometimes receiving a paternal spank, 'what the parents did' was more relevant to his development. Viktor Orbán's mother, Erzsébet Sípos, worked as a teacher for children with special needs, and his father, Győző Orbán, was head at the local mine. Coincidentally, Győző means winner in Hungarian.

*I want to say something about my grandfather. He was forty-eight when he graduated from high school. He didn't need a graduation; he only wanted to prove he could do it. It also became a family tradition. Maybe that's where the love of books comes from, reading the newspaper, and learning. I remember my mother was pregnant with my second brother when she graduated from Gusztáv Bárczi Teacher's College. And in the same year, my father also graduated as an agricultural engineer, also with an adult's head. I remember when I was a kid that everyone in the family always went to school.*

As Orbán recalled in this interview, everyone at home always studied, and when he needed a book, his parents bought it for him. His parents' attitude followed the findings of *Freakonomics*: when parents care about their children, they flourish in the right direction.

> *The best four years of my life so far have been the time I spent at the club MÁV Előre IFI. MÁV Előre was then a team playing in the national cup, NB I. It meant honor playing football there. Not blessed with any football talent, it meant working a lot to get into the team. […] When I changed soccer teams, I always changed cultures.*

So what was the real cause of Viktor Orbán's successes? The underground interpretation is that he did not have enough talent for football. He had to train to get onto the team, even though his technique was lacking. He could only compensate for his lack of football talent with diligence, by practicing several hours every day for many years. He had no other choice but to train. If he did not do so, he would lose his place on the football team and lose his friends. He had the power of self-sufficiency: he foregrounded the workout in his mind, visualizing it on the mental plane. It was then that he could absorb the essence of the sport: everything depended on diligence and how hard you worked for it. Hence the general principle of the work-based society, which not only guides Orbán's economic policy but all his policies; his work-ethic made him the terminator of Hungarian politics.

**THE NEXT PARABLE IS ABOUT ARNOLD SCHWARZENEGGER AND VIKTOR** Orbán. The two terminators, who both gave a higher sense of meaning to training. Both programmed the sport's movement pattern into an algorithm that operates their thinking. The career built on bodybuilding's reps, reps, and reps, the workout plan built on self-discipline, and patience, made Arnold Schwarzenegger—

to become a bodybuilding champion from an Austrian village, then a movie star, Governor of California, and a role model.

Orbán built his power on the paradigm of football and the training-principles of top athletes—the story of the chosen leader and the ruler. Their mindset of sports is the way of overcoming the drawbacks of their lives. Schwarzenegger breaks out of poverty as a bodybuilding champion. Orbán overcomes the deficiencies of his football talent and transfers that skill and power into college, and further into politics.

My starting point is Viktor Orbán is that authentic, and I assume that he is a sportsman. My worldview—call it biased if you like—is that in the long run, you can only train persistently if you are authentic, and since Orbán has made himself by training hard, he cannot be a fake.

Sports success deceives most people by veiling the effort that went into the results. A world-class "athlete," like the two-time Kossuth Prize-winning pianist master Dezső Ránki, practices six to eight hours a day, even though he has been on the top for over forty years. We suppose that being gifted is enough and that the rest comes by itself. Paul Lendvai used to emphasize that Viktor Orbán is one of the most talented politicians. Perhaps by highlighting Orbán's talent, Lendvai can shirk responsibility for his side's loss because Viktor Orbán does not owe his success to an ability that only a few possess. If success is a matter of work, you cannot shrug off the opposition's burden of responsibility, and there's no moral basis for whining.

When the liberal intellectuals decided from fear in the early 1990s to break up with Orbán, they did not recognize the athlete in his character. They saw talent floating on the surface, but they did not see the immeasurable effort that he put into fighting for it. They started with themselves, who attained their knowledge at home, who never had to break out of the world of ignorance and climb into the realm of literacy. And since they did not consider physical exertion vital, they never assumed a workout mindset. They treated Orbán on the same level as themselves, not realizing that Orbán was putting in a tremendous amount of hard, sweaty work.

An example of sincerity is Viktor Orbán's thesis on Solidarity which is entitled *Social Self-Organizing and Movement in the Political System—a Polish Example*. Dr. Mihály Samu, head of the department that evaluated the work wrote that: "The technical background of the dissertation, its theoretical, conceptual system far exceeds the standards of a dissertation. The study of the problems of social movements and socialist civil society, measured to literature on the subject, is novel and individual. Orbán describes Solidarity: the senses in which it was political, municipal, and unionized."

Orbán is gifted, but that's not why he became a historical figure. It is due to his relentless effort and disciplined self-sacrifice, and he campaigned with mental strength and honor until his own collapse, rather than achieving everything automatically as many people think. Only those who go through tough workouts understand him. He who challenged himself, who didn't complain 'I have no time,' 'I'm not in the mood,' 'I have no money,' 'maybe tomorrow,' and pushed himself to his limits. Behind every champion and athlete is self-sacrifice, an honest workout program. One does not have to be a pro athlete to experience this secret, but one who has not lived it through will look at success through a different lens.

# 25

# Die Hard

How will others perceive you? The science of writing an external narrative is the alchemy of modern marketing, in other words, of storytelling. Seth Godin says with a tinge of irony that every marketer is lying, or to be precise, has a lie worth listening to—*All Marketers Are Liars*, or, *All Marketers Tell Stories*. That's the art in it—to turn belief-based storytelling into a brand.

The purpose of branding is to create a positive impression, whether you were born with a swoosh logo, a computer with an apple, a safe car, or a paper cup with a green siren. For example, somewhere in the world, somebody hears "Just Do It." and immediately a movie starts playing, they hear an inner voice and the feeling of victory fills their heart. Anyone who sees a green logo in a metropolis immediately smells freshly roasted coffee beans, tastes a delicious latte on their tongue, and imagines a cozy atmosphere—they don't first think that it's all just overpriced hype. Whoever you are, you want others to have a positive image of you, a credible story, and last but not least, that your shareholders are satisfied with the earnings report at the end of the quarter. Credibility, authenticity, predictability, coherent behavior, reliability, trustworthiness, memorability, all are qualities that good marketer (politician) pays attention to. And, of course, the emotional thread cannot be ignored, because we all make an emotional decision with a choice. At most, we try to back it with the reason that we deserved that chai latte because, after all, we worked hard for it.

Mihály Babits said that, "Hungarians do not think so much with words, but with pictures. Hungarian literature is scarce in flowers of rhetoric. The Hungarian rather uses real flowers, real pictures, real memories" and that, "Outstanding humor, as one of the main features of our literature, is instead peasant wisdom along for the ride: the calm observer's superiority over the player."

A polished identity grants Orbán fluidity. It is much more difficult to say something simply rather than elegantly, and to top something with wit while remaining straight to the point. Anyone who is not familiar with modern art says that he himself could have painted a Pollock. At first impression, Orbán's character is simple and self-explanatory. It seems too simple to admit that it works. While the ordinary politician uses democratic jargon, their core message births arguments and sparks fervor. On the other hand, Orbán's speeches comprise pictures, witty sentence-fragments, power-ups, truth-sentences, silence, and that's all. He focuses on visual elements, some of which appear in a non-verbal form, as opposed to delivering speeches with abstract concepts. His statements are so simple and are ornamented so lightly that only those who know how to communicate appreciate them. What makes excellent and clear communication complicated is that everything must be self-explaining.

THE TWENTIETH-CENTURY STORYTELLING GENRE IS THE HOLLYWOOD FILM. One of the iconic trilogies of the film industry, which promotes American culture and nationalism is Rambo, a feature film from the Reagan era that helped rebuild the American people's self-esteem after the Vietnam War. Kincsem is about self-esteem, too, which attempts to address the trauma of the War of Independence of 1848 through the story of the magnificent Hungarian horse, which defeated the Austrians. Viktor Orbán drew my attention to the fact that Andy Vajna was the producer of both films.

Perhaps it is no accident that Orbán has entrusted the most famous Hungarian Hollywood producer, the brilliant self-made man, with the right-wing media's and his government's communications. One of the many secrets of Viktor Orbán's popularity is that the media portrays his life as if it were a Hollywood movie. Vajna was the producer of *Nixon*, several episodes of the *Terminator* series, *Die Hard*, and the *Renaissance Man*, to name a few productions with Orbán-like characters: the surviving hero, the big-time statesman who opposed communism, and the team-building leader. Orbán's personal social media channels also work with stories; the team consciously builds and shapes the Orbán character.

During Andy Vajna's tenure as the Government Commissioner of the Hungarian film industry, two Hungarian films were awarded the Oscars: László Nemes Jeles' drama *Son of Saul* in 2016, and Kristóf Deák's *Sing*, which won an Oscar in 2017.

Hollywood screenplays build on the same paradigm. In his classic book *Screenplay*, Syd Field describes the structure of the Holywood plot. Each film has a beginning, a middle, and an end. Two plot points separate the three blocks, which redirect the narrative action. The function of the beginning is to set-up the story, introduce the characters, and take the viewer to the first plot point. From here, events take a new direction, and the central part, also called Act II, is where the confrontation takes place. This leads to the second plot point, which reveals the solution, foreshadowing the action in the final part of the film.

The last scene of the imaginary movie *Becoming Viktor Orbán—The Road to Victory* (a movie that has only screened in my head, so far at least) is the two-thirds landslide of 2010. The first plot point is the speech at the reburial of Imre Nagy, and the second plot is the speech given by Ferenc Gyurcsány at Őszöd: two key turning points that lead to a solution. The narrative is compelling because both the reburial speech and the Őszöd speech are about the doom of the communist status quo. The reburial speech forced the first regime change and ushered in the first Orbán government. The Őszöd speech brought about the second regime change and the two-thirds victory.

Let's have a closer look at the story with the help of Blake Snyder's *Beat Sheet*.

In the opening image, we see the house in Felcsút, the legendary grandfather Mihály Orbán appears, and we see the young Viktor Orbán practicing on the football field. The theme states that communism falls, foreshadowing the message of the film, the change in the status quo, and the loser-winner narrative. The story will be about change. In the set-up, we see the formation of the Association of Young Democrats, and we get to know the characters (János Áder, Tamás Deutsch, László Kövér, Lajos Simicska, József Szájer, and the future wife of Orbán, Anikó Lévai). The set-up gives an insight into the life at Bibó College and provides highlights of Hungary at the change of regime. The first plot point is the protagonist's speech at the reburial of Imre Nagy. It is the catalyst and events now take a new direction.

Next is what Blake Snyder calls the *debate*, the protagonist's dilemma whether to become a politician. (Orbán was not sure at first that he would become a politician.) Fidesz gets into Parliament, and Orbán becomes a Member of Parliament. The B story is about the beginning of Viktor Orbán's spiritual transformation and his conversion from anti-clericalism to Christianity. Viktor Orbán's journey to the Reformed religion will be the sideline of the main story. "Fun and games," is when Orbán fights and becomes Prime Minister—finally Fidesz rules. Through life pictures, we get to the midpoint.

The midpoint of the film is the 2002 elections, the defeat. "Bad guys close in." From here, the narrative of the bad guys win continues, first Medgyessy, then Gyurcsány, the 2005 referendum on dual citizenship, followed by the 2006 election. "All is lost" as Blake Snyder puts it, and the characters catch a whiff of death. We get to the emotional bottom of the story. All is lost, this is the 2006 election defeat. It is the "dark night of the soul," where the spiritual struggle begins. What's the meaning of life?

But suddenly we break into the third part. The second plot point is the Őszöd speech and the scandal that leads to the solution. In the scenes of the finale, Gyurcsány tries to survive, followed by Gordon Bajnai, while Orbán stays wise and calm, preparing for the takeover. The A and B stories meet. Everything happens for a reason—two stories, the conversion, and the politician's mission make ends meet. The movie's finale concludes with the election night in 2010. Hurray, we won! A happy ending.

Each screenplay is about the protagonist's transformation. The plot has two turning points, there is a secondary thread that touches the plot's main thread, and one is captivated about whether the protagonist will overcome the obstacle. And, as always, the story ends happily. *Harry Potter* is the story of Orbán's, just like *Star Wars*, *Robin Hood*, or Orbán's favorite, *Once Upon a Time in the West*. The latter became the narrative of the left-wing press and media.

NEXT UP, MOZART'S THE MAGIC FLUTE. THE DIRECTOR OF THE IMAGINARY production is Imre Kerényi (a former mentor of Viktor Orbán), starring Károly Eperjes (Orbán's friend), screenplay and set design by Mária Schmidt (founder and director of the House of Terror Museum) production manager Árpád Habony (Orbán's spin-doctor), and executive producer Andy Vajna.

Orbán's story is Tamino's. Young Orbán (Tamino) faints from

the poison of a snake symbolizing the communist dictatorship. George Soros and his left-liberal intellectuals (Queen of the Night and her three ladies) save him. Soros provides a scholarship and the left-liberal press pampers him. Pamina symbolizes Hungary, who captivated by the national-Christian ideology in the person of József Antall (Sarastro). Orbán realizes that he was misled. He converts from a liberal politician to a Christian Democratic politician. Being deceived by the evil left-liberal spirit, Orbán must now fight for Christian values to save Hungary from dark forces. The three quests are the sovereignty of the country, defense of the national union, and the advancement of Christian values. By rescuing Hungary, peace in the whole kingdom—Europe—will be restored.

The first chord of the overture is about the young politician. The second is about a frustrated politician who has lost two elections and has fallen into the pits. The third is about moral purification, the stand of trial, and order being restored with a two-thirds majority in Parliament.

# PART THREE

## IDENTITY

---

*"We are who we were, and we will be who we are,*
*God help us so!"*

(Kelemen Mikes)

# 26

# The Orbán Identity

The screenplay of our lives is our narrative; the character of the protagonist is our identity. Man's identity affects both external and internal stories. If our lives are an imaginary movie, the change in the protagonist's character provides the plot. It is the basis of the relationship that exists between our inner self—as the protagonist of our own lives—and tales, novels, films, or role models. A well-written script lets you experience the story and identify with the protagonist.

We inherit one part of our identity; another we choose ourselves. Anything can be an identity-shaping force that helps you draw out the character of your inner protagonist. Some of the most important elements of identity are one's roots, family, country, nation, and ethnic group; one's worldview, religious belief or lack thereof; one's sexual identity; cultural background, traditions, and subcultures; one's social ideas or movements, companies, brands, and social groups; one's mentors, historical figures or celebrities that serve as role models.

*Where I come from is uncultured, has a lack of cultural tradition. It was a working-class, nothing to do with farmers, yet we kept animals, but peasant culture had long disappeared from the village, neither was a blue-collar workers' culture. Not a middle-class culture, either. I came from such an uncultivated place.*

In the life of Viktor Orbán, *the lack of culture*, the lack of traditions became a blank slate upon which he engraved his own identity. It is the bedrock identity of a community and a nation upon which he can raise its entire political order. Viktor Orbán's identity is his political vision—the reimagined Hungarianness.

Outsiders are half-joking, half-convinced that Orbán's cult is a religion. No doubt about it, in his communication, he reveals ritual elements and symbols known from Christian ceremonies, but this is not the root of his sympathizer's so-called religious belief. Answers lie more in the connection of Viktor Orbán's identity to the identity of the other person. Voters may not know why they connects to him since the connection is established in the subconscious. The master key opens the hearts of many millions of people who find a common denominator in each other's identity.

The first node of his identity is football, the emotional world of sports. America has had a profound influence on him since his youth, a counter to communism—freedom, protest, and beat. His deeply engrained respect for history has shaped his political identity and career. He encounters Christ as a mature adult, and then he chooses his religion—*protest* Protestantism—and is confirmed in his church during his first term as Prime Minister. His wife, Anikó Lévai (b. 1963), is a devout Roman Catholic. He has a bold idea of the Hungarians, while only as an adult he locates his roots in Transylvania's Szeklerland. Behind the forces that determine his identity are mentors, role models, and the identity-forming forces that intersect to weave his character.

Orban's elements of identity are built on the background knowledge of the recipient, from which the narrative evolves. A spirit of victory touches the deep desires of the people. He is empowering the Hungarian people's destiny, historical tragedies, and traumas with a message of faith, hope, and love. He is a victorious revolutionary and a freedom fighter. As the captain of his government, who lifts burdens off people's shoulders, he must do the work. Our job is to cheer him on and pray. He is the main character you identify with, the inventor, the incomprehensible genius who succeeds at home.

How does he see himself, and how do others see him? He began to build the two stories by himself, and his complete identification with the character he constructed allowed others to take in his story. The method is always the same: to become what you imagine. At first, it seems rhapsodic and revolutionary, but Orban's life is in fact evolution and not revolution; ballad, not rhapsody. Craig Damrauer's statement about modern art fits him: "MODERN ART = I COULD DO THAT + YEAH BUT YOU DIDN'T."

# 27

# Worldview

One lesson that became apparent during the Hungarian change of regime was that there was no unified worldview about the love of a homeland. In 1990, after forty years of communism, the majority elected the national-conservative József Antall, in 1994 the communist Gyula Horn, in 1998 the Christian-nationalist Viktor Orbán, in 2002 the reformist-communist Péter Medgyessy, and 2006 the neoliberal Ferenc Gyurcsány and in 2010 Viktor Orbán again.

Does this seem absurd? It's just identitylessness. Viktor Orbán may have realized that to govern in the long run, the political community he led must buy into a shared worldview. If we share the same worldview, we speak one language. It is how confidence is established. For Hungarians to have a shared worldview of their homeland, we must first have a collective national identity. Therefore, Orbán began his work by drawing his own on a blank slate and began to shape the identity of his political community with the image of a character drawn from his actions—and built a shared worldview. Uniting the right-wing means not only that Orbán has formed one large party out of many small ones, but that he has united voters in a unified worldview regardless of their right-wing party affiliations.

**ONE CAMP = ONE FLAG = ONE WORLDVIEW**

The Orbánian program of politics is a new worldview about patriotism: a strong belief in Hungary. The fundamental vision is that three prerequisites provide power: a united nation, sovereignty, and Christian values. The Hymn (See the full text of the Hymn in Chapter 34.) as a prayer embraces Christian values, the engagement with an enemy means a battle for independence, the suffered past and future is Trianon. Viktor Orbán's policy is to tell the same story every day, again and again: God's blessing on the Hungarians, offering them a protective arm to fight the enemy, joyous years, and bounty to come.

There is no program for government, but a program for a worldview. The clever resourcefulness of Orbán's government led to the merger of the Ministry of Culture and the Ministry of Health. The Ministry of Human Capacities (EMMI) is a ministry of worldview representing a distinct worldview and organizing education, culture, health, and social affairs accordingly. It is no accident that these four areas trigger most of the polarized reactions because these are the four areas that are based on a worldview. By appointing one person to lead the ministry, decisions will be predictable and consistent, bringing voters' worldview into sync with government measures. Moreover, trust builds as a result of this integration.

Ferenc Gyurcsány is the worldview-counterpart of the Orbán policy: for him, love of the homeland implies that Hungary, as part of a utopian United States of Europe, gives up its sovereignty, abandons Christian values, and views Transylvanian Hungarians as Romanian citizens. His party's brand image, the colors of the Democratic Coalition, reflect this radical difference (light blue, yellow, and purple instead of Hungary's national colors red, white, and green). Three hundred and eight thousand people voted for this vision in the 2018 Parliamentary election. Viktor Orbán's got nine times as many votes: two million and eight hundred thousand;

every second person voted for Orbán, while the rest could not decide between the seven major parties in the opposition.

The lesson of the 2018 elections is that Viktor Orbán's tribe has a unified worldview and the opposition voters—the remainder in the minority—still do not. By the time we reach a consensus on what we consider a national minimum; therefore, Hungarians will hold the same as Americans in America is a matter of ten to fifteen years.

Viktor Orbán has no strong challenger because there is no better alternative to the worldview of Orbán's patriotism—no alternative to national unity, a democracy based on Christian culture, and sovereignty of the country. The American founding fathers, too, had no better alternative to this recipe.

# 28

# Grand Master

Freemasonry exerted its most significant influence on humanity through American politics. Fourteen of the forty-five Presidents of the United States were Freemasons, including George Washington, the first President of the United States. Nine of the signers of the Declaration of Independence were Freemasons. The ideology of American democracy took many ideas from the philosophy of Freemasonry. From here, it is understandable why not telling the truth in the United States is the greatest crime. Anyone who has traveled to the United States recognizes the strange questions on the ESTA questionnaire, for example, "Do you seek to engage in or have you ever engaged in terrorist activities, espionage, sabotage, or genocide?"

Freemasonry also creates a worldview. The unified worldview of its members gives the outside observer the impression that an invisible power controls the world from the background. When two people share the same worldview, they will make decisions based on similar principles, so their actions remain coherent. The strength of the United States also lies in the fact that its citizens, regardless of party affiliation, are united for America's interests. They have a unified worldview of their country, knowing that they need to remain united to the outside world, which is in the common interest of all. Viktor Orbán also wants to achieve in Hungarians such a stable worldview that looks at national union and the interest of the country's sovereignty, with a Christian all-seeing eye.

**FREEMASONRY DEFINES ITSELF AS A MORAL SYSTEM, VEILED IN ALLEGORIES** and illustrated by symbols. At the time, Masonry was a disruptive innovation that challenged the status quo. Its ideology is the unity of brotherly love, the autonomy of lodges, and monotheism. The Bible is an essential supply of Masonic lodges in the Anglo-Saxon rite.

The purpose of Freemasonry is to build the invisible temple of humankind. Freemasonry is a diverse, progressive movement interwoven with the ideas of Enlightenment. It defines itself as a philosophical, philanthropic, and progressive institution. In today's eyes, Freemasonry is an exclusive networking club and personality development tool for men. Freemasonry has taken the tools of masonry to the spiritual sphere and created the toolkit for building the invisible temple of humankind. "The square, to square our actions; The compasses, to circumscribe and keep us within bounds with all mankind." With a masonic trowel, the master spreads the cement which binds all the parts of the building into one common mass, symbolizing the spread of brotherly love and its cohesive power. The level expresses the equality of the lodge members among themselves and before God.

The origins of Freemasonry date back to the period of medieval stone masonry. According to one theory, it was an association of the most skilled stonemasons. Another hypothesis says free masons were a community of Gothic cathedral builders who worked independent of guilds and were free to move from construction site to construction site. Freemasons recognized each other by secret signs and handshakes, and masons and their apprentices kept their master trades of their craft in secret. In 1717 four lodges formed the first Masonic Grand Lodge in London. Here is how Freemasonry evolved, also called speculative masonry because the organization reinterpreted medieval masonry tools (compasses, levels, plumb) as allegories.

Because of their secret ceremonies and disruptive behavior that threatened the status quo, countless malicious conspiracy theories spread about Freemasons.

Freemasonry initiates new members through specific rituals. Through initiation, apprenticeship, fellowcraft, and the master degrees, the candidate experiences the secrets of Freemasonry through a secret drama play and ritual. The furnishings of the lodges and the dressing of the members are subject to strict formal requirements. The purpose of the meetings is to exchange thoughts. Religious and political issues cannot be discussed in the lodges. Anglo-Saxon regular Freemasonry requires its members to have a belief in a higher being called the Grand Master of the Universe. Atheists may also be members of irregular lodges under the authority of the French Grand Orient. We mentioned that two of the best-known symbols of Freemasonry, the compasses, and the square, are the symbols of straightness, sober living, and moderating our desires. Although Freemasonry is not a religion but contains many elements that resemble religious liturgy, its members usually believe in a transcendent superior being. The initiation rituals are reminiscent of the temple building of Solomon, the King of Israel in the Old Testament, the system of symbols originate from ancient masonry, while other elements are universal symbols of humankind.

Many elements of the Magic Flute are inspired by Freemasonry, although the Masonic symbols and Enlightenment ideas remain veiled in the opera. To some interpretations, the Queen of the Night is Maria Theresa, who banned Freemasonry in Austria, while Sarastro's character was modeled on Ignác Born, a Viennese scientist of Transylvanian origin.

The articles of the Constitution of the Hungarian Symbolic Grand Lodge are called the *Fundamental Laws*. (The new Hungarian constitution is also called The Fundamental Law.)

Article IX on Masonic Circles states that "Freemasons, who
are ordinary members of the lodges under the Grand Lodge if
they do not have a lodge at their place of residence, may form
their masonic circles..." Compare this to 2002 when, after losing
the election, Orbán proclaimed the organization of *civil circles*,
independent from the Fidesz party structure.

It is also said that critical issues in the Orbán course are decided
in the football stadium's VIP 'lodges.' Now, here is a quote from
Viktor Orbán's 2019 Tusnádfürdő Speech:

> *We have lived the last nine to ten years with the mason's trowel*
> *in one hand and the sword in the other.*

Some of the most outstanding figures of Hungarian
intellectual life were Freemasons.[x]

Some people admit that Apple is also a religion. Steve Jobs's
appearance, personality, and presence reinforced his prophetic

---

[x] Some names, but by no means an exhaustive list, include Endre Ady (poet),
Gyula Andrássy (Prime Minister), Elek Benedek (writer), György Festetics
(aristocrat), Alfréd Hajós (Olympic swimmer), Ferenc Kazinczy (public
intellectual, a leading figure in the modernization of the Hungarian language),
Lajos Kossuth (Governor-President of the Kingdom of Hungary during the
revolution of 1848–49, he was initiated as a Freemason in Washington DC), Dezső
Kosztolányi (poet), Sándor Kőrösi Csoma (orientalist), Ferenc Liszt (composer),
Ignác Martinovics (philosopher, writer and a leader of the Hungarian Jacobin
movement), Ferenc Móra (writer), László Ravasz (bishop of the Reformed
Church), Aladár Schöpflin (writer, public intellectual), Áron Tamási (writer),
and Sándor Wekerle (Prime Minister). The late Grand Master of the Hungarian
Symbolic Grand Lodge, Géza Supka, initiated the Festive Budapest Book Week.
Ferenc Széchényi, the founder of the National Museum, was also a Freemason,
and his son, Istvan Széchenyi, did not join the society but subsidized Freemasonry,
and was therefore honored as a "Freemason without an apron." Freemasonry and
Reformation would be unthinkable without one another.

mission. As a charismatic evangelist, Jobs expressed his vision of technological advancement in a style that charmed audiences. He always stepped onto stage in the same black turtleneck. Product presentations (keynotes) followed a particular choreography—a rite. The liturgy began with a witty introduction, followed by and introduction of the newest device, its list of features, and, in due course, the disclosure of the price. The last episode of the show became Jobs's trademark, the *one more thing*. The Apple tribe's brand loyalty exceeds all rationality. Does this explain why consumers are choosing more expensive Apple products with fewer features or with similar features? How are they able to camp at the entrance of Apple Stores before the release of a new product? Just like Apple's competitors, the left-wing came to the same conclusion that so many are voting for Orbán because they are sheep. What else could it be, if not religion?—they say. According to Orbán's materialistic opposition, only religious spirit can persuade the masses, whom they call amongst themselves "brain dead" and whom they consider to make irrational decisions.

Jobs learned a great deal about the cultivation of a cult from Freemasonry. Viktor Orbán's politics may influence people for the same reason, because the central element of his speeches is an allegory, and his politics contains many symbolic elements. From his annual evaluation speeches of the country to mass events, the highlight of all events is Viktor Orbán's speech, usually closed by the Hymn, analogous to the place of the Our Father in Christian liturgy. With Orbán, construction work is at the heart of its mission as well: building a strong Hungary. Each of his speeches feature symbols illuminated with allegories, metaphors that give the illustrated events, persons, or abstract concepts a second, hidden meaning.

*Today, Hungary is more like a ship whose parts have been replaced with success. No leakage where the gutters are held secure.*

*Hungary also needs to know that, although it is a member of the European Union, flying the western flag, the global economy today is blown by the east wind.*

*We've been through it a few times, so we've learned that it's not dangerous to sail in the whirlwind of history because whirlpools can pull larger ships deeper than ours...*

*The spring wind is flooding the water, but it also seems to inflate the flood of immigrants.*

In the introduction to her book on biblical symbols, Katalin Dávid writes that "a symbol always denotes or represents something: itself, it is not about it, but what it is referring to. [...] Symbol, metaphor, analogy, allegory, emblem, etc. it veils the relationship between image and meaning to varying degrees. [...] The question is, do they understand what the emblem refers to? Is there a social convention to understand the meaning conveyed by the image? And does the community communicate with the emblem? If these are given, the symbol is alive [...]"

The educational significance of symbols is to facilitate orientation. Apple was a pioneer in making certain features more natural to understand through small images and small icons. The Microsoft Windows operating system also employed this concept, which has since become a paradigm for every computer program. Many elements and gestures of Orbán's politics are also symbolic. The first sentence of the Fundamental Law has profound symbolic content, which is quote from the first line of the Hymn: "O, God, bless the Hungarian!"

*I reveal the historical secret that the first line of the Constitution
is credited to József Szájer, who, along with Ferenc Kölcsey [who
wrote the Hymn], cut the Gordian knot by citing the Hymn.
How should we illuminate our relationship with the almighty
of God beyond the references of Christianity? Without being
offensive to modern European religious freedom approaches.*

The First Orbán Government's Millennium Celebration Series
and its relocation of the the Holy Crown into the Parliament
Building, the Orbán era's memorial policy, the House of Terror
Museum, the Table of the Fundamental Law are all symbolic. It
is salient to mention that after the passage of the Fundamental
Law, each governmental institution installed a table where people
can read the new constitution. The dual citizenship granted to
ethnic Hungarians living outside of the national borders can be
interpreted as a symbolic gesture towards all Hungarians and as a
symbol of patriotism. As Prime Minister, in 2010, his first foreign
trip went to the Vatican to Pope Benedict XVI, in 2014 to Poland,
and in 2018 to Austria.

Not only does Orbán's life follow the paradigm of the
Hollywood screenplay, but also the paradigm of becoming a
master. Just as masonry is a craft, so is the practice of politics.

The three degrees of Freemasonry are the apprentice, the
fellowcraft, and the master. The seeker enters the lodge through
initiation. The symbol of the apprentice is the rough ashlar, with
a chisel and gavel he transforms his character into a perfect ashlar.
The speech at the reburial of Imre Nagy was the inauguration
rite, followed by eight years of administrative work on Orbán's
'fellowcraft:' his first term as Prime Minister. You learn to win,
and you learn to lose. The third stage, the ritual of becoming
a master, deals with the mystery of death: during the initiation
drama, the candidate dies and is reborn as a Master Mason.

"Think of death! Going to the best school in life, which soon becomes acquainted with death! It is the apprentice's job to work on raw stone, for the lad to learn how to work in the community. To face death in the hour of darkness is the art of the master!" For Viktor Orbán, the defeat of the 2006 election is death, and his 2010 victory is rebirth. In 2010, Orbán returned to politics as a 'grand master.'

# 29

# Know What You Want!

At twelve, my parents sent me to a private school instead of a public school. It was a tradition that Edward Teller visited the school every year and taught an unusual physics class for the juniors. At the end of the lesson, one could also ask the greatest living Hungarian-born scientist.

— What is the most (important) thing in the world?—I dared to ask. The words of Ed Teller still ring in my ear:

— **KNOW WHAT YOU WANT!**

Since then, these words come to mind almost every day. What do we want from life? What is it worth getting up for, a life worth fighting for and sacrificing? I find myself exceptionally fortunate to have been able to grow up with people, learn from them, and to have role models who knew what they wanted.

If one were to rank the books published on Viktor Orbán by source value, László Kéri's book of interviews would top the rankings. The backbone of the content are the conversations between the author and Orbán, recorded between the summer 1993 and January 1994. A former teacher of Bibó College interviewed his former student. They published an edited version from fourteen hours of audio material. Kéri interviewed Orbán after the change of direction of Fidesz and this text is essentially the only authentic source from which we can meet Viktor Orbán.

Later Orbán books also refer to this work.

Let me quote the book's preface: "'This book is about a politician whose future is still riddled with mystery. As I now see it, without him, it could be hard to imagine the Hungarian political life of the following decades,' wrote Pál Bodor in the summer of 1993. 'But we also know that leaders of changing times usually disappear after half a decade. Why would he be the exception? Viktor Orbán is threatened only by singing himself too early,' notes László Lengyel in a heated January 1994. What's for sure? Viktor Orbán can be loved and hated. You can trust him, you can admire him, or you can be afraid of him. What is absolute and irrevocable is that he was a crucial player in the transformation."

In retrospect, the most exciting thing about the interview is that Viktor Orbán's policy has hardly changed since 25 years ago. In the first half, he talks about himself:

> I'd rather say I was an independent kid. [...] Didn't have all the
> skills to be a boss, but I was strong enough to stay independent.
> If you liked it that way, I didn't belong to anyone.

Here is the deal: Hungary must be strong enough to remain independent. It is that simple: for twenty-five years, he has made consistent decisions because he has planned his vision of fifteen million Hungarians according to his narrative. The secret is that if you identify with the politics you represent 100%, you can always tell the truth from your heart. Many things can be interpreted and understood different if we assume that everything we perceive is an imprint of Orban's personality, from the memorial of the German occupation, through the stadiums to the Hungarian and Szekler flags on the Parliament building.

"Art in art" describes how Orbán's political system evolves

out of his identity. He expressed his political vision through his character. At first, he became the future he imagined. At first, he planned his internal narrative and then translated it into the language of politics. The vision, the external description, is personalized by Viktor Orbán himself and makes the character visible through action. When Orbán reinterpreted, "What Makes for a Hungarian?" he did not want to change people but he did somewhat shape his communication to the souls and innermost desires of Hungarians.

# 30

# What Makes for a Hungarian?

By transformation, Orbán's Hungarian character is the positive version of the typical Hungarian negative traits—an inversion of Hungarianness. It is a story built on people's worldviews that created the belief that Viktor Orbán was the spiritual heir to losing battles and bloodbath struggles for freedom. He was eventually victorious because he did not carry on the historical legacy but reinterpreted its meaning. From here, you can understand it is not that the people's perception is to be changed—in this case, reinterpreting the national mythology—but touching their expectations. The underground narrative is that Orbán created a new Hungarian identity out of the desires of the Hungarians.

Orbán's Hungarian identity turned three typical Hungarian traits on its head—from 'it does not matter' to vim, refraining from action to action, from disunity to pulling together. (Football may have inspired all this. One of the most comprehensive books on the evolution of football tactics, *Inverting the Pyramid*, suggests in its title that from the 1880s, the layout of the players took the shape of a triangle set on its tip and gradually turned into a standing pyramid.)

According to the Urban Dictionary, *ungarn* means "strange ppl with strange language." Are these folks Hungarians? "Hungarians are open-eyed and open-minded people. His culture has been in line with Europe's for nine hundred years"—wrote Mihály Babits in his essay *On the Hungarian Character*. As Babits pointed out one of the first features of the national characterology is Hungarians are "rather convinced of their inferiority." By contrast, the narrative of Viktor Orbán's first government was a quote from István Széchenyi: "We dare to be great, and it is not that hard, but we must also be wise!"

Let's start with vim. "The Hungarian likes to talk about the prince who 'went to try his luck' during the looting of corn. However, the Hungarian is the one who doesn't like to try his luck." On the other hand, Péter Szijjártó, Minister of Foreign Affairs and Trade, is the archetype of the character who is trying his luck, the inverse of the comfy diplomat.

Babits, whose quoted essay appeared in 1939, well before the 1956 Revolution and War of Independence, writes of the rebellion: "The myth of the 'rebel Hungarians' is just as fabricated. The Hungarian is not a rebel. The "rebel Hungarian" was just defending what was his own... His constitution, the continuity of his national rights, the principle of legal permanence. [...] They were always called rebels by his enemies; he never called himself that way."

The first change of regime was not about rebellion, and the constitution was "just changed," even though most of the paragraphs have been replaced. Thus, the transition could remain peaceful. Viktor Orbán's government amended the constitution by replacing the old with a brand-new law. This symbolic move expressed the rebellion and interpreted the 2010 election as a revolt of the Hungarian people.

*We were among the first, or perhaps the pioneers, to rebel in 2010. We proclaimed, and with seven years of hard work, built our own Hungarian political and economic system, a Hungarian model tailored to our flesh, our taste, our traditions, our instincts, and our reasoning—the System of National Cooperation.*

As Babits says: "So, this meaningful statement, that 'Hungary is a nation of warriors,' needs balance. It's more expressive to say, 'Hungary is a nation of politicians.' But not in the sense of being politically active — its greatest political achievements are not political acts. Its most significant political act is always refraining from action. Not a doer, but an observer. A calm observer and ever knowing when not to do, or not worth doing. Its position already shows that. Taking action can only make things worse. Its only self-defense is caution. So, it seems sluggish, single-minded: to wit, has no intention in being pushy. If there's an oriental feature in Hungarians, it's a lazy, contemplative nature. And I confess, I am surprised that the greatest and most significant national characterology denies this through. [...]

There are swift nations all around us, agile, and even obtrusive nations. It sets Hungarians apart from everyone else, this contemplative carelessness. We've shown the world several times, but we soon got turned off: it's not worth doing. [...] It's not our conquering adventures that are unique; other nations would have done it just like us. Ending these adventures is what's characteristic."

If there is something that defines Orbán's politics, it is shining power. For Orbán, politics is about doing, and he makes his political character visible through action. Doing is always about strength, the nation's cohesive force, the country's economic vitality, and its sense of security. The effort to overcome the migration crisis shows strength at all three levels. On an ideological level, halting migration can protect Christian values and the nation's identity. Physical defense of Hungary's and Europe's borders is the most definite pledge of security. A sound economy does not need immigrants and runs well without migration. "In Hungarian literature, the problem of the homeland is always the problem of doing," and Orbán renders these verbs in the past tense.

Our worldview has some positive traits we can build on. Such is the "obsession of the hedge" (in Hungarian, this metaphor refers to a person who meticulously protects his property with a fence): "understanding this peculiar susceptibility of the Hungarians to fence and hedge themselves." [...] "The Hungarian did not shed his blood for the stranger. When he was defending 'European culture,' he was defending what was his. He has defended his own country, his own Christianity." This trait makes it easier to understand why migration and border protection enjoys society's overwhelming support. And why the family is at the center of the government's program. "The foundation of [Hungarians'] love for their nation is the love of their home and family."

HUNGARY'S LEGAL CURRENCY IS THE FORINT. THE DENOMINATIONS OF PAPER money bear the portraits of historical figures representing the values of the Orbán era. The one thousand-forint bill features King Matthias, the ten thousand-forint bill features Saint Stephen I, while the highest denomination features the politician "… who is the most uniquely Hungarian among us, Ferenc Deák. In fact, no matter how surprising it may be, this realistic attitude makes Hungarians a perfect fit for politics and diplomatic roles. According to Mikszáth, a famous novelist, the Hungarian peasant was born to be a diplomat. A good trait for a good diplomat is nothing should "impress" him: the nil admirari. His judgement must not be dazzled or influenced, either by an outside impression or by a too intense emotional backlash. You don't have to worry about this for a straight and genuine Hungarian. He is the one who calmly excels on the floor of Europe's great diplomatic halls, albeit a child of a distant, small nation whose fate depends

largely on the politics, and often on the benevolence of the larger
and happier nations. The one who shines and charms like Ferenc
Rákóczi or Gyula Andrássy, who coldly observes the relations and
secret intentions of the great and uses them against one another
while engaging them all by his calm and sincerity."

*The insane dream of the communists to mold us into homo
Sovieticus instead of Hungarians can never return. And now we
are standing here and astonish to see the forces of globalism are
knocking on our door and busy to mold us into homo Brusselicus
instead of Hungarians.*

**THE TYPICAL HUNGARIAN TRAITS TEND TO CHARACTERIZE ORBÁN'S**
opponents. "'Passive resistance' is the Hungarian way of life."

The reason for the opposition's failure is "we are not blaming
ourselves, but each other. Discord is a common human trait. And
yet, the Hungarian division is quite a strange one with special
forms and distinctive motifs"—I quoted Mihály Babits again.

So far, no one has delivered Hungarian politics a safer and
sounder starting point than Orbán. It builds on that which yields
Americanness: Christian values (In God We Trust), sovereignty,
and national union. "We hold these truths to be self-evident,
that all men are created equal, that they are endowed by their
Creator with certain unalienable Rights, that among these are
Life, Liberty and the pursuit of Happiness."—This is the most
beautiful and most quoted phrase from the *Declaration of
Independence*. Christian values protect life, sovereignty guarantees
liberty, national union grants the power of community, and a
prosperous economy—this gives happiness.

*Thinking about timeframes, we want Hungary to be among the
top five countries in the European Union by 2030. Among the*

*five best countries to live and work. Let's be among the top five most competitive countries in '30. Stop the demographic decline by 2030, connect Hungary with the rest of the historic land, and take the highways to the state borders. Hungary should become energy independent by 2030, which has become an important dimension of security, and Paks [name of the nuclear plant located in the town bearing its name] should be ready, and new sources of energy should operate. Let's suppress the most common chronic diseases, build the new Hungarian army, and start the industrial construction works of Central Europe. [...] 30 years ago, we thought Europe was our future, and today we think of us as the future of Europe. Go for it!*

"The flag of Hungary shall feature three horizontal bands of equal width colored red, white and green from top to bottom as the symbols of strength, fidelity and hope, respectively." Fidelity (in Latin: fides) is backed by strength on one side and hope on the other.

# 31

# Soli Deo Gloria

Two major groups of Hungarian society have a more or less stable view of the world: Christians who practice their religion (Catholics, Reformed people, Lutherans) and Jews. Christians tend to support right-wing parties, and many with Jewish identities support left-wing liberal forces. The rest of society will vote here and there, depending on which side offers it more benefits. There are social groups that share a similar view about a particular issue, but they are too few to form a political community.

Most Christians who practice their religion belong either to the far-right or the national middle-class tribe. One difference between the patriotic-nationalist middle-class and the far-right is that the former derives its identity from St. Stephen on a Christian basis and sharply separates the pagan pre-conquest period from later Christian state formation. The latter interpret Christian-Hungarian culture, incorporating pagan elements with the Holy Crown doctrine.[xi]

xi Formulated in the Middle Ages, the doctrine of the Holy Crown is a Hungarian Medieval tradition and concept of Hungarian statehood. By substituting the state theory that did not yet exist, the principle created the Hungarian statehood independent of the king. Besides the ruler himself, the Holy Crown's "fictitious body" was the Kingdom of Hungary's territory on the one hand and the ruling class on the other. For a long time, this system formed the basis of Hungary's historical, unwritten constitution, on which the theory of the Hungarian state evolved.

In the twentieth century, the far-right used the symbols of the Hungarians to incite hatred, trying to monopolize the red and white striped flag of the kings of the Árpád dynasty, the double-cross in the coat of arms and the drama of Trianon. Orbán considers every Hungarian an equal part of the nation. He uses patriotism in a positive sense and not for exclusion, whereas for him, national union is the starting point of the national consensus.

In Hungary, Jewish identities tend to prefer left-wing liberal forces. It is a peculiarity of the Jewish people to separate religion and identity. Many Jewish people define themselves as liberals, sometimes atheists, while the Jewish foundation is the Torah, the five books of Moses. The *Jewishness* of left-liberal intellectuals is, therefore, more of an identity without affiliation to traditions and religious principles. Still, it gives self-awareness and a worldview. Members of the left-wing and their sympathizers are linked to each other by the casual nature of liberalism. The ideas' loosely cohesive force unites them, with no charismatic leader to lead them.

The underground interpretation of the Orbánian Hungarian identity is that it has two elements. Based on the Christian system of values, the *religious arm* of the Hungarian identity builds on the model of Judaism. The *arm of roots* builds on the self-conscious patriotism of Transylvanian-Hungarians.

Orbán's Christianity only embraced the Christian order of values, not the mandatory compulsion of religious orders. Christians in Fidesz are not the same: not everyone practices their religion, and those who do are divided between two major churches, the Catholic and the Reformed Churches. The Lutheran Church is more balanced in terms of politics, with one half supporting Orbán, while the other the opposition. The overwhelming majority of Catholics and Calvinists back Orbán.

For non-believer liberals, Christianity is a cultural phenomenon. Because of distortions, they consider the government's attempts to support churches as incompatible with the principle of separation of state and church.

### "WE BELIEVE IN THE POWER OF LOVE AND TOGETHERNESS."

Orbán's Christian identity enabled him to touch the whole of Hungarian society. He did not begin as a believer, but as an anticlerical, then converted to and was confirmed in the Reformed religion. But there is a critical detail, his wife, Anikó Lévai, is a devout Catholic. By this fact, Orbán could reach out to Catholics. He understood the cult of Holy Mary and the power of the Vatican, the wisdom of the Jesuits, and the piety of Csaba Böjte.[xii]

He committed to the Reformed religion only as a mature adult and was confirmed during his first term as Prime Minister. In 1998, on the night of the election, after Fidesz won, Viktor Orbán thanked his supporters for praying for him. The symbolic gesture marked the end of the liberal anti-church era of Fidesz. We know from his biography, Forward!, that he has come a long way in saying that he is a Christian, a believer. As a politician, Orbán has testified to his faith many times. Its government, uniquely in Europe, elevated Christian values to constitutional levels.

A prayer chain and a thanksgiving mass are regularly organized for Viktor Orbán. Regardless of the weather, hundreds of thousands of people listen to his speeches live, many with crosses

---

xii Csaba Böjte is a Franciscan monk, founder of the Saint Francis of Déva Foundation. The purpose of the child rescue organization he founded is to support children in the mild conditions of Transylvania, often on the brink of starvation. It provides 2500 deprived children in its institutions and hundreds more in the foster care system.

and a Virgin Mary's medal hanging on their necks. Not only do they hear, but they listen and become one with it. On March 15, 2018, the seventh *March for Peace* (a mass demonstration organized by the Civic Alliance Forum, standing up to the Orbán government), the third major campaign event before the two-thirds victory, was held. At the end of the speech, according to the usual choreography, the crowd sings the Hymn. Orbán broke the earlier tradition and did not sing, but recited the Hungarian Anthem, like The Lord's Prayer or a Hebrew blessing, which elevated the event to ecumenical worship.

*All we have to do is ask for God's help. Now, not singing as we usually do, but in prose, in verse, as taught by Ferenc Kölcsey. We haven't done this before, let's try it together.*

NON-BELIEVERS ARE THE MOST VOCAL ABOUT CHRISTIAN VALUES IN Orbán. They think they understand Christianity because they, too, have read the Bible. Contrasted, there is a picture in their minds that Christianity is a supplement, a self-explained psychology, a well-constructed tale, and, of course, each of them knows at least one Pharisee who is always worshiping in the temple. As a devout Catholic, I write about Orbán's Christianity from a personal perspective, and I want to convey an unofficial theological opinion.

I do not assume that liberals are wicked. It is merely that they view Orbán's Christianity from 'default to lying'—not defaulting to truth. Let me start by saying that the Hungarian left-liberal side behaves rude and offensive to Christians. Their manifestations are full of mocking terms that I would not bring for free publicity. Anyone who does not respect the religious beliefs of others has a zero legal basis for speaking on Christianity because, through his statements, he has violated the primary command of

Christianity: love one another.

One of the essential teachings of Christianity is the right to free will. Everyone decides upon their own lives, i.e., they must take responsibility for their actions. Therefore, the most profound Christian passages of the Fundamental Law are not those which, for example, protect marriage as the union of a man and a woman, but those on responsibility. "Hungary shall observe the principle of balanced, transparent and sustainable budget." The Fundamental Law also regulates the amount of state debt. "Everyone shall be responsible for him- or herself and shall be obliged to contribute to the performance of state and community tasks according to his or her abilities and possibilities."

Christianity does not teach that all people should have the same amount. One of the famous parables of the gospel is a story about talent. Everyone is given a different amount of talent by the Lord, which requires him or her to use it according to his or her abilities. Where Orbán recognizes talent, he entrusts tasks. It does not contradict Christian teaching if one receives more, the other less. Helping the poor and the weak does not mean that everyone must live in poverty.

And what is often forgotten is that Jesus also says, "I am sending you out like sheep among wolves. Therefore, be as shrewd as snakes and as innocent as doves."

LET'S COMPARE THESE TWO NUMBERS: 1.313 BILLION AND 15 MILLION. Pope Francis is the leader of 1.313 billion Catholics, at the forefront of a two-thousand-year-old organization that spans continents—the Pope behaves accordingly. Viktor Orbán is the Prime Minister of fifteen million Hungarians, and it is his duty to represent the interests of the Hungarian nation.

The different approach of Pope Francis and Viktor Orbán on migration confuse Hungarian Catholics. Because God created all men in His image, there is no difference between one man and another in the eyes of the Holy Father, which is Pope Francis' position on migration, the Catholic worldview, and the official Catholic attitude. As a general principle, refugees should be admitted, and those who have fallen victims should be assisted. We, Catholic believers, see the Pope as the earthly governor of Christ. The supreme doctrine of our Church declares that the Holy Spirit inspires the voice of the Holy Father. As Vicar of Christ, the earthly representative of Christ, he stands above politicians, represents a universal (Greek: katholikós) organization that spans continents. Neither can he appear partial. He speaks up in defense of the dignity of the human person, not in a political debate. That is the job of politicians.

It is also confusing to Hungarian Catholics that Pope Francis communicates competently with the laity. He knows that dialogue between believers and non-believers must be based on a shared worldview. Therefore, the Holy Father expresses his thoughts on humanity to the world by separating the mystery of religion from the universal values of humanity. It emphasizes common-sense arguments that can resonate with those who do not believe in the teachings of the Church. Non-believers, therefore, "believe" in the Pope's words because those words express views in tune with their worldview. If we think about it, Viktor Orbán also introduced Christian values in a way that is compatible with the worldviews of non-believers.

When the Pope makes a statement on environmental protection or divorce, he does not change the Catholic Church's position. Still, it expresses the Catholic opinion in a way an atheist worldview could accept. It surprised the right that liberals found the Pope's words authentic, and Orbán's inauthentic. Right-wing media concluded that liberals ensnared the Pope. However, it is just that the Holy Father's worldview is up to date. In the Vatican, they know how to communicate, not only in Fidesz, and unlike Orbán, the Pope did not harm the liberals, albeit he would not have the means to do so. The perceived antagonism between Viktor Orbán and Pope Francis is, therefore, a misunderstanding. Orbán's policy on migration, protection of the home, and the sovereignty of the nation are in line with the teachings of the Church.

I QUOTE FROM SELF-HELP GURU, KEN BLANCHARD'S BOOK, LEAD LIKE Jesus, a story about the famous American preacher John Ortberg:

"Ortberg, a gifted storyteller, smiled at the audience and said, 'Let's assume for a moment that two thousand years ago you were a gambler. I know a number of you don't like gambling, but bear with me for a moment. Let me ask you who would you have bet your money on to last: the Roman Empire and the Roman army, or a little Jewish rabbi with twelve inexperienced followers?' Everyone smiled as John went on to say, 'Isn't it interesting that all these years later we are still naming kids Matthew, James, Sarah and Mary, and we call our dogs Nero and Caesar? I rest my case.'"

Isn't it interesting that 'isn't it interesting' is not just a narrative of Christianity?!

*Who would have thought a year or two ago, that history would throw itself into prophecies. Laughing at the prophets of liberal politics. Vigorously insisting on the benefactors and defenders of the international ruling order, globalists, liberals, influential people sitting in ivory towers, and TV studios, the mobs of the media, and their bosses.*

The talented young man bursts into public awareness with miracles and wonders, and soon gains a following huge crowd, recruiting a team of twelve people from ordinary people. Despite success and miracles, everything collapses at a sudden, and then the miracle happens. He will rise and be immortal.

*I think there is always a higher sense of what happens to a man. What this higher sense is not clear today. Today, we still feel grief mixed with grace. To answer what was the higher meaning of what happened tonight, well, this answer needs time, and time will come. [...] We know that having faith, hope, and love will also grow stronger from the pain.*

Isn't this narrative is what the Christian worldview is about? Is it a coincidence why so many Christians find Orbán's life authentic?

The symbols of Jewish-Christian culture and Christian holidays play an essential role in Viktor Orbán's Christian Democratic politics. In 2010, the second Orbán government decided April 16 to be the Memorial Day of the Hungarian Victims of the Holocaust. Good Friday became a holiday in 2007. Pál Schmitt, President of the Republic of Hungary, ceremoniously signed the new Fundamental Law of Hungary on Easter Monday, April 25, 2011.

Every decision Viktor Orbán's government makes must stand the test of three conditions. Does it serve the unity of the nation? Foster families? Enforce Christian values?

*Soli Deo gloria* 'Glory to God alone,' is the first and most essential Calvinist principle, one of the Five Solae: Glory to God alone, Scripture alone, by Faith alone, by Grace alone, and Christ alone.

Viktor Orbán could stop the migration crisis in 2015 because he alone had two-thirds among the Prime Ministers in the European Union: it is how two-thirds enabled a mission. In a broader sense, this mission is about Europe's future vision, and

more narrowly about Hungary's. It will determine whether
Hungary remains a member of a community of strong nation-
states, that will preserve its cultural roots, or whether it melts
into an imaginary United States of Europe, a liberal empire built
on Kant's common sense.

Viktor Orbán introduced Christian liberty in his 2019
Tusnádfürdő Speech.—Don't do unto others what you don't
want done unto you. According to Orbán's Christian Democratic
vision, the *illiberal* state creates the conditions for a "square,
sincere, and meaningful life."

This Christian liberty is the basis of national thinking because:

> *nations are free, we cannot subject them to the laws of global*
> *governance; empires suppress nations and are therefore*
> *dangerous and undesirable.*

The underground interpretation is that Christian freedom is a
program of common sense.

# 32

# Transylvania

A t the time of the first change of regime, Hungarians in the motherland did not have a unified worldview about patriotism. The Transylvanian Hungarians did.

We know Viktor Orbán's life, where he was born, who his parents were, what and where he studied, and his family. A library of studies has been written about his political system, and anyone can read his speeches and political statements. When I wonder what shaped his worldview, I look for the "Jungian" tree, the roots sprawling beneath the earth, the unseen, that's nourishing the visible, the fruit. From the root of Orbán's identity, one can understand the origin of his world view about Hungarians.

The most exciting transformation of Viktor Orbán's political evolution—as an underground interpretation—is how he transformed from "a genius of the West" into a "genius of Transylvania" and was reborn from the fusion of the two. By genius, I refer to Béla Hamvas's essay entitled *Five Geniuses*, in which the writer divided Hungary into five parts and gave a description of them.

**TWO HIGHLIGHTS:**

• *Genius of the West—civilization, progression, everyday work-ethic, social division, intensive cultivation, reason, constant learning, doing, practicality, loyalty.*

• *Genius of Transylvania—chasm, deep controversy and
bridging it, humor (grotesque), versatility, duality, compassion,
complications, smart practice, high life requirement, taste,
refinement.*

The genius of the West characterized Viktor Orbán's first term
as Prime Minister, and the vision was István Széchenyi's "Dare to
be Great!" As Hamvas wrote, "Széchenyi wanted nothing more
than to spread Western culture to the whole country, to create
an intense cultivation, to integrate the whole of Hungary into
Western bourgeoise."

A symbolic act of the era and Orbán's spectacular diplomatic
gesture to the Pope of Rome was to ferry the Holy Crown to
Parliament solemnly. The Catholic Széchenyi inspired the
political program of the first Orbán government. As mentioned
earlier, during his first term as Prime Minister, he was confirmed
a member of the Protestant Reformation. During the eight years
between 2002 and 2010, the reconstruction of the right-wing, his
political identity matures, and he discovered and identified with
his Transylvanian roots and a new historical figure on the trail
of the Reformed religion. This historical figure is the Protestant
Transylvanian duke, Gábor Bethlen.

There is a symbolic weight of the so-called Tusnádfüdő
lectures. Every year, the Prime Minister attends the Bálványos
Summer University and Student Camp, a one-week event that
concludes with a one-hour speech in which Orbán outlines his
political vision. Particularly interesting, as the Hungarian Prime
Minister, he speaks formally in Romania about the political
concept by which he governs Hungary. However, the case is not
contradictory because, for historical reasons, we, Hungarians still
consider Transylvania part of Hungary: its inhabitants are not
Romanians but Hungarians, whatever their passports may say.

Compared to his first Prime Ministerial term, which began in 1998, a new Viktor Orbán came to power in 2010. From here, the genius of Transylvania characterizes his conduct, which, in combination with the genius of the West, conceived a unique duality. Besides the concrete signs, beyond the Hungarian and Szekler flags on the Parliament building or the dual citizenship granted to Hungarians living outside the border, Orbán's policy is also characterized by a new direction concerning symbolic elements.

He moved the Prime Minister's Office to the Carmelite monastery in the Buda Castle area, thus separating himself from the Parliament as the legislative branch of power (as suggested in his interview 25 years ago). The architectural symbolism is the fusion of the Catholic past of the Carmelite Monastery and the purity of Protestant design. Orbán's political vision between 1998 and 2002 was a middle-class Hungary and from 2010 onwards a strong Hungary.

From the middle of the sixteenth century, the Kingdom of Hungary was torn into three parts: part of the kingdom fell under the influence of the Habsburgs, another was occupied by the Turkish Ottoman Empire, and the third part, Transylvania, became sovereign in the form of a principality.

Gábor Bethlen is associated with the name of the Transylvanian duke, the golden age of Transylvania, and a unique form of state. He built a Protestant sovereign realm.

The US presidential system—not considering its checks and balances—is comparable to the Principality of Transylvania. Bethlen is the closest figure in Hungarian history to Viktor Orbán. His Protestant religion is the same as Orbán's, as well as his constitutional system based on centralization, guided by sovereignty, and he governed in Transylvania, halfway between Byzantium and Rome.

Bethlen was the first genuine self-made man ruler of Hungarian history, who "evolved from a private individual to a true sovereign." Gyula Szekfű, in his monograph on him, writes: "from his social class, he willfully-willingly, used the circumstances to rise to the remote height of the ruler." The first parallel with Orbán is the Reformed Protestant religion with the difference that Bethlen derives the ruler's duties and rights from religious orders. Bethlen's political vision was a strong Transylvania, standing on the three pillars as of Orbán's— Christian values, unity, and sovereignty.

Therefore, Bethlen is also called a *Protestant Sovereign* because his Christianity is founded on Reformed beliefs. Two means represent its sovereignty: "the liberation of Transylvania from the Hungarian Holy Crown [...] the other is the Protestant supremacy against the Catholic Hungarian king ..." In Orbán's political system, sovereignty echoes, the symbolic expression of which is the move of the Prime Minister's Office to the castle, symbolically and spatially elevated above all institutions. Orbán's *Christian liberty* defines the illiberal state, which may even be a reinterpretation of Bethlen's Protestant sovereignty. Bethlen's self-made obsession and the duke's concept are closer to that of the US presidential institution than to the dynastic inherited kingdom.

There were no checks on the Bethlen government, with justice, military leadership, and finance all controlled by one hand. Transylvania organized its economic policy along centralization, with the goal of "bringing in more money in and producing more goods."

The historian monographer highlights Bethlen's "letter-writing and persuasive talents," "the genius he was born with," the fact that he was "barely educated" and he absorbed his technical skill of power "during his work in public affairs."

"The normal course of action is not to defend yourself, citing the accusations, because he is innocent ... [...] From here, the tendencies often fade, even if you are pushing many tendencies into the same statement that leaves its readers in obscurity. From where derive the contrasts of accusation, the pros, and cons of an argument. A friendly threat or statement, the contrasts of love of peace and lethal self-sacrifice, and their almost rhythmic accumulation. [...] Bethlen's whole style is characterized by the ability to lead the satire, after a moment's sneering smile, into a serious reflection of political purpose. As if he were to forget the prick he had just given."

According to him, he is "the first servant of his subjects," who "alone wants to raise his people to a higher material and spiritual living standards." "He is responsible for the well-being and survival of the population. He is the ruling duke, and he cannot share this work with anyone. [...] Most of his sub-leaders, like his diplomats, are simple people by his fortune, and whose loyalty he therefore counts. [...] He was not looking for friends, not great talents, or bright knights, but for the simple people who executed his orders. Instead of them, he is here to think."

Bethlen lived a simple lifestyle, with "hardly any passions" and spent little time with his family. "To the depth of his soul, he was a political character, and what he touched became political at the same time."

The character of the Szeklers is their perseverance in their Hungarian identity: their indomitably solid character and adherence to traditions. For Viktor Orbán, Transylvania may have been the last major force that shaped his identity. Not only did he choose religion for himself in the present and not only did he reimagine the Hungarian vision, but he also wanted himself a *past*.

Transylvania "Between Europe and Byzantium"—Viktor Orbán between the German Chancellor and the Russian

President. The crude personality that liberals reproduce is the echo of Transylvania. Here, too, nature comprises hard-edge contradictions, with the mountain peaks overgrown with dense forests, giving way to open valleys and plateaus, overcast and raining at unpredictable times and then the sun shining unexpectedly through the clouds.

"The Transylvanians have several opinions at the same time, and even if they contradict each other, he is very at home in these intricate contradictions." Therefore, the Tusnadfürdő speeches are symbolic: he shares his political vision and vision with the Szeklers. They are the real *hinterland*. The people of Pest listen to their stomach first, their heart second. For Transylvanians, the heart comes first.

Opposite Orban's Felcsút House (in Hungary) is the Pancho Arena. Designed by master-architect Imre Makovecz, the stadium evokes the atmosphere of the altar of the Virgin Mary pilgrimage site in Csíksomlyó (Şumuleu Ciuc). The landscape of Felcsút also reminds us of the *Csík County* (Comitatul Ciuc). The closed-door world of Transylvania repeats itself in the Transylvanian-style house. A hospitable symbolism of the Szekler Gate breaks the unfriendly rigor of Transylvanian-style homes with its dense lattice fencing. (The characteristic feature of the Szekler gate is the carving (possibly painting) decorated with folk motifs and the dove-top, built on the top of the gate.) Viktor Orbán's house in Felcsút is Transylvanian in style, and even in the character of Viktor Orbán, we can discover these style features.

Lonely and family-friendly at the same time, aloof and direct, and vigor is also recognizable in his character. The red-black combination of the Szekler flag and folk art represents this. Red is the symbol of power and blood, and black is the symbol of earth and mourning. The star on the flag symbolizes unity, and the moon symbolizes hope. Power, loneliness, unity, hope:

behold the character of Viktor Orbán.

In the words of Béla Hamvas: "The Transylvanian man is more polished than the man of the West, the South or the East. He is more mature, more whole, cultivated, finite, more individual, more crystalline, and more recognizable."

My underground assumption is Viktor Orbán's statesman archetype is Gábor Bethlen. Orbán reinterpreted his power system by the paradigm of the United States but through Gábor Bethlen's Principality. The Christian liberty of the illiberal state can also be interpreted as a rethink of Bethlen's Protestant sovereignty.

The character of the *ordinary* man behind the statesman is *Ábel*, from Áron Tamási's trilogy.

> *This meant that I would leave no one to guide me anymore,*
> *but that I would act according to my will and wisdom. And my*
> *goal will be nothing but duty first and then my growth and the*
> *prosperity of my house. But how I should start and accomplish*
> *this growth, I did not think about it now, but I hoped for the*
> *future. All I have to say to myself is that just as an animal has*
> *to fight with its claws and teeth, so mans's with his mind.*
> (Abel in Woodland)

Áron Tamási's Ábel trilogy is one of the most beautiful stories in Transylvanian fiction. One can understand the person behind Viktor Orbán.

# 33

# 1100 Years in the Heart of Europe

Members of the Fidesz generation of politicians understood the importance of the nation as mature young adults. They understood the significance of national belonging, and it was this realization that determined Fidesz's political vision in its fundamentals. The title of this chapter cites a significant source of contemporary national literature. The *1100 Years in the Heart of Europe* is the travel diary, enriched with quotes and data, of a thirty-year-old man, Zsolt Bayer (b. 1963), who traveled through historical Hungary. "A young man's epiphany..."

In his lecture and book, *Don't Hurt the Hungarians!*, József Szájer does not interpret the political space in terms of right-wing and left-wing political ideologies, but as a confrontation between the nation-state system and a new globalism. Orbán's conflicts with the European Union are derivative of Orbán's conflict with opinion leaders who want to conform to the world view of the liberal mainstream that dominates the European Union.

> *The fact that we like to think in the nation, in community,*
> *or that we believe it is beneficial for countries to have borders.*
> *We find that you have community obligations besides rights.*
> *According to Timmermans and the like, it is a provincial,*
> *authoritarian, and alienating attitude. Our way of thinking,*
> *which distinguishes between citizens and non-citizens,*
> *Hungarians and non-Hungarians, in addition, to favor the*

*former, is hopelessly exclusionary.*
*We take pride in our thousand-year-old national*
*accomplishment, for surviving and being "a nation that*
*shall thrive on its homeland." It is, in the liberals' view,*
*incomprehensible and even chauvinistic in a world where*
*everyone ought to come together by multicultural bonds. They*
*cannot comprehend that we feel safer at home rather than in the*
*world. They can't understand why we cling to our tragic heroes,*
*to our national, intellectual resources. (József Szájer)*

The cause of division among Hungarians is that voters' worldview split the weight of the nation. Viktor Orbán could align at least half of the country into an array along national values. By this, he nailed the hidden desires of the Hungarians, backing it with the well-established system of football. Yet this is not an ideology, but rather a useful rationale. He did not force a new worldview on people but declared well-functioning fundamental truths. Although the truth builds on Christian worldviews, it seeks to avoid worldview differences that would divide people.

In America, both Republicans and Democrats represent national politics, and this is the bedrock of cooperation between the American people, which has resulted in them always putting their country's interests first, and their parties' interests second. That's why American democracy can function as a system because it thrives on national cooperation. I think that this explains why Viktor Orbán is not willing to compromise on the question of the nation. Because without national unity, America would not have succeeded.

Mihály Babits says the circumstance that from the outset, we have been thinking in the nation is because "the existence of the national spirit precedes the very existence of the nation." It is why the nation has become a central element of Orbán's policy.

The belief in a strong nation is at the heart of Orbán's story, accepted by millions of people. The vision of Orbán's politics is that Hungary's only chance of survival is if it remains as is—as the Hungarian nation.

"One of the most popular historians of our time may define the thinking of the Hungarian Prime Minister"—an article published in the right-wing daily newspaper *Magyar Nemzet* (Hungarian Nation) showed that the acclaimed Israeli Yuval Noah Harari inspires Viktor Orbán.

One of the central ideas of the bestselling book *Sapiens* is that humans—Homo sapiens sapiens—has conquered the animal species on the planet because of their ability to create and believe in fictional stories. These shared stories enabled cooperation. For example, according to the historian, money is a fictional story that everyone believes in. Religion or mythology is something that can unite many people. The author, Harari, views not only Judaism, Christianity, Islam, or Buddhism as religions, but also Nazism and Bolshevism. Football too exists because the parties must accept the rules of the game, and they enjoy the game because they believe in it. Otherwise, it would be impossible for twenty-two people to chase a ball for ninety minutes.

The System of National Cooperation works because it thrives on the story of (re)uniting the Hungarian nation. It features cooperation while functioning as a system. There is logic behind it, furthermore, based on another fiction: football.

According to Andy Grove, the greatest Hungarian of Silicon Valley, culture is a system of shared beliefs and values that determine how we "settle at long last the price of thought."[xiii]

xiii We consider István Széchenyi—his alternative name—the greatest Hungarian. The "greatest Hungarian of Silicon Valley" is my tribute to Mr. Grove, one founder of Intel and a founding father of the digital revolution.

Simply put, culture is a shared worldview and value system. "People and the nation are united, but only such a group of people is a nation which has gained a historical status." (Béla Hamvas) National unity is the basis of all the shared national cultures. It gives the power of the community. Which in turn, is the trademark of Hungarians—liberty.

"In a word, I could describe it. However, one has the feeling when you are about to greet a dear, familiar acquaintance. Liberty is the word." (Gyula Illyés: Who is Hungarian.)

Liberty, as the universal value of Hungarians, created two kinds of cultures within society, that are predicated on different worldview. These two cultures express the opposition between the nationalist and leftist tribes:

*On the one hand, there is a modern, left-wing, and ultra-individualized liberal view, and on the other, an integrative liberalism with different value propositions regarding the nation, the role of the state, and the Church.*

In Viktor Orbán's politics, the national idea originates from liberty. It is the most crucial difference between Orbán and far-right populists. Extremist-right ideology uses the nation to justify the superiority of peoples and verify dark ideas. In Orbán's case, it is the nation that ensures liberty.

*The years around 1848, when Hungary became a modern nation-state, can be considered as the era of liberal politics and*

---

The term "settle at long last the price of thought" is a phrase coined by Attila József in his famous poem By the Danube, literally meaning it's time to organize our collective affairs: "And settling at long last the price of thought, / This is our task, and none too short its lease."

*liberal politicians, from Széchenyi to Kossuth. Liberalism has
always been present in Hungary, there have always been one or
two prominent writers and thinkers — a line that can be well
shown in intellectual history. All this turned into politics in
1848. This whole era is nothing less than the domestic political
realization of European freedom thinking of that time. Later,
liberalism remained the dominant force of Hungarian politics,
as the Austro-Hungarian Compromise (1867) was also prepared
by liberals. So, we can look back on liberal traditions of political
history that we can be proud of.*

Orbán's concept of liberty interprets freedom from the point
of view of power. That is how sovereignty will have significance.
A strong country is free to decide its future because it is sovereign.
Sovereignty ensures freedom from outside influence, the principle
'my house is my castle' in practice. Migration restricts Hungary's
freedom, weakens its power because mass immigration changes
the ethnic composition of the country, loosens the national
character of the nation-state, and creates parallel societies. A lack
of border controls undermines security and reduces the internal
strength of the country. Border protection, on the other hand,
increases the country's power and authority and ensures that
Hungarians can live in freedom in their homeland.

Freedom also means the liberty of ethnic Hungarians living
abroad. The pursuit of autonomy aims at developing the
empowerment of Hungarians living in Szeklerland or Vojvodina.

*Liberal philosophy and politics are organized around individual
liberties. In contrast, here in Central Europe, people may be
harmed just because they belong to a particular ethnic group.
Therefore, they may be denied the rights necessary to maintain
their cultural identity. Liberal thinking must, therefore, be*

*expanded in our region because there are rights attached to a group, not derived from the individual, or at the very least difficult to derive from individual rights. Remaining in the political realm, preserving traditions, the right to use the language, and multilingualism in street signs are difficult to articulate as an individual right since they address an ethnic group.*

The worldview of Orban's patriotism thrives on three pillars that every second person can accept as a fundamental value: national unity, sovereignty, and Christian values. All three pillars stand on the bedrock of liberty, forming a shared culture, much like what John Doerr wrote in 2018 in his book *Measure What Matters*—"culture eats strategy for breakfast." A shared culture means that we try to overcome challenges together. According to Dov Seidman, the real question is not what we do but *how* we will do it. Therefore, today's leaders inspire us, and we follow them of free will.

*Fidesz is an opportunity, and I am part of that opportunity. An opportunity for the country, an opportunity for the voter. If the voter wants to take advantage of this opportunity and entrust us with the responsibility of making decisions that affect his or her life, then this should be considered an implicit agreement. It is about trying to achieve results under defined conditions for four years. And the voter may say after four years, "I apologize, this contract has not been fulfilled, and Mr. Orbán, do not regard this as an insult, but next time I will agree with someone else." I think we are trying very hard to keep this obsequious behavior far from ourselves. It has its roots in Eastern European culture, to seek patronage among voters—unfortunately, a profoundly paternalistic approach. Besides, this is a difficult time for the country, and unpopular decisions must be executed.*

*Anyone who measures whether the people like a decision,*
*whether they themselves are popular—well, they will make*
*mistakes. While the people will continue to love him, he will*
*ruin the country. We need to let everyone know that Fidesz and*
*this young man are working for the country. That's enough for*
*me. If I can make them understand it, I'm balanced.*

The System of National Cooperation embodies Viktor Orbán's political culture: how the country's rise is a strategy of strength training. Collaboration among those of shared beliefs, emotions, and values is, therefore, about strength, the ability to overcome obstacles. Orbán's political culture may cause a loss of interest in an individual's freedom or in individual institutions, but only if they are part of the executive branch and restrict cooperation. The education system, or the research network of the Hungarian Academy of Sciences, is also part of the executive branch, whose institutions are part of the national effort. Metaphorically speaking, without the synchronization of its muscle fibers, the country could not maximize its efforts.

József Szájer: "With his sharp eyes, Zrínyi also recognized that the threat to the Hungarians also had a metaphysical dimension, that a lazy, sluggish attitude to our own country's affairs was a greater problem than the conquering enemy."

It is not just a real political, military issue with our armed forces, but also about ourselves, our self-esteem. In the subtitle that I borrowed from Zrínyi's book, the word *áfium* refers to opium, a drug that was already known at that time to destroy a person's mind. Losing your mind, your sense, is worse than slavery. Inactivity, inertia, feeds our minds delusions, misconceptions, or *áfium*.

Imre Kerényi (1943-2018), the former mentor of Viktor Orbán, was responsible for the spiritual strengthening of national awareness. As *the Prime Ministerial commissioner responsible for the establishment of conscious national thinking and related tasks for the preservation and development of Hungarian cultural values*, his first task was to promote and disseminate the new Fundamental Law (constitution) adopted in 2011 and taking force in 2012. The government made the new Constitution available to the public at the *Table of the Fundamental Law* between September 2011 and September 2012 at municipalities and government offices. Kerényi is associated with the National Library series launched in 2012, and the Hungarian Chronicle launched in 2014.

*Áfium* and *antidotum* are old Hungarian terms, áfium meaning a narcotic substance, the antidote of which is antidotum. According to the metaphor of József Szájer, "The main antidote to the opium of utopian globalism is the fostering of the national bonds that connect us, the wise national building that takes care of the world and our environment. [...] Do not hurt the Hungarian! Here too, the closing phrase sets the direction for the patriots: Volenti nihil difficile! (Nothing is impossible for the willing!)"

**WITHOUT A COMMON CULTURE, THERE IS NO SHARED VISION. WITHOUT** vision, there is no cooperation. Without cooperation, there is no system. Without a system, there is no team play. Without team play, there is no victory. Without victory, there is no politics. Politics is therefore based on culture, because culture is the bedrock of the worldview—we have been here for 1100 years. Orbán's politics is storytelling based on the worldview that has emerged from liberty.

> *In Hungarian. That my mother tongue is Hungarian, and I speak Hungarian, I think, I write, is the biggest event of my life — nothing compares to it. (Dezső Kosztolányi)*

*To me, one is Hungarian who cannot withstand obscurity,
either in prison or in thought. One is Hungarian who loves the
intellect, who only releases his passion when the word is no
longer used to accepting the truth. All peoples are communities.
A good Hungarian is a human being, a good member of the
Hungarian community. (Gyula Illyés)*

*We are a nation in the old, spiritual, legal, moral sense of the
word, not a race among the raging races, nor a miserable little
effort in the fearful battlefield of the great powers. Don't we
just want to be like that? We must remain a nation, a soul, a
free man, a nobleman, a creator, in an eastern tranquility that
defies everyone, in a spiritual power that does not feel behind
anyone. We do not need transformation. We need to emerge from
ourselves, rather to return to ourselves. (Mihály Babits)*

*Love of country is a matter of quality. (Péter Esterházy)*

# 34

# Here You Must Live and Victor

The calendar represents the identity and history of Hungarians through three national holidays. The 20th day of August is dedicated to the memory of the state's founding and its founder King Saint Stephen. Founder of the Christian Hungarian state, St. Stephen is one of the first Hungarian Catholic saints, a prominent figure in Hungarian and European history. His significance is that he organized the country of the Hungarians, the principality formed by the union of Hungarian tribes, into a united Christian state.

The other two national holidays celebrate freedom. The 15th of March commemorates the 1848–49 Revolution and War of Independence—a cornerstone of Hungary's national identity. With its social reforms, it became the initiator of civil transformation, and its struggle for self-defense became part of national mythology. The spirit of enlightenment, progress, and innovation inspired the spiritual background of the 1848 Revolution. The Hungarian people revolting against the ruling feudal Habsburg status quo set the stage for the heroic struggle and the will to win. Although the revolution was stifled in blood, the nation still identified with itself.

The three most important symbols of March 15 are the national-colored cockade, "We shall vow, / Shall vow that we must be enslaved / No more now!" (Sándor Petőfi's National Song, translated by Alan Dixon) and "Long live the freedom of

Magyars! / Long live the nation!" (Kossuth Song).

The 23rd of October is dedicated to the memory of the 1956 Revolution and War of Independence. The 1956 Revolution and War of Independence—the revolution of the Hungarian people against Stalinist terror and the Soviet occupation—began with a peaceful demonstration of students from Budapest on October 23, 1956 and ended with a crackdown on the resistance of armed rebels on November 11.

On October 23, like March 15, Hungarians celebrate the people who fought for their liberty. Like the Revolution of 1848-49, the Revolution of 1956 ended with a tragedy. During the 1956 Revolution, hundreds of thousands of Hungarians left their homeland and started a new life abroad. Most of them settled in the United States—*Hungarian-born* became an international trademark of world-class quality.

Besides our national holidays, there are eleven memorial days in the calendar. They include the loss of Hungarian independence, the drama of Trianon, and the memory of the victims of totalitarian dictatorships.

March 15 and October 23 pay tribute to the martyrdom of the hero who sacrificed himself for the nation. It is the battle of the oppressor and oppressed, independence, and slavery, the culmination of a centuries-long struggle in which fortitude has prevailed. Hungarian history in the modern age is a series of failures and tragedies rather than a success story. The first change of regime was a turning point that allowed Hungarians to turn their backs on fate. Viktor Orbán's second regime change in 2010 fulfilled this opportunity.

Ferenc Kölcsey wrote the external narrative of Hungarians in his poem *Hymnus* in 1823, which became the official national anthem of Hungary.

Poetic translation by William N. Loew:

*O, my God, the Magyar bless*
*With Thy plenty and good cheer!*
*With Thine aid his just cause press,*
*Where his foes to fight appear.*
*Fate, who for so long did'st frown,*
*Bring him happy times and ways;*
*Atoning sorrow hath weighed down*
*Sins of past and future days.*

Literal translation by László Kőrössy:

*O God, bless the nation of Hungary*
*With your grace and bounty*
*Extend over it your guarding arm*
*During strife with its enemies*
*Long torn by ill fate*
*Bring upon it a time of relief*
*This nation has suffered for all sins*
*Of the past and of the future!*

Mihály Vörösmarty wrote the internal narrative of the Hungarians in his poem *Szózat* in 1823, which is the second most important national symbol of Hungary after the *Hymnus*.

Lyrical translation by Watson Kirkconnell:

*Oh, Magyar, keep immovably*
*your native country's trust,*
*for it has borne you, and at death*
*will consecrate your dust!*

*No other spot in all the world*
*can touch your heart as home—*
*let fortune bless or fortune curse,*
*from hence you shall not roam!*

Literal translation by László Kőrössy:

*To your homeland without fail*
*Be faithful, O Hungarian!*
*It is your cradle and will your grave be*
*which nurses, and will bury you.*

*In the great world outside of here*
*here is no place for you*
*May fortune's hand bless or beat you*
*Here you must live and die!*

We can also say, in 1823 and 1836, two people wrote the self-fulfilling prophecy of the Hungarians. Everyone knows the end of the story: 1848, the bloody revolution and war of independence, two lost world wars—Trianon and the Holocaust—, forty years of communist dictatorship, and in 1956, another bloody revolution and war of independence. We are divided—separated by walls—into *kuruc* and *labanc*, countryfolk and urban dwellers, nationalists and liberals.

Only one man who dared to change this. He said your destiny is not carved in stone, and the wall could be torn down.—Just a crucifix instead of a double-cross. Two flags on the Parliament are more than one. From now on, you can count on the nation and not just yourself.[xiv]

xiv Kuruc and labanc are terms coined in the 17th-18th century. Hungarians

**CHANGING OUR INTERNAL NARRATIVE WAS ONCE A FIELD OF PSYCHOLOGY.**
The ever-expanding universe of psychology, however, nowadays includes not only classical, therapeutic psychology, but so-called positive psychology. The latter does not use the methods of psychology in the therapy of mental illnesses, but to support the positive development of the healthy ones. The American export-product of applied psychology is coaching. Contrary to the dogmatic view of psychotherapies, this promises a rapid and profound change. The coach helps the client with questions to find their way out by themselves. Hundreds of motivational gurus and self-help books are convinced of the salvation of their method. The philosophy of *everything is decided in your head*, to self-fulfilling prophecies, says that a prerequisite for changing the external narrative is to change the internal story first.

All motivational and self-help methods start from the same scientific realization. One builds a wall that restricts or prevents him from fulfilling his abilities. Therefore, all coaches begin by breaking down this wall by changing their client's internal narrative. The eternal advice of one of the most potent gurus, Napoleon Hill, is to repeat the positive thought you desire many times a day. Anthony Robbins advises us to look for a role model, and then to model our inner narrative by repeating his pattern.

---

fighting for independence called the Habsburg loyalists "labanc." The word labanc comes from the word to flutter in the wind, named after the long-hair wig worn by the Habsburgs. Labanc was primarily the name of the German Habsburg-based troops and the Hungarian party leaders of the dynasty who were in Hungary during the Thököly uprising and the Rákóczi War of Independence. The kuruc were the Hungarians facing them. In colloquial language, labanc has a pejorative meaning of somebody who is a traitor. A kuruc on the other hand, is a Robin Hood-type freedom fighter who breaks the law for the higher purpose of his nation. The most anti-Semitic online portal reserved the name kuruc in their domain name, implying that left-wing and liberal Hungarians are traitors opposed to the far-right Hungaros.

One of the founding fathers of positive psychology is Mihály Csíkszentmihályi, a Hungarian-born psychologist living in the United States and best known for his bestselling book *Flow, The Psychology of Optimal Experience: How to Find Happiness in Life, What Gives You Pleasure, How You Can Give Meaning to Your Life*. When we experience flow, "we act freely, for the sake of the action itself rather than for ulterior motives, that we learn to become more than what we were."

If you want your nation to believe the same, Hungarians must be given a new internal narrative. In 2011 the Parliament adopted the new Fundamental Law of Hungary and the National Creed. (The text of the new Fundamental Law entered force on January 1, 2012.) "We, the citizens of Hungary, are ready to found the order of our country upon the common endeavors of the nation."

*The National Creed*, inspired by the *Declaration of Independence*, contains the essential elements of Orbán-coaching:

St. Stephen, independence, intellectual achievements, defending Europe, Christianity, and culture. Values, and how-s: human dignity; cooperation; family and nation —fidelity, faith, love— work and achievement; helping the vulnerable and the poor; security, order; the serving state; historical achievements, Holy Crown; defending our identity is a fundamental duty of the state; anti-communism and anti-fascism; "our current liberty was born of our 1956 Revolution."

The purpose of the "workout plan" of national cooperation is to overwrite the internal narrative—"spiritual and intellectual renewal"—and shape the external story—"make Hungary great again"—so that the world can believe in us.

In 1823 and 1836, two people wrote the internal and external narratives of Hungarians. And Viktor Orbán was determined to change both. Not only did he dare to oppose the story of ill fate—he reversed it.

*In the great world outside of here is no place for you?*
He who is strong has and will.
*May fortune's hand bless or beat you?*
The weak country is beaten, the strong is respected.
*Here you must live* and victor!
**STRONG HUNGARY**—this is the goal of training.

# PART FOUR

## TRAINING

---

*"Hello darkness, my old friend*
*I've come to talk with you again."*

(Paul Simon)

# 35

# It's Not Every Four Years,
# It's Every Day

To illustrate the athlete's desire to win, I borrowed the following gag from cognitive psychologist Steven Pinker: Donald Trump, Emmanuel Macron, and Viktor Orbán are sitting in a doctor's waiting room, and each is told he has twenty-four hours to live. They are asked how they plan to spend their final day. Donald Trump says, "In a Twitter message, I say goodbye to the American people, appoint a new president to head my companies, play golf with the kids, write my will, and spend the night with Melania at the Trump Tower." Emmanuel Macron says, "In a video message, I say goodbye to the French people, hold a brief government meeting in the Élysée Palace, eat a delicious dinner with Brigitte, watch the Eiffel Tower at sunset, and spend the last night making love." Viktor Orbán says, "I'm going to see another doctor."

THE EASIEST WAY TO ILLUMINATE VIKTOR ORBÁN'S CHARACTER IS TO FIGURE out his biggest fear. It's the same as with all most successful Olympic athletes: he cannot stand to lose.

At the Beijing Olympics, Michael Phelps' biggest rival, Milo Čavić, told a newspaper he thought it would be good for the sport if Phelps lost his eighth gold medal, after the seventh. The Serb was driven to be remembered for taking the eighth gold medal from the American. In the final, it took a hundred seconds for Čavić only to achieve the silver medal, though he swam better than anyone in the semi-finals who had an Olympic record. Čavić stated that he accepted Phelps' victory because "there's nothing wrong with losing to the greatest swimmer there has ever been."

Anyone who wants to understand Viktor Orbán must understand a character willing to put ten years of relentless training into a gold medal. Such an attitude is unusual in the world of politics because there is a fine line separating him from dictators. Still, the line exists, though it's not easy to recognize. A dictator gains power, then eliminates competition and kills the rules of the game. Orbán only changed the rules of the game and retained the competition. The thin line is called the athlete's mindset.

The previous two-round electoral system in Hungary was not an analogy of the semi-finals in sports competitions, because in sports you cannot add the semi-finalist athlete's results to the results of the finalist. In both rounds, the athlete's performance counts. In contrast to the past, the rules of Orbán's democracy are based on sport: training is more important than small talk at the coffee house. There is no second round where voter tactics and bargaining between party interests can override a politician's performance to the benefit of a less talented but more resourceful political competitor. Election preparation can begin the day after the previous election. It is a different question why only Orbán can take advantage of this opportunity.

There is a critical difference between Milo Čavić and the Hungarian opposition. The width of a hair separated Čavić from a gold medal. The opposition was light-years away. In the same way, Čavić was relentless and pushed himself to the Olympics, and when he failed to take home the gold, he elegantly said, "People, this is the greatest moment of my life."

"He is the most focused person I have ever met..." "The most interesting and complex person I know. Your ability to dream, plan, and work for success has inspired a generation and redefined what is possible in the world. Your name is synonymous with excellence."—The coach wrote in an acknowledgment to his student.

"We will ask for more effort, more focus, more persistence, more toughness, more training, more creative thinking, more problem-solving, and more honesty than you've ever put forth. These are the hallmarks of champions," said Bob Bowman, head coach of the US Swimming Team, on the first day of the Olympic preparations, 1068 days before the Rio Olympics. To pose a poetic question: why does Orbán's opposition think they can get away with a few months if an Olympic team needs at least 1068 days of preparation time?

Bob Bowman was the coach of Michael Phelps, the twenty-three-time Olympic champion swimmer and the most successful athlete of all time. I quoted from The Golden Rules in the paragraph above. If we ranked the politicians of the democratic world by the number of times that they won a two-thirds majority for their party, Viktor Orbán would be the most successful politician of all time.

In a top-performing athlete's mind, only a gold medal exists. So, ask yourself the question: how good do you want to be? Do you want to be good enough or the best in the world? The US Olympic Committee's slogan is a good starting point:

**"It's Not Every Four Years, It's Every Day."**

# 36

# What Is Training?

*The fight is won or lost far away from witnesses—behind the lines, in the gym, and out there on the road, long before I dance under those lights.* With this sentence by Muhammad Ali, I would like to highlight the meaning of the next few chapters for the reader: the importance of training.

Viktor Orbán spent at least ten years in political training, first getting into government and training another eight in the opposition. From high school, he needed to spend four years of hard work to get to college and to overcome the disadvantages of being a country boy. And before high school, he had needed to study well to get admitted to a good school. By 2010, twenty years of "political sports training"—plus fifteen years of self-directed training—were behind him. Thirty years of hard work preceded Orbán's overnight success.

The most important rule of sports is that success is the result of work done. Although practice cannot replace talent, talent is worth nothing without practice. In competition sports, repetition is of primary importance. Training teaches you that if you fail at first, it doesn't mean that you will never succeed.

*There were gifted people around me, far superior to my abilities. Here, too, I experienced what I had in football. Much more talented than me, but then they fell out. As I went forward in learning or football, my much more able companions were left behind at once.*

Physical training refers to a regular effort to achieve a specific sporting goal. We can also say that training is a systematic effort to overcome disadvantages. The disadvantage is that some are better than you. Disadvantage sets your goals for you. Disadvantage does not make it impossible to achieve a goal. It only makes the goal difficult to achieve. In the words of an unknown sage, disadvantage makes difficulty difficult. While an important feature: you can overcome it—with willpower, diligence, perseverance, motivation, and above all, planning.

My underground understanding is Viktor Orbán wants to change the Hungarians by training: we will become world champions if we learn how to play, cheer, and win as a team. Therefore, football is how to set the country on a new track. Dual-politics and the winner-take-all principle are the hallmarks of American democracy. The team-based logic of American democracy is no accident: American football, baseball, basketball, and hockey are among the most popular sports. Why did the iconic piece of American fashion become the baseball cap embroidered with the logo of the wearer's favorite team's logo, or work jeans and T-shirts? And why did athletic shoes first become commonplace in America?

It is from America's team spirit that Viktor Orbán's concept of democracy follows, namely that political competition is determined by team readiness, player talent, and work, not by the press or other outside forces. From 2012, this mindset was raised to a constitutional level, which Orbán's opponents complain about for obvious reasons, because their positional advantage did not stem from their talents and their desire to win, but from the sympathetic, liberal-dominated institutional system. In the olden days, the mediocrity of the socialist-liberal side was counterbalanced by the liberal media, the prestige of atheist-minded intellectuals, and the two-round electoral system that supported political bargaining. The new system forces parties to unite, cooperate, and train. In fact, not only parties must do this, but all social groups.

In this new "sports democracy," the stronger team wins, the more organized, and better trained. Viktor Orbán built himself and Fidesz by training. You can understand this way of thinking from the principles of strength training, not only the vision of a strong Hungary but the difference between a strongman or a strong man. A strongman is a pejorative term that refers to a person to be feared and unfair. A strong man is always fair, reliable, and trustworthy.

Training is an excellent tool for rewriting a narrative. The developmental effect of exercise is that physical and physiological changes associated with training change one's internal story: the power of training transforms a country lacking in self-confidence into a confident nation-state. This changes the external narrative: a strong nation-state gives the impression of a different country in the world than a country that lacks self-confidence. The external narrative changes too. More people believe in you.

SOME TASKS HAD TO BE DONE, GOALS THAT HAD TO BE ACHIEVED. *Goals made sense, and nobody ever put into my mind the doubt that they might not make sense. Doing high school, going to college, getting a diploma, running the four hundred meters in sixty seconds, passing the Cooper test in level time—wouldn't that be a good idea?*

Every workout must have a purpose. What do you want to get from your workout? What are the needs that can be met through training: reducing government debt, writing a new constitution, stopping illegal immigration, winning an election? In a broader sense, the goal of training is more self-confidence and self-esteem, better quality of life, more energy, overcoming difficulties, finding the purpose of life, accepting ourselves.

The purpose of training is always specific. 'I want to look better' is not the goal. To win a football championship cup is more like, because whoever gets there has a dream come true: he has a strong club, a steady team, and financial success. Assuming responsibility for organizing the Olympics is symbolic because it requires building a country capable of catering to the world. It takes at least fifteen years of effort before the country—one by one—celebrates victory with the world.

If you know the purpose of your workout, you can create a workout plan broken down into smaller units with specific exercises and measurable milestones. You must know what steps must be taken, which corrections are needed, where more strength is needed, where endurance needs to be built: in short what more you need to do. A training plan includes nutrition and recovery, and you should be prepared for any injury or lack of motivation.

The training plan should be broken down into smaller units and practiced. Anders Ericsson writes in his book *Peak* about the importance of deliberate practice. Practice is not enough. When Viktor Orbán was elected Prime Minister at thirty-five, he had been preparing for at least ten years, at the Bibó College, during the Opposition Round Table and eight years in Parliament. He learned how to express himself clearly, to speak effectively. By then, he had hosted thousands of public forums and read hundreds of books.

Viktor Orbán has been using the same method for at least twenty-five years, systematic training, day by day. As an outsider, it is much easier to say that Orbán is a dictator than to face the fact that he did not just work hard but went along a plan, and when the situation seemed hopeless, he never gave up.

This absolute rock-solid belief—*Drive*—is lacking on the other side and adds to the success of the method. Another world-class athlete, Churchill said, "Success consists of going from failure to failure without loss of enthusiasm."

When viewed from point of view of training, the opposition ignored the law and lost. Because Orbán's system works like a sport, there can be only one winner and the winner takes everything. Therefore, the victory must build on training principles, and preparation begins the next day. It works like the Olympics, not like an exam period.

Orbán's opposition has purposeless policies. Sometimes the opposition attack the system, and sometimes they attack each other due to their lack of foresight. The period between the first day of the four-year parliamentary term and the closure of the next election should be divided. There is no team. They bargain at the last minute, a few months before the competition. Then the campaign begins. The opposition does not understand the rules of strength development because if they did, they would do the same as Orbán: unite the party, unite the right-wing parties in one alliance, and then expand the united party's organization.

For four years, the Orbáns have been building, shaping politics in a systematic, predictable, and consistent manner. They know that an Olympic athlete does not prepare for the Olympics in three to four months but throughout his life. Again, in the words of Muhammad Ali: "Champions aren't made in gyms. Champions are made from something they have deep inside them. A desire, a dream, a vision."

# 37

# Strength

Viktor Orbán gained power along the lines of competitive sports training principles. This strategy has transformed Hungary and continues to do so to this day. The electoral term is always one long workout cycle, with a championship every four years that decides which party is eligible to exercise power. The parliamentary election is one turn, and the winner takes it all. Politicians who personify the future vision of their parties stand on the starting block. The goal of the workout is to win the election. The strongest competitor with the strongest vision wins. The goal of the workout is to build strength, which is measured by the strength of the story and how well it is integrated with voters' worldviews. Whichever party's vision most people believe in will win.

> *The situation is that in the campaign we are facing, we have to deal with external forces. Over the next nine months, we have to deal with the Soros mafia network and the Brussels bureaucrats in the battle, and we have to fight the media they operate.*

In sports, strength means that one can overcome substantial resistance with the help of muscular strength. The maximum force is the maximum amount of effort, for example, how much weight someone can lift doing a bench-press. The speed of the force exerted can characterize the speed of muscle contraction. Endurance refers to how long a person can perform a given muscle activity, remain active for an extended period, and its ability to resist fatigue. In martial arts, speed-strength and endurance-strength are more critical than maximum strength.

> *Physical strength has always been important in our family,*
> *and it is still so. My younger brother is an amateur bodybuilder*
> *[Áron Orbán], my older brother [Jr. Győző Orbán] took it to the*
> *wrestling youth team. My dad [Győző Orbán] did sports too,*
> *and he could bench press 160 kilos when he was forty-five. For*
> *us, this is necessary to take a person seriously.*

You can also approach strength from a political point of view. The politician who is the most popular is the strongest. The party that can beat its competitors is the strongest. A country that can overcome great resistance is strong. Voters will vote for the party with the strongest vision for them. A 'strong country', a 'strong vision' has a different meaning for all people, but all people share the same belief that they will decide based on their worldview, beliefs, and emotions.[xv]

---

xv  Based on Maslow's hierarchy of needs, we know that all people are motivated by the same needs in order of importance, hence the name *Maslow's pyramid*. At the bottom of the pyramid are the most fundamental needs. Above these fundamental needs lie belonging and love (e.g., togetherness), and above those are the needs for esteem: the needs of prestige and feelings of accomplishment. Finally, the need for self-actualization lies at the top of the pyramid. Let's have a look at Viktor Orbán vis-à-vis the needs pyramid with some examples for each level. Reducing utility costs is the basic necessity, handling migration fosters security, national values serve the need for belonging while raising wages for educators and healthcare workers benefits recognition. Supporting small and medium-size businesses cultivates self-realization. Starting a family covers all levels of the pyramid, which is why the government prioritizes the support of families. According to Christian values, the purpose of marriage is the birth of children and a family is the building block of the nation and expresses togetherness.

The purpose of Orbánian strength training is to convince the voter to have the conviction that Viktor Orbán's power is invincible.

ONE MISCONCEPTION ABOUT STRENGTH TRAINING IS THAT STRENGTH requires big muscles. Before 2010, Fidesz was not a Hercules-sized party; compared to the socialist mammoth, the right-wing's resources were meager. Yet they proved to be stronger in the end.

One of the biggest myths about fitness is that you can only increase your strength by increasing your muscle mass. Improving the synchronization of muscles and muscle fibers will increase strength without increasing muscle mass. In this way, the more organized and agile David of Fidesz could defeat the Goliath of the socialist-liberal coalition with its high muscle mass.

There are three ways to develop strength. The first is to increase the number of fibers in synchrony within the muscle: more muscle fibers are involved in the effort, while the thickness of the muscle fibers remains the same. The second is to improve cooperation between the muscles that make up the muscle loop. The third way to build strength is to achieve muscle fiber hypertrophy: thicker fibers can exert more effort. As a result, strength training does not always lead to gains in muscle mass. For gymnastics or martial arts, it is not beneficial to gain muscle mass, as opposed to bodybuilders who are pumping to achieve considerable muscle mass.

This is precisely how the Orbán's strength training works in practice. First, the "muscle contraction" within Fidesz had to be synchronized. It was necessary to develop a disciplined organizational background. The party can have one leader and one direction.

The second step is to establish synchronization between the right-wing parties—the loop of the helping muscles. Four or five different parties were competing on the right in 2002 from which Viktor Orbán created a synchronized party alliance—besides establishing civic circles: involvement of new muscle fibers—as the basis of the organizational background. The third step is to thicken the muscle fibers. By hypertrophy, we mean increasing the party's organization and the financial hypertrophy of the national side.

> *A campaign is the event when one experiences that nothing is possible if you are alone. You can be anyone's favorite person, you can be any popular, you can be a celebrated speaker, but if you do not have real supporters who work around the clock, put up posters, distribute flyers, then you will have nothing. Without a party organization and building on the media alone, one cannot run a successful campaign.*

Anyone who wants to understand the success of Fidesz must understand by analogy that there is only one way to build power. Whoever wants a strong party needs a lot of muscle fibers, those muscle fibers need to be in sync, and the thicker they are, the more effort they will exert.

# 38

# Grit

One says that it's not worth it anyway. The other one would take shortcut. The third one begins properly. The third is the true worldview of training.

> *After 1956, some, realizing the situation, switched sides: I was talking about November 4th and the next year. Others left because they had to leave or thought they had to escape. Some did not switch, did not flee, but stayed at home. Bibó symbolized this behavior. I do not want to contrast his behavior with Imre Nagy and other members of the political elite, but this is far from obvious. And this is the attitude: not to go away, to take what you need and stay at home, this is decisive for the way folks come from the countryside at Bibó College. Because Bibó could have gone. [...] I do not want to look sentimental, but this was part of a mindset that focuses on freedom but accepts political realities and knows that philosophical results cannot be put into practice. [...] The "here we have things to do, we won't go" attitude became the ideal both for Fidesz and the college.*

There are three ways to relate to training. Most give up before they try—'it's the same anyway.' The second group are those who hope to be smarter than everyone else and can take shortcuts—getting results with less work. They try to imitate the other, which will usually end up ruining the workout instead of achieving the best version of themselves. And there is the third group, one in a thousand people, who recognize that there is only one way to go: work, push hard, and do more. This fraction of a thousand are the ones that the rest are trying to imitate, or palely imitating because they are trying to avoid the suffering that accompanies true effort. You can understand the success of Viktor Orbán in the essence of a good workout: you can't cut back on the work. That's the secret of training.

These three attitudes are present in all areas of life. When faced with a problem, we either give up or try to solve it with as little effort as possible, seldom do we solve it for ourselves the proper way. This is also a watershed between Viktor Orbán and the left-wing liberals.

From the beginning, leftist governments offered hope for an easy life. In 1994, Gyula Horn, appealing to the illusion of the Kádár era, said that upon his election to office he would ensure that "professional expertise" would run the government. In 2002, Péter Medgyessy's 100-day program irresponsibly distributed the financial reserves conserved by the first Orbán government. When his popularity declined, the Socialists answered by forcing Medgyessy to resign, replacing him with the fresh Gyurcsány, who acted the Tony Blair character. In the meantime, the country took out loans to pay back social welfare incentives. "Divine providence, the abundance of the world economy, and hundreds of tricks that you need not know helped us survive. But there's no more. Nothing."—I quoted from Ferenc Gyurcsány's Őszöd speech.

I would also like to quote three of the twelve demands of the 2018 opposition student demonstrations: "Cap the maximum number of compulsory classes for students at 30 hours per week in high school, and 25 hours in elementary school! Don't increase the length of the school year in any way! Abolish zeroth class lessons [note: lessons starting at 7 am], do not begin teaching before 8 in the morning!"

Before the 2018 Parliamentary elections, the Socialist program had the slogan of "The rich shall pay!" The moral view of the left-liberal side is that whoever is wealthy must pay more taxes, who can earn ten times as much money, should not pay ten times as much tax, but more. The frustrated crowds on the streets think that the government should take away money from hard-working and educated people and redistribute it to their pockets.

It is a left-wing belief that people who succeed under the Orbán government owe their wealth to corruption rather than hard work. Because of my social background, I have many relatives and friends who have built businesses worth millions of dollars. While they sympathize with Viktor Orbán, nothing could be further from reality than that their success resulted only from having connections. Instead, they have endured hard work to prosper, and have sacrificed many evenings of television and comfort, even summer vacations, to spend all their time building their businesses.

Viktor Orbán always chooses the hard way. The country, which the Socialists have indebted, was recovered not by imposing austerity measures on the population, but by levying sector-specific taxes, abolishing private pension funds, and issuing government bonds abroad. He has recapitalized the nation in a legitimate way, transparently in front of voters. His attitude towards Hungarian culture runs along a similar line: an independent Hungarian voice instead of copying the West.

The way Orbán systematically built up his power is the exact method that competitive athletes use. On the surface, analysts see government measures, but, under the surface, Orbán is putting together a worldview. And this worldview, a story based on people's beliefs and emotions, has the effect of being populist or extremist. While that's not what happened. Hungarians did not have a shared identity, and Orbán decided they should have one.

Orbán's system is considered a dictatorship because it is solid. The only thing that the opposition did not realize was that this construction is built on the bedrock of athletic training, the method of systematic effort, destruction, and recovery. Yes, destruction...

That's what super-compensation is about—another law of conditioning.

# 39

# Destruction

A good workout has a disruptive effect on the body. The purpose of training is always change, which can be triggered by stress, so the body has enough time to adapt and recover after each workout. Systematic exercise is, therefore, a destructive activity that breaks down the body's steady state to rebuild it stronger and more efficient. The body's adaptation process is called super-compensation. To achieve and maintain super-compensation, you must vary and harden the intensity of exercise, its frequency, duration, and extent of stimuli.

The mechanism of action in training works on the cycle of destruction and recovery—just like Orbán's government. It is indeed the "systematic destruction" echoed by the opposition. Without this, strength building will not work. The financial stability of the country has been achieved through stress, such as the destruction of private pension funds, sector-specific taxes, and residency bonds.

These measures harmed the interests of some but ultimately prevented the country from depending on the International Monetary Fund, thereby increasing the country's liberty. The result of changing the retail tobacco business was that the concessionaire could become financially more stable (mostly Fidesz loyalists won the permission to operate tobacco retail shops). In 2019, the subordination of the research network and institutional system of the Hungarian Academy of Sciences to the government was not a restriction on the freedom of science but a cessation of the left-liberal status quo. Science funded by tax revenues must adapt to the government's program, as results from the electoral mandate. Freedom of science is not restricted, yet the government only regulates the operation of institutions maintained on public money. If you want a muscular country, you need to synchronize cooperation between the government program, higher education, and R&D. The Hungarian state does not need intellectuals that are disrupting the unity of the country. This principle is not fascism, but common sense.

Super-compensation is a result of stimulus during exercise, and the body's response to these triggers, the body's ability to adapt to the harder workouts. One must step out of one's comfort zone. It is why many people confuse exercise with fatigue. Exhaustion at the end is an integral part of a workout, but fatigue does not make a workout. Destruction does.

The principle of super-compensation in training science is why Orbán takes on conflicts. There is no gain without a clash with the European People's Party, without putting the pedal to the metal. Because of such destructive activities, Fidesz suspended its membership in the European People's Party. But it takes time for recovery, and the body is rebuilt at a higher proficiency than before. Orbán has remained in the party alliance and has been even more respected.

Here is the most beautiful part of a workout, the watershed. This is that one is always challenging oneself to overcome yesterday's self. That should be a little better understood, at least by anyone willing to do it.

Now I want to quote from my book, *The Self-Made Workout*:

*Getting to the turning point involves work. Not easy, but worth it. The success of each turning point depends on three things: motivation, action, and repetition.*

*With the coordinated work of the muscles, joints, tendons, ligaments, and nervous system, general fitness, and motivation, they all, together, reach a turning point. The driving force behind our motivation is the desire to win stronger than ever to change the status quo that governs our lives. The second step is to turn the internal drive into action. An action plan requires a strategy, a strategy a mindset.*

*The first step in the action plan is a crazy plan that will take you from zero to one. The strategy requires a disruptive mindset of climbing the two mountains and crossing the chasm with the principle of super-compensation. Faith and the inner dialogue of man with himself play a decisive role in bringing ourselves into action. The third element of the workout is repetition, so we can continue to grow, combining motivation and doing and their dynamic cycle.*

*Knowing what you want can only be achieved through goals. Increasing goals require increasingly intense repetitions that, with due diligence, will produce the desired results. Start doing it. As Lao Tzu said, "A huge tree grows from a tiny sprout; A nine-story high terrace is built from heaps of earth. A journey of thousand miles begins from the first step."*

*There is no motivation without a goal, but without motivation, you cannot reach a goal either. There is no workout plan without purpose and motivation. There is no workout without a workout plan. The goal can be achieved through specific steps— good training.*

# 40

# Reps, Reps, Reps

"There are no shortcuts—everything is reps, reps, reps." So, as Arnold Schwarzenegger says, the first law of training is regularity, and this is the rule that most people violate. The success of a workout depends on the difficulty task of persevering at regular intervals. To persuade one to act and not only so, but every blessed day. It's not a matter of genetics or magic.

> I went to school in the morning, had two or three hours in the afternoon to get ready for the next day, and then went to work out. I had four trainings a week at the MÁV Előre. And it took up my whole afternoon. By the time I got home, it was seven in the evening. Once again, I sat down and learned something, had dinner, talked to my parents, and then go to bed. That's how it went for four years. I was living a disciplined life.

Regularity means regularizing habits appropriate to the purpose of the exercise: either reinforcing new habits or replacing bad habits with new ones. Whether you're setting up a new pattern or trying to overwrite an old one, you'll certainly need one thing: willpower.

In the words of János Arany, literally translated:

*The fight ahead of you, the track ahead of you,*
*Your powerless despair, the strong stands.*
*And you know what strength is?—Will,*
*Which sooner or later reaps amber.*

Willpower is the invisible strength and stamina required to overcome a challenge. Like muscle conditioning, you can systematically support and develop it. First, we need to identify the habits that govern our lives, so we know what to change. Where can we intervene to break the status quo? Second, we need to know ourselves better—if we understand what drives us, what the motivational points behind our decisions are, what our personality type is, and what representation language we use, we will know how to motivate ourselves.

The liberal attitude is the celebrated self-realization of the individual, and the Orbánian philosophy is team play. The Hungarian liberal mindset is the attitude of being selfish and critical, debate disguised as reasoning, and over-complication instead of simplification. Viktor Orbán harvested amber for not only knowing thy camp but also identifying the habits that dominated his liberal opponents, recognizing the motivating points behind their decisions, the driving force behind their actions. He recognized his opponents' lack of willpower, their attitude to bypass physical discomfort. Therefore, he has built a system in which one cannot thrive without willpower. And the one with the highest willpower wins. No one else must put in more than Orbán did: his entire life.

One must also practice the ability to pull together, which does not happen by itself. Companies do not spend fortunes on team building because of some fad. At Viktor Orbán's, teambuilding is called the movement of civic circles and the *March of Peace*. The patriotic national tribe has been at least eight years in the making.

It wasn't an overnight success. The arduous part of politics is uncomfortable. It is not possible to take shortcuts. Reps, reps, and reps of monotonous construction work, nationwide rallies, or the taxi of participants to events lead to success, not the path paved with the "good intentions" of journalists.

A drop in the ocean was a television political talk show called *Straight Talk* (the title recalling BBC's *Hard Talk*). Thanks to an aggressive hostess, the show was one of the opposition's leading lighthouses for eight years until the end of 2016. The show built along training principles, it was systematic and consistent: it clashed opinions, of opposition parties' and politicians. Hence the critical left-wing attitude that dominated the show, no one could have dismantled the opposition more professionally—in my private opinion. In fact, the opposition was/is satisfied with the quality of left-wing broadcasting. And the right-wing is grateful for the two-thirds, which would not have happened without the left-wing media. Because, exercise can indeed be done badly. The story will also fail if you systematically follow a bad workout plan, not just if you don't have a workout plan in the first case.

By criticizing each other, the opposition parties have earned the image of the *argumentative opposition* in the public opinion. Whether or not this image is good, it is for the reader to decide.

> *Taking an image of a debating party—even if there is otherwise a legitimate political debate—breaks the whole picture, and people will say these folks do not differ from the others.*

(I didn't say this; Orbán did, not now but twenty-five years ago, and he got a two-thirds majority, not anyone else.)

Here, too, it may not solve this subject from the perspective of liberal pluralists. According to the liberal dogma, debate and criticism are positive. Not in the world of professional sports. There, public criticism is not part of the culture because criticism destroys the athlete's self-confidence. In sports, one must be very careful about criticism. Alex Ferguson says two words bring the athlete to the top: "Well done!"

*But we held together but closed our rows, shoulder to shoulder, we were honest with each other, and we always got out of struggle. That is why we are up, and the liberal left — always betraying each other — is down there. It is what Ronald Reagan called the eleventh commandment. Yes, the eleventh commandment is needed in politics. That sounds like you don't say bad about your Fidesz mate. This will have to be practiced. And as our domestic opponents are disappearing and we are left without a severe opponent, this eleventh commandment is becoming more and more critical. The attacks of our adversaries less and less hold us together. What keeps our community together are the bonds of camaraderie.*

According to Aristotle, "We are what we repeatedly do. Excellence, then, is not an act, but a habit." In the first place, it is not Viktor Orbán that opposition could not defeat. But themselves.

VIKTOR ORBÁN, HOWEVER, OWES HIS SUCCESS TO HIS ABILITY TO overcome himself. Igor Janke's book, Forward! draws the curve of an overnight success, narrating Viktor Orbán's story "through the eyes of a Polish journalist"—a narrative of triumph. However, the narrative is at least as inspirational when viewed not from the side of victory but from the point of failure: how does one recover from a defeat.

"I've failed over and over and over again in my life. And that is why I succeed," said the 1963-born Michael Jordan. First, he was not chosen for the high school team and later was not chosen for the university team. Yet today, everyone celebrates Michael Jordan as the hardest working role model in sports history and the best basketball player of all time. "Mental toughness and heart are a lot stronger than the physical advantages you might have. I've always said that, and I've always believed it."

Viktor Orbán was not the strongest kid and the best student. His dream was to become a football star. He gave up on this dream because, despite all his efforts, he could only become a mediocre player. He graduated from law school, became a Bibó collegiate, and was given the opportunity to be involved in the political transformation of the change of regime. Everyone considered the young man who spoke at the reburial of Imre Nagy to be the most talented young politician. Yet, in 1990, he could gain only 5% of the vote. He has almost failed to overturn his party's conservative turnaround, with just one hair in the 1994 election keeping his party in Parliament. His personal work could compensate for Fidesz's disadvantage. He learned how to deal with people and to speak memorable. He defeated his political rivals in 1998 and was elected head of government at 35, but despite his momentum, Orbán lost his power in 2002. The day after the fall, he began to rebuild the right to prepare for the next election. Although socialist Péter Medgyessy was overthrown by his party two years later, in 2006, Orbán lost. After the second defeat, his party mates began to question his suitability, but he did not give up. Today, it is easy to connect the dots in the context of the Őszöd speech in the rearview mirror, but that Orbán could recover there and then was far from obvious. After Gyurcsány's speech leaked, he remained in excellent self-control.

He learned something from everything and never said why it couldn't be done. Failures made him what he had become.

Overcoming difficulties has enabled peak performance.

His opponents also confront the fact that he seems to be able to turn a hundred and eighty degrees. I think that this is one of Viktor Orbán's best qualities: he is capable of change. Learning from mistakes means you change bad innervation. He could change his relationship with the churches, with Russia, and with himself. He realized that untrained intellectuals lacked willpower, here was their weak point. And he ruthlessly defeated them. He also realized that the right-wing lacked the willpower to cooperate, so he was relentless and practiced until he enabled cooperation. And when he did, he defeated his yesterday's self.

*Relentless* is a serious word. It was not by chance that Tim S. Grover gave this title to his book. Here is where he sees the essence of the cutting-edge character. The author of *Relentless* has worked with unstoppable world-class names like Michael Jordan, LeBron James, or Kobe Bryant. You make good and big decisions under extremely high pressure. You gain until you become irreplaceable— as Grover puts it, a cleaner—when everybody presses the emergency button, everyone is looking for you. You do not compete but find your opponent's weak point and attack. The opponent should fear you rather than like you. There is no failure because the goal can be achieved in many ways. And after you win, you don't celebrate or lean back. Viktor Orbán's character is also that of the relentless Michael Jordan's.

Bob Bowman's coaching advice is that short-term goals lay the foundation for long-term success. Dream big, take risks, and live your vision every day! Fate strengthens you. And when the time comes, deliver confident performance.—Viktor Orbán's character is a confident Michael Phelps's too.

Muhammad Ali: "It's the repetition of affirmations that leads to belief. And once that belief becomes a deep conviction, things begin to happen." Exactly so.

EVERY ATHLETE'S INTERNAL NARRATIVE IS THE SAME: 'I WILL BE THE best.' In the world of top athletes, 'everyone is worse than me' is not about superiority but self-esteem. It is not an inferiority complex or trauma that fuels the desire to win, but the belief that I will be the first in the race because I have earned the job through victory. My goal is to be the best in the world.

Viktor Orbán's national policy must be interpreted through the spirit of leading athletes. Most people misinterpret it because there is a thin line separating this "sports nationalism" from nationalism, the desire for a "national gold medal" from dictatorship. Orbán says, 'let's be the best.' Nationalists say, 'we are the best.' Orbán does not say, 'we are the best, and we can sit back,' but that 'we can only be the best if we do not sit back.'

The goal of nationalism is to use the myth of national supremacy as a means of self-destruction for the unsportsmanlike destruction of rivals. Orbán's national policy is about sportsmanship and a great competition—about a nation that earns influence not through birth privileges or exploitation of other nations, but through labor. This policy is about winning, work, and diligence. Let's become a nation worth looking at. In this task, he motivates Hungarians as a coach, giving Hungarians their self-esteem back, the belief that they can do it. To make his nation the best version of itself—SELF-MADE.

# PART FIVE

## STARTUP

---

*"Let's dare to be big, and not that hard,*
*but also be wise!"*

(Count István Széchenyi)

# 41

# Zero to One

W*e choose to go to the moon in this decade and do the other things, not because they are easy, but because they are hard, because that goal will serve to organize and measure the best of our energies and skills, because that challenge is one that we are willing to accept, one we are unwilling to postpone, and one which we intend to win.* I quote from John F. Kennedy because both the purpose of training and the goal of politics must be specific and *crazy*: a challenge. Indeed, technology startup companies were born with such expansive visions.

Two young guys in their twenties—Bill Gates and Paul Allen—come up with an idea to write an operating system for personal computers: this became Microsoft. In a garage, a computer freak and a charismatic hippie—Steve Wozniak and Steve Jobs—build a desktop computer: it became Apple. Larry Page's and Sergey Brin's vision was to organize the world's information and make it universally accessible and useful: this is how Google came into being. In a dorm room, a college student—Mark Zuckerberg—codes an application that could connect everyone in the world to a single network: this has become Facebook. Bill Gates, Steve Jobs, Larry Page, and Mark Zuckerberg all started from zero. They had a crazy idea and believed they could make it happen. They all started from nowhere, just like Orbán and Fidesz.

To put it simply, Viktor Orbán has always thought like the founder of a startup: with limited resources, he wants the greatest success possible—strength, confidence, renewal. The mission of this unique startup is to change Hungary.

To make a difference in our lives, we need a workable plan. We must break down the status quo in our lives and build a new one instead. It is essential to understand that we are starting a business, not starting a war. A war has no winner, and the only difference is at most that the extent of the loss is not the same between loser and winner. Unlike a war, business is about building. Growth. Creating value. It is our free will to choose the political vision, not because others are forcing us.

**EVERY SUCCESSFUL STARTUP HAS GONE FROM ZERO TO ONE. ITS** founders dreamed up something that did not exist before. On an imaginary scale of ten, they did not move from two to three, from nine to ten, and not even from one to two, but from zero to one. That's why Peter Thiel gave his book on startups the title *Zero to One*.

What is a tenfold improvement in people's lives? For example, compared to mail, email is a tenfold improvement. Digital photos instead of analog photography. Compared to a cassette Walkman, a digital music player with "a thousand songs in your pocket." It is said that Steve Jobs was a revolutionary innovator because the products he launched introduced the zero-to-one concept: the personal computer, the touch-screen smartphone, the digital music player, the tablet, and the air thin laptop. For Steve Jobs, innovation meant saying no to 1,000 things.

The most important message of Viktor Orbán's twenty-five year-long political career is this, without exception. If we look at the ideas that the various parties have come up with, there is no single point that would beat Orbán's level of innovation. No other party could outline a vision.

# 42

# Think Different

Here comes the crazy one who wanted to change the world. Though from a poor family, his parents did their best, so he went to college. At twenty-one, he started a great venture with his friends. After sudden success, he lost everything he had built so he could start all over again, wiser this time. "Sometimes, life hits you in the head with a brick. Don't lose faith," he said. Despite his ruthless leadership style, he was beloved. A cult creator and a role model to millions. His vision changed the lives of everyone as he disrupted the status quo, rewrote the rules of the game, and the business he built grew stronger year after year. On one of his famous campaign posters, under the iconic logo of a fruit, a slogan faded in: Think different. He concluded his other brilliant campaign video by saying, "… And while some may see them as the crazy ones, we see genius. Because the people who are crazy enough to think they can change the world, are the ones who do."

Steve Jobs was the historical figure who had one of the biggest influences on the technology revolution. Significance of being able to change the way we live. Personal computers and smart devices that provide an easy-to-use and enjoyable user experience are part of our lives. The technology revolution is not only thanks to Steve Jobs, but he is the person who personified this era in one by its most significant achievements. Apple, his heritage, is one of the most valuable companies in the world today.

Steve Jobs and Viktor Orbán both come from impoverished family backgrounds, and the path to break out means learning. Although Jobs did not graduate from university, both men laid the foundations for their future in college. Jobs's stepfather had a decisive influence on his stepson. Orbán, his legendary grandfather, Mihály Orbán played a significant impact. As a child, there were problems with both their behavior—they were self-governing, rebellious people. As a seeker of God, Jobs's path lead him to Buddhism, and Orban's path led to confirmation in the Reformed Church.

Success finds them both at a young age. Orbán will become Prime Minister at thirty-five, Jobs will be twenty-five when Apple goes public, and its shares are worth $256 million. Then they both lose what they have built so far. The board of directors fire Jobs from Apple and he leaves the company he founded in 1985. Orbán loses the elections in 2002—even though he had higher chances at winning than the opposition—and loses to his rival in 2006 too. They both lay the foundations of their return at this stage of their lives and become masters of their respective crafts.

Jobs founded two companies, a new computer manufacturer (Next Computer) and an animation film studio (Pixar Animation). Ten years later, Jobs returns to his company as part of Apple's acquisition of Next Computer. In the years following Job's return, Apple launches a series of revolutionary products based on Next and Pixar technologies: the iMac, the iPod, iTunes, the iPhone, and the iPad. To date, these products represent Apple's economic strength.

In his eight years in opposition, Orbán reorganizes civic circles, unites the right-wing forces, builds his media apparatus, prepares his team, and ultimately defeats his opponents by a two-thirds landslide victory. In the coming years, he will revolutionize politics, give Hungary a vision, establishes the country's financial independence, and introduces a new constitutional law—the second regime change, and in 2014 and 2018 he wins again by two-thirds majority.

Viktor Orbán's life, personality, and way of thinking are like Steve Jobs in many ways. The most exciting features are those that, like Steve Jobs, made him an outlier. How does one create value from nowhere? How does one break out of hopelessness? And how does a loser become a winner?

They are both masters of the art of doing (or making things happen, of realization)—practical people with strong theoretical backgrounds. They share an outstanding ability to speak in public and private, and they can engage their audience. A glittering lifestyle attracts neither of them, and they do not change their lifestyles, they live in a puritan manner. Orbán and Jobs hold outstanding associative abilities, which provide both of them insights, recognition of important issues, quickness in decision-making, and the ability to simplify: "He [Orbán] can be very suggestive in debates."

As a leader, Steve Jobs could squeeze the impossible out of his staff. During the development of Macintosh, Job's biographer Walter Isaacson mentions that he created a 'reality distortion field.' When his engineers said there is no time, or that the task is impossible, he ordered that it must be done. And they always succeeded. He brought out the maximum or even more of his people. Orbán did the same. "You take the initiative when others get scared. When others think 'we are too small for this, we will fail anyway,' he goes to the task and does, or at least does everything to accomplish the goal."

Compared to his opponents, despite much more limited resources, he could win by street length. How did he do it? He dismissed educated SZDSZ members from the Parliament, liquidated the left-wing media, and had the courage to confront George Soros. How much self-confidence does it take to break down such walls?

In 2005, Steve Jobs, founder of Apple, was asked to speak to graduate students at Stanford University. Jobs selected three dramatic chapters from his own life and summarized his philosophy of life through these examples. (I've listened to this speech at least fifty times, it is so inspirational.)

The first story is about connecting the dots: how seemingly unrelated events form a coherent chain. One cannot look forward to connecting the dots until he has looked back. You have to believe that everything that happens to us eventually will make sense. For Jobs, this outlook boosted his everyday life.

The second story was about getting fired from his own company and losing everything he had built up. You wouldn't have thought that such an even would be to your advantage later. The last story was about death. Jobs got pancreatic cancer, which was fortunately diagnosed in time for him to live another nine years. When confronted with the disease, he stated time is finite, and let us not waste our lives in others. "And most important, have the courage to follow your heart and intuition. They somehow already know what you truly want to become. Everything else is secondary." [...] "Stay Hungry. Stay Foolish." He concluded.

Cal Newport, a young scientist at MIT, emphasizes in his book, *So Good They Can't Ignore You,* that Steve Jobs is not a natural fit for the 'listen to your heart' narrative. He argues that for a long time, Jobs didn't know what he needed to do, was drifting toward computing by accident, but that had the will to learn and was good at what he was doing. Viktor Orbán spoke in his early interviews about how many doubts he had about his career in politics. At twenty, he did not wake up to being a Prime Minister but he developed a mission that required diligence and a lot of positive feedback. Newport's advice is to master the craft, that is, to choose something that interests you, learn the craft of your profession, and be the best at what you do. Andrew E. Czeizel, a world-famous Hungarian geneticist, said the same idea: talent is only an opportunity, practice makes genius.

# 43

# Apple and Orange

The striking difference between Viktor Orbán and Steve Jobs is that, on the outside, Jobs was a more friendly character. His packaging was better, with the goggles of Mahatma Gandhi and John Lennon, in sneakers, with a sense of style without being too casual. The simplicity of modern design and Apple's democratic philosophy has caught the taste of liberal opinion leaders. Yet the parallel between Apple and the two charismatic founders of Fidesz is real. Steve Jobs realized his vision through Apple to improve the lives of mankind. For Orbán, Fidesz, and then the government created the framework for the lives of Hungarian people to be able to change in a positive direction.

Both the Apple and the Fidesz logos bear fruit. Byte into an Apple. "If you get bored with bananas, choose the orange!" Apple's "1984" campaign, already a cult brand in the 1980s, might have inspired Hungarian rebels and Americaphile youth to come upon the analogy of the biblical apple in the communist system borrowed from the movie *The Witness*—for *Hungarian Orange* (the orange actually was a lemon).

Apple standardizes its products with the prefix "i" (iMac, iPod, iPhone), and Orbán does the same with "national." Apple's philosophy is the so-called controlled consumer experience. Control means Apple produces its hardware and software. Based on the example of a personal computer, a PC operates democratically, with components freely assembled, multiple manufacturers competing for multiple operating systems, and countless software programs for operating systems. (The most well-known operating system is Windows, which the vast majority of PCs run on.) From the outset, Jobs insisted on getting the full package and keeping the user experience under Apple's control. Experts say the closed-loop, controlled user experience is one of the main reasons Apple has become one of the most valuable companies in the world. Another benefit of the closed system is that Apple's various devices—computers, tablets, smartphones, smartwatches—now work in sync. Steve Jobs favored the less democratic concept.

Orbán built his system on a similar method. "Hardware" is the legal system, "software" is the political worldview. Apple also produces hardware and software, so third-party developers can only develop applications in a controlled way as Apple pre-filters all applications. The advantage is that the system is more stable and is guaranteed to work well. In IT, security is a matter of due diligence, but Orbán is attacked for not wanting to let immigrants into Europe uncontrolled. For computers, a firewall is an essential protection against unauthorized intruders. Don't fences and border guards do the same?

Just as Apple has nothing left to chance, so does Orbán's state of disciplined logic. Here, 'controlled user experience' also means that the state sets not only specific constitutional frameworks, but also reflects national ideology in as many areas of life as possible, and centralization is a general principle. Orbán's critics see this as a restriction of their freedoms, which is why Orbán's system is mistakenly labeled as autocracy. As with Apple, centralization, and integration is a market advantage, so centralized units and integration between them can provide a stable Orbán system. Such integration takes place between foreign and trade policy, the government and the National

Bank, family policy and tax policy, or coordination of national resources—culture, education, health, social policy—around the world. As a market leader in hardware and software, Apple wants to grow into services—home-made shows, news, games—to cement its market advantage. For Orbán, from 2018, course building, a self-made culture, has become a trend.

When on April 1, 1976, a "rebel" and a "squarehead" set up their first venture in a garage, they were still joking about changing the world. When Viktor Orbán and László Kövér founded the Alliance of Young Democrats on March 30, 1988, how seriously did they think they would be able to destroy communist rule and rewrite the constitution of the country in just over twenty years?

# 44

# Disruptive

Born in 1981, two decisive historic achievements influenced the world in which I live: the Internet and the regime changes which were led respectively by two emblematic figures: Steve Jobs and Viktor Orbán. The former represents the digital revolution, the friendly PC, life-enhancing smartphones, connect machines and people to the Internet, and the spread of digital content. Just as the world would be different today without Steve Jobs, Hungary would be different today without Viktor Orbán. I'm talking about my country, about all the things Viktor Orbán and his politics touched, whether as head of government or in opposition, his impact has been decisive from the change of regime to today.

If we consider the Internet the number one and unrepeatable opportunity for humanity's development in the modern age, then the change of regime in 1989 and 2010 was a real turning point in the life of the Hungarians. The spread of the Internet and the development of our democratic state under the rule of law took place almost simultaneously. Leaving behind the tragic past of our history, the first change of regime gave us a unique and unrepeatable opportunity: to grow, to belong to the West, and to live in peace.

Just as the Internet revolution has taken on a similar mission at one higher level: democratizing the world, connecting people, giving them the tools that they need to thrive, making their lives more comfortable, productive, and more enjoyable. Share your opinion, share your knowledge, learn, start a business, write a blog, entertain others, be productive, live happily ever after, and push humanity forward.

Viktor Orbán's second change of regime fulfilled the opportunity created by the first.

Clayton Christensen, a professor at Harvard Business School in the 1990s, coined the theory of disruptive innovation. *The Innovator's Solution* and *The Innovator's Dilemma* are essential reading in the technology industry.

Disruption has a double meaning. On the one hand, disruption entails a significant loss of interest in losing its status quo role despite its domination. On the other side of disruption is an innovative, novel, often revolutionary product created by its disruptive innovator. The outcome of the match between the disruptor and the disrupted is up to the user, i.e., the consumer.

The technologies of the digital revolution are called disruptive innovations because they are rebellious, build from the ground up, and rearrange the status quo. As a typical political product of the eighties and nineties, Fidesz was a disruptive innovation: it built on rebellious young people. It eventually could not only overthrow the system, but today, Fidesz has become the status quo. Just as Steve Jobs saw the opportunity in digital technology, Viktor Orbán saw the potential for the collapse of communism.

I want to illustrate the essence of disruptive technological innovation by examples. Cheaper and simpler technology replaces the slower and more expensive: email, digital music, digital photography, video sharing (YouTube), online commerce (Amazon, eBay), online newspapers, Wikipedia, Facebook, Instagram, low-cost airlines, self-driving vehicles, all disruptive innovations. Disruption is a necessary result of the loss of interest resulting from a change in power. More significant, more embedded, those who consider themselves more worthy will struggle to accept changes in the status quo. Inequality of power between the parties makes it challenging to process defeat. Yet we know from one of the oldest stories in the Bible that in the fight between David and Goliath, it is not the seemingly stronger who wins.

Orbán demolished the historical left-wing, and two of the most prominent parties of the first regime change, the MDF (conservatives) and the SZDSZ (liberals). Both fell out of Parliament in 2010. Orbán's victory in all spheres of life (constitutionality, economy, culture) redistributed political power.

Similarly, the Sony Walkman dominated the portable music player market for decades. Walkman, with a single cassette or CD, could hold ten to fifteen songs. When Apple released the iPod, it converted the music on CDs and cassettes to electronic files, allowing 1000 songs to be carried around in your pocket. The iPod was disruptive because it not only replaced previous music recording devices but also because it allowed Apple to replace Sony in this market segment.

*I think the MSZMP [the state Communist Party] didn't take us seriously. They didn't know what Fidesz was. Apparently, we weren't looking for the bargain opportunities that others might have been looking for. We didn't have any connections. For example, I did not meet with the leader of the MSZMP, except for the official hearing. Nor do I remember that an official Fidesz delegation would have negotiated with the MSZMP. They didn't come. We didn't go.*

All disruptive innovations follow the same pattern. There is a market dominated by specific market players. In this seemingly dormant state, a new technology emerges that major players ignore. On the one hand, their customers are not interested in the new technology, and on the other, it would not be viable to introduce it. For the newer technology, no market research data is available that would allow management to make a responsible decision.

Meanwhile, the market share of companies launching new technology is growing at a slower rate. When growth reaches a tipping point, there is a sudden and dramatic increase in demand for new technology. Old technology companies will lose their loyal customers in no time, and new players will replace their lost market position with the latest technology. The new players shape the status quo, but with it, even newer disruptive technologies begin emerging, and the whole process starts all over again.

The pluralist democracy that emerged and replaced the one-party system had a disruptive effect on Hungary. The social forces that changed the system built up their widespread support from a small social base, but by changing power relations and the status quo they were disruptive: they disintegrated the one-party system.

How did a close group of friends become one of the decisive political forces in the change of regime? How did they replace the Horn government in 1998, which dominated political life by a two-thirds majority? How did Viktor Orbán become Prime Minister at thirty-five? Why did the liberal SZDSZ fall out of Parliament in 2010? The SZDSZ has worked since its inception with the most embedded intellectuals: innovative philosophers, social scientists, and marketing consultants. How do we explain that Socialists with powerful social influence and a more extensive organizational network began to fight for survival in 2010? Fidesz could win in the elections in 1998 and 2010, hence, in terms of resources, financial means, and media support, they were far smaller than their rivals. That is why it is crucial to study disruptive phenomena: Why do the bigger and the stronger lose?

From Orbán's point of view, disruptive innovation is exciting in two main ways. The first, when Viktor Orbán became a politician of national renown, Fidesz became a prominent political player as the one-party system in Hungary collapsed. Fidesz, as a political power, emerged as a disruptive party, intent on changing the status quo. Another aspect of Orbán's policymaking is often disruptive. The dilemma does not just concern facing new phenomena (Christensen calls this the innovator's dilemma). Know that by embracing a new idea, you can weaken yourself in the short term, taking risks for a longer-term but stronger impact. When Fidesz switched from liberal to conservative, its popularity declined in the short run.

Second, how did Orbán, as the symbolic successor of the status quo, face the disruptive phenomena of his overthrow? The disruptive phenomenon is not one-way or static. From 2010, Fidesz became the absolute possessor of the status quo in politics in Hungary. It had government power with a two-thirds majority in Parliament and as such was subject to disruptive effects. New parties and political movements want to replace Orbán's movement. Orbán deliberately used disruption to come to power, and then instinctively opposed any disruptive endeavor.

# 45

# Disruptive Democracy

Disruptive technology does not rule out free competition. In fact, the latter is a prerequisite for the former. Therefore, disruptive politics can only be discussed within a democratic rule of law. The adjective disruptive is not a synonym for authoritarian or anti-democratic. Under democratic conditions, Orbán rose to the top in an environment of sports-like competition, with free elections and voter power. Hungary is a member of the UN, NATO, and the European Union, and its legal system recognizes the primacy of international treaties.

Orbán's political tactics are not anti-democratic, only disruptive. They are not autocratic either. They are merely a threat to those interested in the status quo. Many people confuse these. For Orbán, the years following the change of regime were unique because the parties had agreed in advance on the rules of the game so that he could make the most of the opportunity. If there were no rules of the game, Fidesz would never have been a party, and Orbán would not have been a leading politician.

By competing according to the democratic rules of the game, Orbán could take advantage of the opportunities offered by disruption. The more freedom he has, the more chances he has to outperform his opponents. It is easy to see that, if the debate in the European Union were not democratic, Orbán would not have a slight chance to get his ideas through. However, since the parties agreed in advance on certain democratic rules of the game, the status quo of the Germans and French were also subject to these rules, thus exposing themselves to disruptive forces. Orbán goes to the extreme if he needs to, but he doesn't even entertain the idea of leaving the European Union. Many accuse Orbán of preparing Hungary to withdraw from the European Union. Such is the textbook example of a biased 'default to lies' worldview.

Orbán's vision for Hungary stems from disruptive thinking: Hungary is to have more weight in international politics relative to the country's size and population, and Hungary is to serve as a role model. The purpose of any disruptive endeavor is the same. Change the status quo and influence the future according to your vision. A disruptive strategy works only from the inside out. Orbán does not use disruption for its own sake, but to provide Hungary a place on the EU table. So, his idea is not to lead Hungary out from the EU but to strengthen its position. And he did not demolish democracy, only foreign influence.

# 46

## Disruptive Challenges

For Orbán, anything is a threat that amplifies disruptive phenomena: philosophers, NGOs, theaters, churches, taxis, and, of course, the recent expressions of young democrats like Fidesz—to name a few.

Why did George Soros consider it essential to send young politicians to Oxford on the eve of the fall of the communist dictatorship? Why did he support workshops, magazines, and libraries? For the same reason, Orbán was the first to attack philosophers who attacked his politics when he came to power. (He also criticized George Soros as a philanthrope and philosopher.) Intellectuals can play a leading role in disruptive social ideas: they conceive, they verbalize, and they are the first evangelists.

Non-governmental organizations serve as breeding ground for intellectuals, who then could draw attention to social problems and to exert pressure on the power at hand—education, health, human rights, LGBTQ issues, etc. George Soros understands the power of disruption, and he is a keen supporter of NGOs. And Orbán understands the threat in this power, especially if his government is the target thereof. The legal restriction on NGOs is one of Orbán's defenses against disruptive phenomena. It is not a self-serving limitation of democracy, not at least because government-critical NGOs have the same distorted view as the opposition media and the default to the argument that Orbán is "lying."

In Hungary, the Budapest taxi can be a disruptive wasp

nest. It is a nightmare of every politician: the taxi driver who agitates against the government. Orbán's fear is, therefore, not unfounded. Taxi drivers caused the first major political crisis after the change of regime, the so-called taxi blockade, in 1990. Perhaps that is why the Orbán government has done its best to satisfy taxi drivers, banning UBER (which is a disruptive innovation) that democratizes passenger transport, decreeing fees for taxis, eliminating a price-war, and sabotaging the construction of a high-speed rail link between the airport and downtown.

With the exception of the Hungarian Socialist Party, several disruptive parties competed in the 2018 Hungarian Parliamentary elections. The LMP (Politics May Be Different) was created in 2009 to disrupt the dual political system of Hungary divided by the Fidesz and the Socialists. Their vision was for a country without Viktor Orbán and Ferenc Gyurcsány. Their vision of disrupting the status quo is also the name of the party: Politics May Be Different.

Jobbik, a far-right party, and Gyurcsány's Democratic Coalition were also disruptive, the former seeking to change the power over the right-wing, and the latter over the left-wing. The so-called 20th-century parties and the so-called twenty-first-century parties of the opposition speak to this phenomenon.

*Nobody liked the word "party." Everyone saw Fidesz as a movement. In contrast, a movement—at least we thought so at the time—was much more concerned to liberate society. Translating all this into the language of political practice. The purpose of a movement is to activate citizens, not in the name of their own ideas.*

The story of the Momentum Movement illustrates the power of disruptive politics. In 2017, the Orbán government made the

Budapest application for the 2024 Olympics competition an official program. The plans, supported by public opinion polls, were endorsed by a broad spectrum of society and presented to the International Olympic Committee. A minority group of opponents of the Olympics has launched a referendum on the subject. They wanted to collect enough signatures so a poll could decide about the competition, hoping it would be withdrawn. NOlimpia aimed to change the perceived or real social consensus (status quo) to support the 2024 Budapest Olympics. In the status quo, the government interested in holding the Budapest Olympics ignored the referendum initiative and, in the absence of contradictory polling data, believed that voters were not involved in the subject either. They thought the referendum initiative would fail. The initiators of NOlimpia began a diligent and well-organized collection of signatures. The first few days resulted in unexpected successes: they collected many signatures. The government counterattacked instead of airing more arguments, employing force in the opposite direction. Public opinion tipped over to those who opposed the Olympics, and, as with disruptive events, pro-government voters began to switch to the anti-Olympic side. Finally, a record number of signatures was collected, 266,151, instead of the required 100,000. The government beat a hasty retreat and withdrew the *Budapest 2024 Olympic Competition*.

Inspired by the success of NOlimpia, the 20-year-olds turned into a party, began nation-wide organizing, and pushed themselves into the top six recognized opposition parties. They built on a disruptive strategy: copied Fidesz, step by step, in the same way that Orbán had once done. To gain national recognition (Imre Nagy's reburial versus NOlimpia), they won over a small class (Western-oriented youth), developed an outspoken style, shaped cleverly themed communication and fashionable packaging.

NOlimpia's message was also a worldview. It is about the freedom of education. They linked the cost of hosting the Olympics to higher education spending, which fits in with the young people's worldview, and voilá, tons signatures appeared out of the blue.

Momentum is a liberal generational party that consists not of Bibó collegers but Erasmus scholars. The former founders of the SZDSZ (liberal party of the regime change) did not want to reach out only to the young but the free-minded voters. Fidesz was once known as the SZDSZ's little brother. Momentum is now called the Democratic Coalition's. Momentum and the Democratic Coalition are both liberal and anti-clerical parties. They do not want to continue the tradition of SZDSZ in terms of liberal intellect. However, the imitation of the Fidesz rebellion, its jeans and posters, is even more real.

*Voters could feel that we were like them, their sons, their daughters, their grandchildren.*

**CTRL + C, CTRL + V.** The Latin name of the movement echoes Fidesz's *fides*. The Latin *momentum* may have been inspired by Viktor Orbán's "Our Country in Momentum" slogan. On the surface, they are anti-Orbán. Under the surface, they wake up and go to bed with Orbán, trying to imitate him. They cook up everything from the Fidesz cookbook, they create circles, and they tried to make a direct impression like the Fidesz twenty years ago. The decisive difference from the original Fidesz is that they have no charismatic leader, their build is less athletic, and apparently, no one has told them what the Holocaust was (so they are good to deal with the extreme right). Isn't it strange that while at Momentum, they can only play Orbán, the greatest glory is of those who used to be Fidesz supporters? "I was a Fidesz sympathizer too," said the president of the movement.

# 47

# Crossing the Chasm

How will a disruptive technological innovation become a mainstream product? How will a group of friends become a parliamentary party and then institute a change of government? The answer is the same! The pattern followed by successful disruptive technology products resembles the path that ended with the election of Viktor Orbán and Fidesz. Geoffrey Moore's *Crossing the Chasm* is the bible of disruptive marketing.

> *We have struggled with the disadvantage of every small party that has no chance of winning. Citizens like to vote for who will govern. A small party always faces a problem of how to attract voters who know their vote is lost—in this respect. The point of our message was that young democracy needs young democrats. So, this generation we represent should not be left out of the loop [...] That was the first message. In the second half of the campaign, the idea came to beat the Socialist Party.*

To spread technological products, climb two imaginary mountains, one smaller and one larger. The difficulty is that there is a gap between the two mountains—Moore calls this the chasm. So, you can get to the top by climbing the first mountain and then crossing the chasm before you get to the top of the second mountain.

Moore divided people into five groups according to their

relationship to new technology. The first two groups are the early adopters of technology. They are the ones hungry for anything new, always looking for the latest. For them, it does not matter how much the technology costs, but they need to be the first to have it. The next big group is the majority. Depending on whether the new technology is adopted sooner or later, they are called early and late majority. Finally, the so-called laggards, who will only switch when there is no other option.

*Initially, our primary concern was to cross the 4% limit. Later this was changed so that the MSZP [Socialist Party] had to be beaten.*

The first group comprised liberal young people who voted for the Alliance of Young Democrats (Fidesz) in 1990. The first mountain was when the Fidesz got into Parliament, hitting the 4% parliamentary threshold. Then Orbán began to broaden his support, turning from a narrow circle of liberal youth to right-wing conservative, not just young people. This is how he first came to power in 1998. Climbing the first mountain was the era of the liberal Fidesz. The second mountain was the conservative-middle-class Fidesz and the first Orbán government. Crossing the chasm between the two mountains was a period of conservative turn that took place after 1994—this is how Orbán solved the problem without reading Moore's book.

In 2002, Orbán began to reorganize the opposition. The first mountain is the unified opposition right-wing block. Then came the second step, mobilizing every effort to climb to the top. Crossing the chasm is symbolized by winning the disappointed masses after the Őszöd Speech, which made the difference in the two-thirds victory. The peak of the second mountain was the 2010 'revolution' and the two-thirds landslide victory.

The problem with the chasm between the two mountains is that the passage between the two groups is difficult. There are different aspects of who wants to be the first, not the importance of the product being perfect in everything. The majority is concerned with minimizing the risk of change, so the majority will choose the new one when they see references from people like them. They will try it once it works well enough. It is a vicious circle. Technology companies have to use a different strategy to win the first 5% and another for the majority. The gap is always bridged after the enterprise has dominated at least half of the first segment. Then you can expand to a mass market.

For the first time, Fidesz dominated young people and only expanded after they have reached nearly 80% support in this segment of society. To win a majority, they tried to win right-wing intellectuals and churches, key people who authenticated Fidesz, and broadened the party's social background. (My grandmother, by the way, was one of the mavens that helped Orbán reach the tipping point.) After the right-wing turn, the citizen's idea was drawn from this broader pile. Winning churches was also a vital issue because it is an essential point for religious people to trust that the former anti-clerical Fidesz can already be trusted.

Small parties rarely recognize that there are two mountains. That is why the far-right Jobbik, the Politics May Be Different (LMP) and the Democratic Coalition (DK) failed to become governing powers. It's one thing to get into Parliament and another to enter government. Although Jobbik attempted to move from a radical party to a people's party, the problem lies because the majority they favor are supporters of Viktor Orbán, the most loyal audience, while Fidesz is the strongest opponent. The LMP and the DK of Gyurcsány, with their radical outlook, have burned the bridge over the chasm.

Many startup companies go bankrupt after climbing the

first mountain but cannot cross the chasm. It became the fate of Gordon Bajnai's Együtt (Together) and the LMP. It is the experience of Hungarian politics that while a liberal can become a conservative, the far-right has fewer chances to succeed. Neoliberal economic policy, green politics, and Gyurcsány's radicalism do not appear to be the mainstream soon either.

Momentum is the first political group to retrace the Orbán Path. By 2022, they want to climb the first mountain (to gain entry into Parliament) and to do this, they want to win narrower social groups and subcultures: Hungarians under 30, Hungarians working abroad, members of the LGBTQ community, "Soros-victims," and former conservative intellectuals abandoned by Fidesz.

If we look at history, we may not see why Orbán had to climb two mountains. In fact, two times two over the years.

- On June 16, 1989, at the reburial of Imre Nagy and the martyrs of the 1956 Revolution, Viktor Orbán gave a speech, which gained national fame.
- In 1990, MDF gained a simple majority. Fidesz reached 5.4%. (First Mountain: get into the Parliament.)
- In 1994, the Hungarian Socialist Party and the SZDSZ got a two-thirds majority. Fidesz reached 5.18%. (Crossing the chasm.)
- In 1998, Fidesz, the Farmer's Party, and the MDF gained a simple majority. (Second mountain: the first Orbán Government.)
- In 2002, the MSZP and the SZDSZ won a simple majority. (First mountain: united right, strong opposition force.)
- In 2006, the MSZP and the SZDSZ gained a simple majority. (Crossing the chasm.)
- In 2010, Fidesz won a two-thirds majority. The SZDSZ and

the MDF fell out of Parliament. (Second mountain: two-thirds.)

• In 2014, Fidesz gained a two-thirds majority. (Build a castle on the peak.)

• In 2018, Fidesz won a two-thirds majority. (Build an even bigger castle on the height of the mountain.)

When analyzing Orbán's opposition, they have recognized neither the two mountains nor the chasm. Orbán was the only politician who understood this problem and could switch. Fidesz became the status quo because it followed the process to the letter.

**GOETHE'S WILHELM MEISTER'S APPRENTICESHIP IS A BILDUNGSROMAN,** is about Wilhelm's journey of self-realization, who seeks and finds himself in amateur theater. I chose one of my favorite quotes:

*Art is long, life short, judgment difficult, opportunity transient. To act is easy, to think is hard; to act according to our thought is troublesome. Every beginning is cheerful; the threshold is the place of expectation. The boy stands astonished, and his impressions guide him; he learns sportfully, seriousness comes on him by surprise. Imitation is born with us; what should be imitated is not easy to discover. The excellent is rarely found, more rarely valued. The height charms us, the steps to it do not: with the summit in our eye, we love to walk along the plain. It is but a part of art that can be taught; the artist needs it all. Who knows it half, speaks much, and is always wrong; who knows it wholly, inclines to act, and speaks seldom or late. The former have no secrets and no force: the instruction they can give is like baked bread, savory and satisfying for a single day; but flour cannot be sown and seed-corn ought not to be ground. Words are good, but they are not the best. The best is not to be explained by*

words. The spirit in which we act is the highest matter. Action
can be understood and again represented by the spirit alone. No
one knows what he is doing, while he acts a right; but of what
is wrong we are always conscious. Whoever works with symbols
only, is a pedant, a hypocrite, or a bungler. There are many such,
and they like to be together. Their babbling detains the scholar:
their obstinate mediocrity vexes even the best. The instruction
which the true artist gives us, opens the mind; for where words
fail him, deeds speak. The true scholar learns from the known to
unfold the unknown, and approaches more and more to being a
master. (Translated by Thomas Carlyle.)

# PART SIX

## ART

---

*"To see what everybody else has seen,*
*and to think what nobody else has thought."*

(Albert Szent-Györgyi)

# 48

# Art and Values

"*Hungarian genius has two archetypes. Bartók and Puskás. Bartók is lean. Puskás is not.*"

'Like it or dislike it.'—A bad question.

The judgement of a work of art does not move on the scale of like it or not like it. Many works of art I do not like, but they may still be good art. It's the aesthetic quality that matters: not the artist's inner world, but the work he created. The original vision, the energy of the composition, the extent to which it gives back the zeitgeist, the spirit of the age, how it fits into the mainstream. The first step is to set aside my subjective taste and try to analyze it as an outsider. I set aside my prejudices and try to isolate them from others' opinions. What gives the power of novelty? How and why does the artist create something—we can call it change—that profoundly touches people?

**I LOOK AT VIKTOR ORBÁN AS AN ARTIST.**

I'm interested in his way of thinking, the trail he blazes, the art of his politics. What gives its originality? What are the rules that can describe his success? How did it touch Hungarians so profoundly? In what else is he different from his rivals?

Taste is a specific framework for interpreting our worldview. In a narrower sense, it is used to judge an artwork or an aesthetic category. Intellectuals basically have a taste for the world, and they can come to a rough consensus on what is meant by good taste. In Orbán's case, they lay too much importance on the fact that Orbán was/is not "packaged" according to their liking.

The driving force behind the "culture war" is that intellectuals approach the values created by art with their taste and distorted thinking. Whoever respects Orbán as an artist does not have to like everything—you are not obliged to vote for him. I can imagine that some do not like Péter Esterházy's art. However, everyone should appreciate its value, whether it comes from the art of politics or the art of literature. The wounds of a "culture war" can be healed by respecting and acknowledging artistic values. This is the key to end the cultural war with cultural peace.

It took me years to understand that conflict resolution depends solely on whether one considers the other to be honest or lying—defaulting to truth or lies. The division of our country can be traced back over twenty years ago when liberal intellectuals landed on the default position that Viktor Orbán was lying. They made a snap decision and kept with it. Their values were distorted by their prejudices of worldview, group pressure, and fear. All the blows and revenge can be traced back here. Once they behaved unfairly, they triggered a chain reaction and have since been unable to get out of the vortex.

This contradiction could only be resolved by treating Viktor Orbán the same way he would have to artistic value. Only the work matters!

Seth Godin refers in his book, *The Icarus Deception*, to James Elkins, an American art historian who wrote that an artist has three things to learn. First, you need to learn to see. Second, you need to master professional skills. The last step, the tabula rasa, is when you need to create on a blank slate, something that did not exist before.

To see the world as is means that I can absorb the world

without distortions (prejudices, beliefs, etc.). It is the most difficult challenge, and at first, it is does not work. Viktor Orbán sees better than anyone, and no one knows more about power than him.

Without skill, there is no art, which means that everything that exists, that is readable, that which is available, that I know. The fact that Viktor Orbán knows everything about power is an essential requirement. His friends and foes wonder at this. "Very confident, very prepared." I don't want to talk about Orbán's skill for two reasons. There is a library of specialized literature, and basically, all political science works deal with this issue, *kurz und gut*, many people know it better than I do. The second argument is that Orbán is even better at them. In other words, it is useless to analyze Orbán's proficiency since this will not get us closer to solving the mystery. What and from where he seeks inspiration, how he twists and reinterprets is less critical from the perspective of the art. What's interesting is not the order behind the collage. But the picture itself.

There are two starting points for the underground narrative: self-made and training. And the relationship between the two: how the disadvantage becomes an advantage, how *Viktor* Orbán becomes *Victor* Orbán, on his own and by practice. It will make two stories, two narratives built on the worldview: the leader and the tyrant. Viktor Orbán injected both narratives into the Hungarian mind, and both arrived the same intellectual immune response: he can't be defeated. The essence of his art is this: by his own, by democratic means, he has succeeded in turning his own team a winner and making his enemy's collapse—an original vision, a skilled feat, and a new way of thinking, the tabula rasa. That is no longer a matter of politics, but ART.

# 49

# Prospect Theory

Daniel Kahneman's most important discovery was prospect theory, which heavily weighed into his Nobel Prize. This theory describes how individuals evaluate in an asymmetric manner their losses and gains. According to prospect theory, the pain from one unit of loss could only be compensated by the pleasure of earning two and a half units. Thus, contrary to the rational assumption, it does matter if we lose or gain (a loss of $100 is offset by a gain of $250, not $100 as would otherwise be the case based on reason).

Prospect theory may explain why opposition parties are reluctant to reach an agreement. Who would sacrifice his vanity for the sake of the rival party? Who wants to take one step back to increase the chances of the other's victory? Who is risking his/ her guaranteed position in exchange for losing in the battle for change of government? Who prefers a partnership to a secure living? It is a loss to change our habits as well as to give up the parties' independence. The change of government would have to make at least two and a half times more profits so that it is worth it for MPs to say: "Change."

The aim of the opposition politicians' leaders points not entirely in the same direction as that of the opposition voters. Parliament members' basic salaries provide a politician with more than a decent living. It means that anyone who passes the parliamentary threshold can expect a guaranteed dream-salary for four years, not to mention other benefits. Many argue that it is because of the anti-democratic hocus-pocus is the reason why Fidesz benefits from the new electoral law. Nothing could be further from the truth.

The second point is that, in exchange for this payment, there is no government responsibility, one can watch politics from the position of the critic. For all parties to join forces, it would be necessary for all parties to have two and a half times the benefits in their prospects, in other words, to feel at least two and a half times more secure with the new role. It's easy to see why this will not happen.

The third point is the difference in worldviews and the resulting distrust among each other. As a reminder to anyone who has a different worldview than mine, I can easily assume the idea of lying. (Exceptions strengthen the rule: which party in the opposition squarely believes the sincerity of Ferenc Gyurcsány?)

Of course, opposition voters are persuading all opposition parties that they very much want to replace the government. The truth is that they have no intention of changing their comfortable lives. The answer to the question of why opposition voter turnout is so low is simple: people feel that the parties are not telling them the truth, and neither are they honest with each other.

The main rule of electoral law is that the winner takes everything. It is more democratic than before because it lowers the entry threshold. Similar to the US system, where presidential candidates pre-assess their chances in different states and campaign intensively only where the outcome of the election is dubious. You can concentrate your resources, and the system is easier to measure and model. All resources can be concentrated on a single round, and there is no campaign silence.

However strange it may sound, the starting point of the current Hungarian electoral concept is that Fidesz has fewer resources. Orbán never overestimates his dominance, but always assumes that he is weaker. The rules of the game are to allow all players more freedom of movement to mobilize resources and keep fewer districts in mind. The advantage of a one-turn system is that there is no second half, no second chance for the opponent to turn the score.

It is not the feature of the electoral law, but of elections that each person has one vote. You have to choose one of the parties—the one you entrust your future. The magnitude of Viktor Orbán's art is indicated by the fact that every second person entrusted him.

# 50

# Direct to Consumer

Political scientists imagine democracy as a kind of wholesale structure where the "political product" does not reach the consumer directly. For a long time, the world worked if you wanted to sell something as a politician, you had to fight through the mass of gatekeepers first (party platforms, media, intellectuals). It was up to them to decide who could become Prime Minister. The twenty-first century quickly changed this. This is how Viktor Orbán and Donald Trump changed the status quo.

The so-called direct to consumer principle is also the product of this flow. A new wave of sales strategies that deliver products to consumers through digital hubs, thanks to the Internet and its search engine and social media network—including online shopping on Amazon and eBay, travel on Booking.com and Airbnb, television on YouTube and Instagram, and the disruption of the press by bloggers and influencers.

Orbán's politics and opposition parties are fundamentally different. Instead of dealing in abstract dogmatism, I will provide a specific analogy from the world of direct-to-consumer commerce.

"We rely on our own strength and on our own will!", summarized IKEA-founder Ingvar Kamprad in *The Testament of a Furniture Dealer*. "Concentration. The very word implies strength. Use it in your daily work."

IKEA's political analogy is Fidesz. IKEA's mission is to create a home. Its philosophy is a blend of Protestant simplicity mixed with liberty. A self-made business, the product range covers the entire spectrum of society, is a family-friendly place but also popular among singles. They offer a variety of products at different prices, and the store includes a furniture section with A to Z furnishings, a restaurant, and even a donut kiosk. IKEA strongly embodies a national identity, and Ingvar Kamprad, the charismatic founder, has identified the ideological background and product philosophy of the business.

You either take IKEA's design or leave it. For those who prefer traditional style or custom-made furniture, there are many alternatives to IKEA. If we divide people into two groups according to the worldview of interior design, there is a block of IKEA on one side, and everyone can choose between smaller and bigger alternatives on the other, not from "IKEA 2." Design shops, individual craftsmen, are on the market, but none of them covers the needs of the masses as broadly as the Swedes.

In the direct-to-consumer model, you are not trying to sell your product to opinion leaders and wholesalers, but directly to a broad audience of customers. What makes this populism? Someone may associate this with the legacy of fascism since fascist dictatorships have favored the use of mass communication, but I consider it more a manifestation of democracy that a politician wants to establish a direct relationship with voters rather than going on a date with the editor-in-chief of *The Economist* or *The New York Times*.

Viktor Orbán's Hungarian opposition wants to sell it in the Budapest mall scene, which Gábor Demszky's mayorship dreamed up.[xvi] They are less of a manufacturer-to-consumer

---

xvi Gábor Demszky was the mayor of Budapest for 16 years, nominated by the Free Democrats, who gave way to shopping malls, office towers, and the automobile.

principle, trading in imported goods or the craft home rather than branded products. Like a nightmare, the opposition resembles a mall that has seen better times, where shops symbolize parties.

To the left of the entrance is the *DK Fashion Store*. Due to the popularity of fast fashion, they have recently moved to a larger store (joined by the recently closed *Bajnai Clock and Jewelry Salon*), the collections are changed every three weeks, and they range from men's sneakers to women's purses with EU stars. Next to them is *Momentum Books and Café*. The primary source of revenue for the bookstore and new wave café are events organized and café services.

The *Gulyás Márton Contemporary Art Gallery* and the *Two-Tailed Dog Comic Gift Shop* are located on the first floor of the shopping center. In the attic, the *LMP Lifestyle Center* operates with a vegan restaurant and an eco-friendly range of products, and solar panels on the roof power the space. In the basement, we find the legal successor of the late *Magyar Service Point, MSZP*. To the delight of many retired customers, you can still buy parts for a centrifuge made in the 1980s, a dial-up phone, and a dust bag for the Rocket vacuum cleaner (an icon of socialist consumer electronics). The bankruptcy business is kept alive by the lessor's benevolence, though once the entire building was theirs. In the parking lot of the mall, you will find the cozy *Jobbik Fair*, with handmade leather ornaments, traditional Hungarian products, a shop of flame, Transylvanian delicacies, and archery for families. The mall has an in-house radio and a mall-TV. The *Mi hazánk!* provides security.

It's all about art: the owner of the mall is Viktor Orbán.

# 51

# Taboo

After World War II, the Communist Party leadership realized that the social redistribution system could not be maintained. A well-established institution inspired the solution for the lack of funds: the tip. The tip seemed to solve the crisis resulting from the shortage, but it threw Hungarian society into a moral crisis. The institutionalized gratuity is one of the last remaining legacies of communism in Hungary. Today, part of this tip is paid for by citizens and the other part by businesses. Laws deny its existence, but everyone knows that it exists and believe in it. People think that they are favored, or at least not disadvantaged. Businesses are interested in acquiring more government orders through it. Both parties, private individuals and businesses, agree that they must pay the same person: the physician.

The Hungarian social system institutionalized corruption in the form of gratitude money. The Hungarian state guarantees the right to free healthcare in the social security system. One part of the costs are personal expenses (salaries of health professionals); the other part covers the maintenance of health institutions and reimbursement of medicines needed for treatment.

I would like to recall the opening phrase of the Hippocratic Oath: "I will use treatment to help the sick according to my ability and judgement, but never with a view to injury and wrong-doing."

Gratitude money exists because patients and doctors believe in it. The patient's narrative is that whoever pays the doctor is admitted for treatment first, gets better service, receives above-average care, and gets a larger share of the limited resources. The belief behind gratitude money is that doctors do not tailor the treatment of their patients by ability and judgement, but by the thickness of the envelope.

Medicines used for healing make up the bulk of social security expenditure. The market is dominated by a dozen companies that have registered their patented molecules as pharmaceuticals. Due to the high costs and years of licensing the drug, most of the twenty years of the patent's protection have elapsed by the time the compound is marketed as a drug. The pharmaceutical company has a limited time to recoup its costs, generate profit for shareholders, and gain for research, development, and licensing of newer active ingredients.

After the patent expires, the molecule will be in the public domain, and anyone can manufacture it. There is a saying among pharmaceutical companies: "It is not important that the medicine works, but that it is sold." Behind the cynicism lies some truth. Effectiveness is measured by the so-called survival time (not the question of which remedy the patient heals from, but which one will die later). The ability and judgement of the attending physician will allow him to consider which of the many medications available to treat the disease he is prescribing for the patient. On the other hand, the pharmaceutical salesman's worldview is that the doctor does not prescribe the medicine to the patients according to their ability and judgement, but in proportion to the financial motivation of the pharmaceutical manufacturer.

Doctors are not only executives of healing but are also formulators of healing protocols through medical associations and professional colleges. They decide—based on their ability and judgement—what kind of medicine the state should fund. It is in the interest of pharmaceutical companies to sell more and more expensive medicines to the state. This question will be addressed at the afternoon meeting by the doctors visited by the medical sales rep in the morning. In this game, the limited income of social security is overshadowed by the pharmaceutical company—with the help of a doctor. In the end, there is not enough money to pay the doctors who have to look for a salary supplement in the form of gratitude monies and sponsorship.

Besides, senior and more professional opinion leaders at the top of the pyramid are reluctant to let younger colleagues down to the operating table who will not gain experience, will lack experience, cannot make a living, and thus move abroad—where gratitude money doesn't exist.

Gratitude money acts as corruption without actually being corruption. Because both the patient and the doctor believe it, it becomes an automatic part of the process. The patient feels the moral duty of the envelope—'it fits'—so voluntarily gives it, not in most cases due to the pressure of the doctor. Patients usually ask each other how much they give to the doctor. The doctor will take over the envelope afterward, meaning that he will not know before the treatment how much it contains, if any. Society, as a whole, believes in gratitude money, and it is why it works.

The most significant accusation against the Orbán system is corruption. This phenomenon disturbs those who construct the narrative from default to lying. They believe that only Fidesz people in Hungary can win government grants because the system is corrupt. The press that serves their viewpoint feels obligated to report this and confirm to the reader that, yes, the system is corrupt.

A bribe requires two parties, one requesting the undue advantage and the other accepting that advantage. The purpose of the transaction is for the acceptor of the bribe to breach his duty by giving the other party an undue advantage. Since bribery is prohibited by law, it must be kept secret. Gratitude money or a visit to the doctor is not legally a bribe because the doctor cures or prescribes medicine by ability and judgement, he does not formally request the benefit; he only accepts it. Neither the drug manufacturer nor the patient incites the doctor to breach his duty, but rather to make sure things go smoothly.

Let's start with the issue of breach of duty. Viktor Orbán has clearly and unequivocally announced that his government wants to build a strong national entrepreneurial caste. If you like, this is an election program point, one can vote on it. The press also made sure to let us know how much money is in the family's pocket. Viktor Orbán never promised that as long as he was in government, his family would not get a government deal. (In brackets, without exception, we are talking about sophisticated, high-skill companies that most of the angry people are not familiar with anyway. None of them wants to operate a power plant, but it still bothers them if somebody else does.)

The second point—granting or accepting an unjustified advantage—is not justified either. The first frame of the opposition narrative is that a company that is supposed to belong to a Fidesz supporter is submitting a bid. The second is that it has won. Cause-and-effect relationship between the two is produced by maliciousness, assuming that *Orbán is lying*. For them, it follows from the two frames that only corruption can be in the background. While there is nothing to justify this, only the poetic question of fantasy, "what could it be other than corruption?" The most straightforward answer to this question is nothing. The appraiser decided so and was ready, based on his "ability and judgement," like the doctor in charge. The idea here is that the players play their cards in the open. Everyone knows which company belongs to whom. Since everyone believes in "corruption" that only lets Fidesz supporters win, there is nothing more than an applicant to clarify their affiliation. Hence it is not a disadvantage if someone is close to Viktor Orbán, but an advantage. Leftists will give up and never try. The nationalist believes in corruption the same as the patient in gratitude money, because both see a cause and effect relationship between his fate and the money given to the doctor. 'If I don't give him money, the doctor will not heal me.' 'If ours do not win, the enemy can come back.' The patient and the Fidesz supporter are both correct. The doctor really does treat the well-paying clients differently, but there is also evidence that war requires money, and if the opponent has no money, it can be harder for him to fight.

Continuing attacks by left-wing media on the wealth creation of NER (System of National Cooperation) businesspeople has the opposite effect. First, the attack confirms on the other side that they are on the right path because if they are so disturbed by their growth, this confirms the assumption that they would not come back. At the same time, the opposition side is disarmed by "Fidesz corruption" just as the "dictatorship." It is not only political power, but it is impossible to compete with financial superiority. And they get back to the starting point: Orbán can't be beaten.

One more argument. We give gratitude money not only because it fits, but it also makes us feel good. We liked the doc, and we are grateful to have survived the treatment. We give him a human gesture as an expression of our gratitude for him. We do not envy the money, and we feel he deserves it. The heat of corruption news is fueled by envy on the opposition side. But there is no sign of envy on the right. If anything, then they could have come to realize that this "near-corruption" is on a very different basis than the "true corruption." The fact that people are not bothered by the financial success of the Prime Minister's family proves that he is genuinely loved. This love is the foundation of faith in people, the treasure that Orbán has worked for throughout his life. One of the secrets of his art.

# 52

# From the Turul Bird's-Eye View[xvii]

What is sport? The same as politics: a story built on people's worldview. From world-class Olympic peak performers to amateurs trying to lose weight, everyone has the same goal: I can do it! I will succeed! Who, if not me?! When, if not now?!

Internal and external narratives have particular weight in sports. The importance of positivity and negativity is appreciated because sporting performance is a matter of faith in yourself. Whose faith is stronger? Who yearns for victory more? The athlete's narrative is that he will win. Only you can win, no one can take away your victory. This belief will not be easy to build (especially not to keep) because impulses from the outside world override the narrative. The importance of external circumstances influencing the narrative increases; let's consider the stress associated with a competitive situation: you have one chance, in front of cameras and under the pressure of fans, not to mention the psychological pressure exerted by your opponent. I see that my opponent is in better shape, has a better result in the qualifier, is younger than me. Known in martial sports, the psychic breakdown of an opponent, or how to take away faith, is about conflicting narratives. The famous motivational guru Anthony Robbins uses the method of walking over hot coals at the end of

xvii The Turul is a mythological bird of prey, mostly depicted as a hawk or falcon, in Hungarian mythology. It is a national symbol of Hungary.

a self-development course. Because of the resistance of the nerves in the soles and the short-term contact with the hot coals, the risk of burning is insignificant. The idea is participants have to overcome their fears, the wall they have raised within themselves.

In team sports, the situation gets one step more complicated because the team's narrative stands on the narratives of the individual players. A player's stress-relieving ability can affect the group as a whole and everyone is aware of the phenomenon of panic-striking power on the team. The coach or team captain's most important task is to program the inner narrative and write the external story so that the faith of the players and team is rock solid because that is where victory stands or falls.

And here comes the artist again: the real team captain who can build two stories—one in the head of your team, one in the enemy's. Your team's tactics must be put together by scoring as many goals as possible, while disrupting the opponent's tactics, destroying their unity, and luring them into failure. The collapse of the opponent and the performance of their team adds up to victory. There are thousands of tactics, but the strategy is always the same: two stories!

Two stories and one conclusion. Political analysts tend to say almost the same thing, though they use a different wording: not that Orbán won the election, but that the opposition lost it. Only they did not think that their loss of faith had caused them to fail and who had taken away that faith.

Fans also talk about how their team played, well or poorly. Orbán was brilliant in recognizing that his opponent's performance was decisive. The tactics of your team must be designed to weaken your opponent's tactics. If the opponent plays badly, it is enough for us to be good. If the opponent outnumbers my team, but I can weaken them and give my all, I may have a chance of winning. The saying "It's a game of two halves" is to be understood as meaning that not just us we who are better can lose the game, but that I can outperform an opponent who is more likely to be better on paper.

With this strategy, Orbán was able to knock out the Socialist-Liberal parties hence their media's predominance, financial resources, organizational background, intellectual backyard, and urban embeddedness. Only from 2010 onward, was he able to do this. For he had to figure it out, for which he had to analyze two lost elections. In 2002, the Socialists overwhelmed Orbán by making him believe in his victory and by this deceived him. He lost, although he governed well. The Socialist's campaign guru built two victories in the minds of two teams, though this could hardly have been conscious. In 2006, Orbán failed to break the demonic hypnosis, even though he was more likely to win, even though the socialists governed badly and led the country in debt. What Orbán learned from all this is that government work does not influence the outcome of the elections. What does is the narrative of the opponent. He should focus the emphasis on this—this leads to victory.

Viktor Orbán was the first politician to bring athletic training methods to the world of rule and put the football mindset at the center of his politics.

What do your friends and enemies think of you? It's the end result that matters—to believe in you, it makes the difference. Looking for the answer while the solution was right in front of your nose all the time? The flagship fashion label outfits the Hungarian football teams. The sports brand name is a play on words, pronounced in Hungarian as the holy bird of Hungarian prehistory, the word means to reign (also makes sense as a noun). Still, the brand describes the Orbánian innovation, the domination of the opponent, and their own camp. Viktor Orbán's humor, Freud, or the hand of Fate? Here's the last piece of the puzzle:

**2RULE. BELIEVE IN IT—THIS MAKES THE DIFFERENCE.**

**WHY COULD VIKTOR ORBÁN CREATE TWO STORIES AT THE SAME TIME** in people's minds? It is because the weapon of political war is coding the symbolism behind speech and action. The battle is mental and not physical. Political reality is made up of people's minds, and the corresponding narrative feeds on people's beliefs and feelings.

It has become a common practice for left-wing intellectuals to attack Orbán with under-the-belt punches, appealing to people's beliefs and feelings through narrative fabrication. They tried to imprint on Orbán the stamp of anti-Semitism, the personal cult of the dictator, the image of the Godfather. Whatever he does, it will never be good enough for them. Even though the public debt is declining, the economy is growing, unemployment is at a record low rate, and liberals have been washed off the line in three elections, they can only be right. I do not want to generalize. I think there was a narrow group that decided that no matter what Viktor Orbán does, it would be wrong. This is a result of a long process that started more than twenty years ago when intellectuals began to interpret politics that did not exist in Orbán politics.

> *Unfortunately, for many, analyzing politics is nothing more than the ability to read symbols. [...] Today, the logic of what is not revealed, of what is in the background, is, unfortunately, dominated by the reporting of all congresses.*

What's not working out? What's in the background? This question was answered in the 1970s by two American psychologists, John Grinder and Richard Bandler. Originally, the two psychologists asked how excellence could be modeled.

Highly successful psychologists were analyzed to decode the secret code of excellence. It has now become one of the most potent personality development methods in the world. This is the so-called NLP. It is used in many areas, from training athletes, coaching, learning, selling, dealing with phobias, to useful purpose, and manipulation. Of course, it is also used by politicians.

The point of discovery is to think, perceive, and experience the world through the use of our nervous system—and ultimately, store it in the form of images, sounds, feelings. When we communicate, we express our thoughts, pictures, sounds, feelings previously stored in our brains in words. Neurolinguistic Programming (NLP) is a method that helps individuals to get rid of their bad habits, overcome beliefs, break down walls, and overcome themselves. Neuro refers to the nervous system, its linguistic meaning is language, and programming here means re-learning. The revolutionary discovery of the method is that every human being follows other neurolinguistic maps, rules, and the scheme can not only be deciphered but also changed.

Every person has a primary language of representation. Some are primarily visual, others are auditory, and some are kinesthetic. Of course, most people see, hear, and feel, and the primacy of the representation system is what makes them different.

The visual man perceives the world primarily through his eyes. You see pictures and think in pictures. He has to see things first. In the vocabulary of the visual person, terms related to vision are more common, 'I see,' 'it seems,' 'I have noticed that.' The visual profession is design, programming, medicine, or aerial (flight) control.

Acoustic people are informed by hearing. They evoke voices, dialogues, music lovers, who are particularly sensitive to the tone of the other person and usually have a specific organ. In their vocabulary, hearing-related words predominate, 'I hear,' 'said,' in Hungarian, they call dishes a story ('I ask for that story with the bacon'). The profession of hearing people is everything related to music, speech, or listening: performer, journalist, teacher, psychologist, pastor, actor, lawyer—everything you need to hear.

His emotions and feelings navigate the kinesthetic man. He likes to touch everything, hug others, likes physical contact, and always relies on his feelings. We could say they are moody people. They are the least. Their vocabulary often includes expressions related to emotions, 'I get the impression,' 'I feel,' generally less frequent and quieter. Often prominent athletes, politicians, and hedge fund managers are among them. The fourth category is the acoustic-digital people who have regular conversations with themselves—Viktor Orbán.

> Politics also means linguistic fight. You have to create a chessboard: each cube is a meaning or a category and occupy it, on the one hand, so that it can be captured and, on the other, so that the opponent cannot seize it. It is vital in politics to speak louder and louder, national, freelance, and so on.

NLP supports not only demolishing the walls but also building new ones. Orbán could get a sense of the beliefs of the two camps and figure out how to kill two birds with one stone. What he would have to say and do to get the same conclusion across all fifteen million Hungarians: his power cannot be defeated. As the left-wing liberal intellectual punched Orbán beneath his belt, they revealed their weaknesses and taught his opponent their tactics. If they put fiction behind words, this is where you have to attack: through their ears. Viktor Orbán did nothing but reverse the unsportsmanlike tactics of fictitious narrative production and punched his opponents with their weapon: the power of words. If left-liberal intellectuals see themselves as victims, this book blames the victims.

The NLP also states that one can achieve peak performance when he is in a good emotional state. In other words, if you are in a top state, you are capable of everything. If you are depressed, then nothing. It is why the cult of sporting events can play a role because sport is one of the most powerful emotion-generators invented. In addition to changing the emotional state, another practice of NLP is visualization. One imagines a desirable future. Perhaps this is no accident, why Viktor Orbán's speeches are made up of frames.

> In 2010, we gave new outfit to the Hungarian state, cut back
> the wildings, strengthened it where it needed more muscle, and
> began slimming down where it started to gain weight. Friendly,
> healthy, smiling dentures with biting teeth and strong jaws.

ONE OF THE AIMS OF ORBÁN'S POLICY WAS TO BREAK DOWN THE liberal status quo (in the media, independent NGOs, culture, and science) that oppressed democracy. Those who use their position to undermine the politics of Orbán's democratically elected government become enemies. From Sun Tzu's book, *The Art of War*, we can understand what to do: "If you know the enemy and know yourself, you need not fear the result of a hundred battles. If you know yourself but not the enemy, for every victory gained you will also suffer a defeat. If you know neither the enemy nor yourself, you will succumb in every battle."

Gergely Salát writes in the foreword of The Classics of Chinese Military Science: "The Sun-tzu ping fa, the Art of War, has been the most influential military science work of the last two thousand years in China and throughout East Asia. Its main message is that the best thing to win is not enter open a battle—we have to adjust the circumstances so that the enemy loses the battle before the war begins. [...] Because the book does not deal with military matters in the strict sense, but generally deals with tactics and strategies applied in competitive situations, its teachings are nowadays applied in a wide range of life. It is taught at many business colleges, used by brokers, businessmen, diplomats, politicians, lawyers, athletes—for example, before the 2002 World Cup, Master Scolari made the book compulsory for Brazilian football team members (and won the trophy)."

Orbán recognized that the main threat to the System of National Cooperation was the uncooperative tribe of left-liberal intellectuals, who often scoffed at national sentiment and mock at national feeling. The strategy aimed to disarm them. Orbán learned the worldview of this social group—their beliefs and emotions—and adjusted the tactics to that. "All men can see these tactics whereby I conquer, but what none can see is the strategy out of which victory is evolved. [...] He who can modify his tactics in relation to his opponent and thereby succeed in winning, may be called a heaven-born captain."

The left-liberal side considered Orbán's politics a lie, and they were afraid of him. Their belief that he was a liar and their fear combined triggered a reflex of defense against imaginary fascism.

They were doing everything they could to prevent Orbán for power. They considered him stronger, and it forced them to behave in unsportsmanlike ways. Orbán sensed that his opponents were afraid of him, and he had added to their fears while he knew that if he wanted to win, he would have to disarm the unsportsmanlike intellectuals. Intellectuals made their ideological principles into a question of prestige. While underestimating the importance of beliefs other than their own, they disregarded sport and religion. They revealed their weakness. They are sensitive to and influenced by verbal insults.

Thus, Orbán had to do nothing but entertain his opponents with speeches addressed to his followers and by the writings of right-wing columnists.

When we approach the question of the art of war, Orbán defeats his opponents by essentially not waging war. I think we can all agree, and we have no doubt about it that he knows himself. What is more interesting is how well he knew his enemies. They cannot think in an organized, team-based way because their liberal view is individualistic, based on the opposite of team play.

Once Orbán had the opportunity to transform the rules of the game, he transformed individual democracy into team democracy. It had nothing to do with fascism, yet the opposition felt this way, for them blocking the way to power and finding no better expression than dictatorship in their anger. The mistake of the liberal intellectuals led to their moral conviction being overwritten by the narrative that Orbán was dangerous, above all, to them. Eventually, this was said until it became a self-fulfilling prophecy.

**TWO PEOPLE ARE SITTING IN FRONT OF A CHURCH ON SUNDAY. BEGGING.** There is a cross beside one of the beggar's hats, and a kippa on the head of the beggar sitting beside him, and a Star of David beside his hat. The crowd pouring out of the Sunday mass enthusiastically throws money into the cap next to the cross, with just a few pennies in the cap next to it. A gentleman walks to the beggar wearing a kippa:

—Can't you see? It's a Christian church. Here you will never make money with a Star of David!
After the gentleman left, the man with the kippa turns to the one sitting next to him:

—Do you hear that, Ábel? They are trying to teach us marketing.

Simply put, he figured it out well, went through it, did not give up, and did not try to cut the road. Consciously and analytically, he has built a worldview with constant feedback, while this worldview is based on a trivial basic truth, the same as America.

It does not matter what the world is like. It is how you think it looks. The strategy is the art of the parallel stories: 2Rule.

# 53

# Orbán United

Good artists copy, great artists steal. Steve Jobs quoted this saying in 1996, attributing it to Picasso[xviii].

I think the crown jewel in Viktor Orbán's art is how he brought football into the world of politics. As Freemasonry shifted the toolbox of masonry into the intellectual realm, he transformed the world's most popular sport into the realm of politics. America was built on the principles of Freemasonry and took more than two hundred years. Viktor Orbán wants to rebuild Hungary on the principles of football and strength development but within twenty years.

The stadium became a symbol of Orbán's political methodology. The stadium building symbolizes the Carpathian Basin. The field is Hungary, and the national playing team is the Hungarian government. Football is a symbol of political goals, and Europe's leading powers are leading football powers too— where is a keen football, the living standards are high, also. The audience in the stands represents the Hungarians and national unity. Another rule is that countries with a strong national identity (England, France, Germany, Italy, Spain) have become football superpowers. The strong dotation for Hungarian football

xviii According to Quote Investigator, the saying comes from W. H. Davenport Adams, who first used it in Gentlemen's Magazine in 1892, as Harold Evans pointed out in his book.

is a methodological consideration—not an allure, as some mistakenly interpret it—since according to the Orbánian logic, the easiest way to measure the country's success, its national cohesion, and the strength of the economy. It is not a matter of taste but creativity. Viktor Orbán wants to teach Hungarians how to play as a team because he believes that this method will educate the generation that will renew Hungary. It is like the Kodály method in music education. It works.

Viktor Orbán built Fidesz and his government in a similar structure to football clubs—with instrumental success. The most important task of a football club manager is to set up a team, give and take players, set goals, mentor players, motivate the team, represent the club in public and ensure that shareholders—voters—are satisfied at the end of the day. The authors of *Management by Football* analyzed the parallels between business and football clubs from perspective of management. "The conclusion is clear: top football managers operate in a world like that in many ways is similar to that of any other manager. Only multiply that by 100!" Millions judge the work of club managers, and even if you can achieve results, there is no guarantee of how long you can keep your job. "You must deliver outstanding results every time!" Passion and self-sacrifice. Breaking the status quo. Workout and timing.

Why and how can Viktor Orbán manage the processes? Because he interprets politics as a football game, he can think in an abstract, algorithmic way: who is on his team and who is on his opponent's, what the rules are, what the field is like, who the referee is, where his fans are. You do not have to keep in mind specific players and issues, because you can model all political games by football. When a problem comes up, it is enough to replace the players in the formula and give the answer according to the laws of football, which can be only one kind. And since politics is also his own identity, decisions in this regard, too, remain consistent.

*Match is a battle that can be won only then and there. And the moment the match stops, you have to be at the top.*

The question arises in every situation: how can I strengthen my team and weaken my opponent's? Before the match, the parties must agree on the rules of the game. For example, that you need a two-thirds majority to change the constitution of Hungary without any criteria being met, other than securing the votes of two-thirds of the Parliament members. In 2010, the Fidesz-KDNP gained a two-thirds majority in Parliament. In 2012, Hungary's new Fundamental Law was adopted, which is called a "Fidesz constitution" by those who previously embraced the rules of the game. They try to set it up for the demise of democracy.

Football has few rules, and each team is given freedom to score as many goals as possible and to prevent their opponent from attacking. Avoiding the 2010 financial bankruptcy, the *unorthodox* economic policy to establish financial self-determination was about this. Dual citizenship can add more fans, while the autonomy of Szeklerland or Vojvodina can enlarge the field.

For the government, the stakes of the games are the implementation of the government program: economic growth, living standards, prosperity. The government term is similar to a football championship, with Election Day as the final match. Throughout the four-year cycle of the championship, a multitude of obstacles have to be overcome, each difficulty and outcome is a match, such as debt, migration, unemployment, public safety, home-building, economical safety nets, action plans. The country's condition needs to be improved in various areas in order to overcome obstacles. The field for the government can be Hungary, the Carpathian Basin, Europe, or the world market. The referee is different in every situation, sometimes the media, the EU institutions, or the credit rating agencies (Big Three). The rules of the game are outlined by the Hungarian Fundamental Law and international treaties.

For a party, the stake in the final match is the election victory. The audience is the nation. The electoral law determines the rules of the game, the path is the individual electoral district, in the case of the list votes, the national politics. If the government is a party, the opponent is the opposition, so the unity of the opposition teams must be broken, and their chances weakened. How to prevent a goal from being scored? First, they have to believe they have no chance. Second, where should the field incline? As a depositor of the status quo, how can I change the rules, positively influence the referee, weaken the opponent? The simple question is: what can I influence in a given situation to win the match?

According to James Carse, one kind of game is finite and the other infinite. The essential difference between the two is that the finite game is played for the win, the infinite game for the game itself. The game features two teams that agree on certain rules and play accordingly. The stronger team will be the winner of the game. How strong a player is can be judged relative to others. You have to wait for the game to finish. You can say that you are strong if others recognize it. "Let us say that where the finite player plays to be powerful, the infinite player plays with strength."

If we interpret Viktor Orbán's politics as a game, victory for the election gives him power, but his vision is above finite games—another duality. "Infinite players look forward, not to a victory in which the past will achieve a timeless meaning, but toward ongoing play in which the past will require constant reinterpretation." Finite play is about power. Infinite play is about strength. In this endless game, he initiates, and others have to react. For at least 25 years this is the formula:

> *After the first week, it became clear that the public saw us as a supporting team of the SZDSZ. We have lost all kinds of initiatives. An alternative began to emerge in political life, with the MDF and its affiliated parties facing the SZDSZ. If this image remains in the electorate, well, we won't even get 4%. I think it was there that we were able to formulate an independent voice. [...] I have always suggested that we clearly define what Fidesz is and how it differs from the SZDSZ and the MDF. [...] In January 1990, both major parties were concerned that each of the other parties could only determine their place in relation to them. This was exactly what we had to avoid.*

The Feldenkrais Method is based on the relationship between movement and thinking. The founder of the method has compiled a series of exercises that combine judo and yoga that can be used from elite military training to rehabilitation. According to Moshe Feldenkrais, movement determines the way of thinking: if the joints move better, we can think fluid. If Viktor Orbán's success is to be traced back to the laws of football, the mindset inspired by the movement pattern of football is worth a look at Orbán's rivals. Why couldn't they be "at the top?"

Tennis was a popular sport among the politicians of the MSZP-SZDSZ regime. Their practice in politics was modeled on the doubles tennis match. In the Socialist Party, politics was played in pairs, and the party always had several strong politicians—Gyula Horn and László Kovács, then László Kovács and Péter Medgyessy—who complemented each other, as opposed to Fidesz under the hierarchy of Viktor Orbán. The Socialist-Liberal coalition partnership is different in nature than the Fidesz-KDNP cooperation, one resembling an open relationship, and the other a lifelong marriage.

The socialist-liberal equilibrium was dismantled by Ferenc Gyurcsány, who was a runner. Running is typically not a group sport, as the runners' paces divide the starting mass into smaller units over a short time. The Socialists did not reward Gyurcsány's pace, some of them gave up at the beginning and preferred the buffet; some broke away and tried to run with the leader. In 2011, the left split, the Gyurcsány-led "runners club," formed a new party called the Democratic Coalition, and the Hungarian Socialist Party became 'obese' and started to suffer from 'chronic' symptoms.

Bicycles are a popular means of transport for new wave green politicians. The problem with this form of movement is that it does not work in Budapest because there is no social culture and no infrastructure for it. You have to be careful, or else you will be hit by a car, or you will hit a pedestrian. You cannot drive as fast as you want to with public transport, and you sweat which, in a word, is not the most practical. The positive health effects of cycling for 10-15 minutes a day are minimal, especially in smog. The Politics May Be Different movement pattern was inspired by urban cycling: they built politics without strategy, hurrying, responding to it, some politicians being hit, the other overturned, and they had to lash out instead of the planned route.

The analogy of the Jobbik movement pattern is marching the Hungarian Guard (the organization was founded in 2007 and disbanded in 2009). The most significant disadvantage of block-like marching is that it is slow and hard to change direction. When the Jobbik leaders wanted to conjure up a people's party from the far-right party, the rhythm of the swift and sudden reversal of marching was interrupted. One side of the group continued to the right and the other to the left, splitting into two.

"**Uncle Guszti was one of the greatest soccer experts in the world** to date. From a professional point of view, he introduced a host of innovations, and he was able to deal with people very well. He trusted us. He knew the player's abilities, lifestyle, virtues, weaknesses, and judged him by merit. It didn't matter if the player had a bad day. He never selected people based on sympathy or dislike, by club membership or other criteria, but solely the player's abilities mattered. [...] He trusted and built on the people," said Ferenc Puskás about Gusztáv Sebes, the legendary federal captain of the Golden Team.

The most important task for modern club managers is to put together a team. The club's value consists of two main assets: the personal qualities of the club manager and his football team as a whole, not the individual players. These managers and their teams are the fiercest competitors. Alex Ferguson and Manchester United. Viktor Orbán and Fidesz.

Viktor Orbán's most potent ability is leadership. He provides the vision, and he has to make the critical decisions. At first, it may be an astonishing statement, but the most vital decision is to put together a team. A declaration or action is easier to correct than a wrong personal decision. When delegating government tasks, the selection of leaders influences the quality of the entire area, and this is where Viktor Orban takes a street-long advantage over his rivals. The quality of Hungarian politics after the first change of regime was diminished by the fact that none of the political parties could think in a team. Without compromise, and the coalition parties made personnel matters the subject of bargaining. Orbán could take advantage of football because he was able to build a team without compromise. He was able to select the best of exceptionally talented people because they had been chosen on their own merits.

This is why singing about dictatorship is a dead end, because it ignores the world champion team of talent and genius behind Viktor Orbán. In football, you do not compete primarily with players, but with the team. Viktor Orbán is not the invincible adversary, but Viktor Orbán and his team—the machinery that shares a common worldview.

Here comes the finite or infinite play again. When the game is finite, a politician is not even interested in the fact that his or her personal decision may also result in the government failing. For Orbán, the game is infinite. Therefore, he cannot afford not to build a team of the best players. Stress-resistant, knowledgeable, and trusted.

The government has to implement the government's program as a team. Therefore, the government members were selected according to the function of team players: team captain, striker, defender, cover, goalkeeper.

One of the most vital positions is the minister of finance. Orbán entrusted the cash box keys to the most reliable man among the countless candidates who are good at mathematics: a Reformed presbyter with four children and an economist. Mihály Varga is the leader of the Fidesz Economic Cabinet and has been a member of the party and one of the most predictable—authentic—figures in the political generation of the regime change. He was one of Orbán's most faithful supporters, in addition to György Matolcsy, in his "freedom fight for financial sovereignty."

The criterion for selecting a team is that you could look for a person for the function, and with a two-thirds mandate, there is no need to sacrifice personal issues for a political compromise.

In the current world order, competition between countries is as fierce as it is in the market. Therefore, to lead the Foreign Minister's office, Orbán chose a high-performing, predictable manager instead of a classic diplomat. Péter Szijjártó is also a leading athlete, and it is not by chance that he is one of the most influential figures in the government. Economic growth is fueled by investment in the country, and an increase in exports, which will foster prosperity. Prosperity satisfies voters and earns a parliamentary majority.

> *[...] the rule of thumb in Fidesz is that if a person desperately wants a position and is dying for it, he cannot get it. You can't get it because if you are craving for a position, you can only fail—a political, a professional, and, most of all, a moral failure. I've seen just enough. That is why it is important, perhaps the most important rule in Fidesz, that work is distributed here and not positions. And, above all, not the power.*

Orbán's personnel policy always puts players in key positions who are eager to fight for the status quo. Such positions were held by György Matolcsy, who changed the financial status quo. And by Péter Szijjártó, who represents the new wave of foreign policy. Imre Kerényi, who had to overthrow liberal cultural hegemony, was one such figure in the world of culture, or Philip Rákay, who reinterpreted the public service function of Hungarian Television.

In Orbán's system, there is not a single *Golden Team*, but dozens. József Szájer, mastermind of the Fidesz Group in the European Parliament, is one of the founding members of the party. His character blends the rebel John Lennon's with the archetype of the European thinker-politician. Among the members of the European team is the Fidesz founder, forever young Tamás Deutsch, or my former English teacher Balázs Hidvéghi. At the ELTE Radnóti Miklós School, the elegant English teacher, who was still in his twenties, brought Martin Luther King's 1963 *I Have A Dream* speech to the class.

Orbán United's communications team was formed to maintain power and popularity. However, here too, the rule is that one can always make decisions based on one's character, so Orbán has appointed people who have the inner desires closest to the lifestyle everyone wants. Andy Vajna was one of the geniuses who lived the Hollywood dream life—a jet-set lifestyle with red carpet glamor. The magic team responsible for communication are masters of intuition. Árpád Habony or Antal Rogán genuinely resonate with people's desires (both have come from rags to riches as a self-made man).

In addition to the government, the party also has a crucial role, organized at least as sophisticated as the government. Management talents like András Gyürk, Lajos Kósa, Gábor Kubatov, or Szilárd Németh are needed to carry out a campaign. The think tanks, research institutes, and polling organizations working for the party have to deliver reports to the Prime Minister to assist him in decisions—science-based data and analytics. The Századvég Group, the Nézőpont Group, or the Public Foundation for the Research of Central and East European History and Society are the most significant. The background institution of the civic-national intellectuals is the Batthyány Circle of Professors and the Hungarian Academy of Arts, which was promoted to the rank of a public body at the beginning of the presidency of György Fekete.

"In his analysis of the methods and practices of the Orbán regime, independent and prestigious law professor Tamás Sárközy speaks of a 'new conquest'... Sárközy calls attention to a unique phenomenon in Hungary that has been neglected by the Western media. [...] there is no other democratic country in the world where only a small group of ten or twenty former students, who have existed for nearly thirty years, would occupy such high positions in the state. The highest dignities of public law: the President of the

Republic, the Prime Minister and the President of Parliament are three good old friends." According to Tamás Sárközy, this is two-thirds over-government. I call it the art of two-thirds.

**"LITTLE MONEY, LITTLE FOOTBALL, BIG MONEY, BIG FOOTBALL," IS THE** maxim attributed to Puskás Öcsi. Viktor Orbán cut into politics by saying, "we were alone in a situation where we had nothing," for which he was forced to raise financials. The economic background of Fidesz is associated with the name of Orbán's former high school friend Lajos Simicska. Until 2014, Simicska was Fidesz's most influential backer, owning strategic right-wing media—news television *Hír TV* and newspaper *Magyar Nemzet*—and being the biggest winner in public procurement. In the 2018 Parliamentary elections, he was a supporter of Viktor Orbán's fierce opponent of the far-right Jobbik, having lost his business interests after Viktor Orbán's two-thirds victory and subsequently retired from public life.

Money is also a strategic issue for Viktor Orbán, not only to strengthen his nationalist side financially but also to minimize his opponents. "For war you need three things: 1. Money. 2. Money. 3. Money." Part of the football mindset is that not only your team, your opponent, the referee, the rules, the field, and the audience are part of the formula, but also the seventh element, money too. Government policy is as much about the art of domination as it is about the art of making money.

György Matolcsy is the most valuable player in making money, and many consider him—after Orbán—the second genius. His name is related to the so-called unorthodox economic policy. Its innovation is that the country's financial stability was achieved not through the IMF's required tax increases and spending cuts, but sector-specific taxes, government reforms, market-financed bonds, and tax cuts—allowing Hungary to retain its sovereignty.

As of 2010, Matolcsy, as head of the Ministry of National Economy, has led Hungary's financial recovery. The chronicle of the nearly three-year economic 'freedom fight' was written by Helga Wiedermann in her book *Chess and Poker*. The stake of the game was that Hungary's debt by socialist governments would avoid bankruptcy and create the basis for the country's financial sovereignty.

"Whoever is in debt cannot be a free man. He is vulnerable, humiliated, a prisoner, a prisoner of debt, and bankers, he must live as his creditors dictate." György Matolcsy was the team captain. Some of the most important matches: avoiding state bankruptcy, excessive deficit procedure, IMF negotiations. Some opponents include the International Monetary Fund (IMF), Olli Rehn, the then EU Commissioner for Finance, credit rating agencies (Goldman Sachs, Moody's, Standard and Poor's), and András Simor, former chairman of the National Bank of Hungary, appointed by the Socialists. Some memorable goals: the 29 Point Economic Protection Action Plan, elimination of sector-specific taxes, private pension funds, issuance of government securities, conversion of foreign currency loans, utility cost cuts, reduction of bureaucracy, withdrawal of EU funds, growth protection net. Finally, Hungary was excluded from excessive deficit procedure, credit rating agencies upgraded the country to a higher investment-grade status, and György Matolcsy became president of the National Bank of Hungary in 2013.

COACHES AND MENTORS HAVE ALWAYS PLAYED AN ESSENTIAL ROLE IN ORBÁN'S life. In addition to the professors at Bibó College, he was influenced by the highly educated figures of the conservative side. Sometimes they just exchanged ideas; other times, they put a book in his hands. Orbán seems to have chosen a second family for himself, with fathers, brothers, and uncles. There is an extraordinary human relationship between the mentor and the mentee; it is also an exception in politics to establish an alliance between the head of a state and the top intellectuals based on unwritten rules of honor and loyalty. Master architect Imre Makovecz and theater maestro Imre Kerényi also played such a unique role in the Prime Minister's life, and I mention them by name because I knew them in person, and they told me about this.

Zoltán Balog, as a Reformed pastor, was also the spiritual leader of the Prime Minister, who, as we know from Igor Janke's biography, underwent a confirmation and spiritual transformation during his first term as Prime Minister. "For more than half a year, once a week, late at night, after he had finished his government duties, he walked from his office to the Reformed church where his friend, a pastor, had been waiting. They usually talked for 1.5 hours. [...] Confirmation took place in a narrow circle of only ten, excluding the media. His friends claim that Orbán experienced a profound observance."

*If you ask me why I want this confirmation, I have three things to answer. First: I'm late with it, twenty years late. It's always been a part of my life.*
*I forgot about it. I want to be reborn. Second reason: Jesus Christ was always present in my life, even when I didn't know it. Third reason: Since the Lord God has been with me all my life, even when I did not know he was with me. I wish he would remain with me in the future.*

**FOOTBALL CLUBS ALSO TALK ABOUT TALENT DEVELOPMENT, HOW TO NURTURE** the next generation. Here, too, there are countless examples to be given so that I will provide one instead. According to the underground narrative, Peter Szijjártó is the closest to the organic way of thinking, the leading sports-politician character. Born in

1978, at 21, he was the founder of the Fidelitas organization in Győr. At the age of 24, in 2002, he will become a member of Parliament for the first time, just as the Orbáns were at the time of the political transition. He worked in the opposition for eight years—just as much as the Fidesz from 1990 to 1998—from 2010 to 2012, he was the personal spokesman for the Prime Minister, and then he was appointed Secretary of State for Foreign Affairs and Trade. At the age of 35, he became the second-youngest foreign minister in Hungary, just as old as Viktor Orbán at the start of his first term as Prime Minister. One of the most influential people in the government, he heads the strategic foreign affairs and trade ministry.

There is a fifteen-year gap between Peter Szijjártó and Viktor Orbán, which is precisely the midpoint of the political transition between generations. There is a 30-year age difference between the generation of József Antall and Gyula Horn and the first generation of Fidesz, similar to the age difference between the first generation of Fidesz and the new generation of politicians. (I write in parentheses because this is not part of my line of thought, but I cannot fail to mention that Orbán provided a parliamentary office for Gyula Horn. He was politically defeated, and I know from reliable sources that after 2010, Orbán personally arranged for the then severely ill Horn to receive priority medical and human care for the rest of his life. Orbán not only personally appreciated the predecessor of the Prime Minister, but he also helped his family.)

Perhaps you may also be aware of the fact that the new capitalist cast created by the Orbán course comes from Orbán's contemporaries to prepare their children studying abroad for the next generation change. When the opposition underestimated Orbán, they also underestimated the number of steps on how he is ahead of them.

And when it comes to *future talent development*. Of Viktor Orbán's five children—Ráhel, Gáspár, Sára, Róza, and Flóra—Gáspár was born on February 7, 1992. When he was young, he gave up his dream of being a professional football player because of a knee injury. During his spiritual journey, he met Christ on an African mission, and then returned home with his friends to form the charismatic Christian movement called Felház. He is studying law at the Eötvös Loránd University, Faculty of Law, and has taken an oath as a professional soldier. Here is the recipe for becoming an Orbán man: Christ leads, sport educates, law teaches thinking, and the military gives a badge of honor.

THE ROLE MODEL IS A PROVEN TOOL FOR MOTIVATION. IF ONE IS TOUCHED BY the spirit of football, he will sooner or later be exemplified by Ferenc Puskás.

*We never went out on the field, not in a single match, that victory was not the expectation. I even hate the idea of a coach defining decent defeat as a goal. Not a sportsman who doesn't win. Soccer is a special sport, many times—just think of the various cups—that the small team can win against the big ones. I never had a match in my life that I would not go out with a desire to win.*

*For the fan, it is important for the team to win and the player to do their best. [...] So, the footballer has nothing else to do except win the spectator's recognition with his game.*

*I'm Catholic. I believe in God. The Hungarian national anthem begins with His name. I go to church when I feel I have to go. I don't attend long masses, but there are times when the silence of the temple attracts me. I can only pray Our Father in Hungarian because I cannot pray in any other language.*

A good artist copies, while the great artist steals the essence of the thing:

*When there is no harmony, there is no victory.*

# 54

# Functional Democracy

Political scientists interpret the Orbán system in several ways. According to extreme beliefs, the system is an autocracy and dictatorship. More moderate opinions call it a hybrid regime. Viktor Orbán called it an illiberal state and later explained it as Christian freedom. The term illiberal was coined by Fareed Zakaria in 1997, who used the adjective in his published article in *Foreign Affairs* and it was not intended to be a compliment.

I am not a political scientist. I try to read the world outside the rigid dogmas of political science: a phenomenon cannot be interpreted in isolation, but it is always intertwined with other phenomena. My writing does not describe Viktor Orbán as isolated from the tides of the world, like political science does. At first, I look for the type of person closest to his character, and from this perspective, I play what I see. Starting from the self-made kind of man, I also describe the profession of a politician in a new way, which I find more exciting than the ideal type of ancient philosophy and the Enlightenment.

If good marketing is storytelling based on people's worldview, as Seth Godin says, politics should be about storytelling based on a worldview of patriotism. Viktor Orbán's politics builds a worldview, conditions people's beliefs and emotions. Because, as Muhammad Ali said, "It's the repetition of affirmations that leads to belief. And once that belief becomes a deep conviction, things begin to happen." Undeniable, things do begin to happen.

The question is, what causes this? If not fascism and autocracy, what is the miracle?

**THE NAME OF THE MIRACLE IS DESIGN. IN THE FOLLOWING, I WOULD LIKE** to include this field in the interpretation of the Orbán system.

Design in everyday language is a dirty word. Many people think of it as a luxury problem. If a Hungarian says something looks *designy*, they usually mean that it is ugly. In a narrower sense, design is the appearance, form of an object, and is not hocus-pocus. In a broader sense, it is a mindset: form follows function. Less is more. Solution-oriented. I see design as one of the great achievements of the twentieth century. Design is not decoration, not mere craftsmanship. On the contrary, it should be associated with high technology, mass industrial production. For example, the design of logos, cars, electronics, furniture, touch screen interfaces, or product packaging.

The first designers were architects, and industrial design became an independent profession in the second half of the twentieth century. Design has principles and a language. A good design object is not only beautiful but also useful. Not only does it look proportional, but it is at least as durable. A good designer is skilled in designing and knows the industrial background needed for production.

A good politician is familiar with the tricks of design and technology to manufacture power—Freemasons working with compasses and squares also designed and built, not without any success. The result of their work became the United States of America.

Many underestimate design. 'Why do you need all that planning stuff?' they say. Indeed, they may be right because a well-designed object is self-understanding. Politics design is as sophisticated as product design, and everything has to be self-understanding. "All this is true, but it is not that simple because there is nothing more complicated than simplicity. These very everyday activities can only be built into politics if they fit into the political narrative, and their effects are cumulative. It must also be borne in mind that distrust of the parties makes it difficult to launch a well-intentioned movement too," writes Zoltán Lakner in his book *Four Turns*.

The Orbán political design also works like design—only to a great extent. We need to plan how we can transform Hungary to make it as functional as possible and to look its best. We focus our attention on our goals. With a pragmatic approach, we strive to build the already broken path, force it into shape, and give it an element of beauty. Let's strike a balance in a peaceful, even rhythm.

Design is also about storytelling. Its worldview is harmony between functionality and beauty. The same thing characterizes Orbán politics: functionality, also called solution-oriented. The equivalent of visual beauty is the unity of national sentiment. The harmony between functional legislation and the value system behind them is the unity of the Fundamental Law and the National Creed.

Functionality can be characterized by objective criteria, while beauty is a matter of taste. Orbán's system works well, including the economy, public security, and public administration. The national value system behind government measures, the education and cultural policies that stem from it is more a matter of taste and more easily divide people.

Functionality and beauty can also be interpreted from the perspective of strength: durability and number of units sold—a two-thirds majority in Parliament and 2,824,206 popular votes.

THE IDEAL OF FUNCTIONALITY AND BEAUTY IS NOT JUST THE WORLDVIEW of design. It is at least as much as fitness'.

The ideal of bodybuilding is Hercules, with his enormous and well-defined muscles. For a bodybuilder, sport is about the appearance of the muscles, the body that commands authority. Bodybuilders pump their spectacular bodies to an impressive size during brutal workouts. The main difference between weight lifting and powerlifting is that in bodybuilding competitions, it is not the lifted weight that determines the final result. For bodybuilding athletes, the level of definition, symmetry, and proportion of the muscles matter.

Fans of functional training give less to the look; they are more interested in the strength and usability —the functionality—of their body. Functional training is often coupled with military themes and training in tactical gear. One of the essential training tools is the kettlebell, a particular dumbbell from Russia, essentially an iron ball with a handle on the top, used in elite military training just as well as in underground gyms.

Calisthenics is a Greek word meaning 'strong' and 'beautiful.' The ideal type of calisthenics physique is the statue of the ancient Greek athlete, rediscovered in the Renaissance and reborn in the sculpture of David by Michelangelo. The body radiating strength is not characterized by the size of the muscles but by their proportional shape. The new wave version of calisthenics, street workout, is more geared toward compact builds; smaller muscles are often more elaborate than those of professional bodybuilders, indicating the high level of strength development of the sport.

Today, the two significant branches of fitness are bodybuilding and functional training. In modern fitness clubs specialized for bodybuilding, we find weights and all kinds of machines, as opposed to a functional gym with few equipment, placed in a large hall with pull-up and dip bars, kettlebells, Plyo cubes, and a bench. While a bodybuilder will train each muscle on a separate machine and with different weights, a functional training session will be based on just six basic movement patterns (pushing, pulling, swinging, carrying, squatting, and everything else: get ups, rolls, etc.).

The ideal type of American democracy is bodybuilding. Because of the elaborate sophistication of the rule of law institutions—the magnificent ratio of checks and balances, the spectacular military muscle mass, and the authoritative economy—the United States is a model for those who want to be muscular. The striking appearance of Hercules will fascinate the world and give them reason to fear him. However, steroid-inflated bodybuilders look strong, but in reality, they are not always the strongest. Because of their enormous muscles, they are not always able to perform vigorous movements and may be embarrassed by their bodyweight exercises. Just as America can be inflated with the intellectual steroids of the enlightenment, the idea of an open society based on a liberal worldview, or the stock price bubble of listed corporations.

However, muscle size cannot be increased indefinitely, the steroid will eventually cause health complaints, and the bubble will burst. The steroid injection of open society is illegal immigration that undermines the cultural power of the nation-state, and the lowering of the stock market bubble is a stock market crash. George Soros is one of the most respected experts in both areas.

ORBÁN'S DEMOCRACY IS BASED ON THE ANALOGY OF FUNCTIONAL training patterns: a functional democracy.

In Viktor Orbán's functional democracy, it is not the spectacle of the institutions, but the coordinated work of the institutions— the "muscles"—the so-called movement pattern gives power to the government and the country. Single muscles are not involved in the effort, rather the whole body. Movement patterns of pushing and pulling between the ruling party, the Parliament, the government, and the administration are based on national strength development.

The swing of foreign trade and diplomacy will boost Hungarian exports. Government mobility allows the Prime Minister to work in the full range of (joint) movement. The Ministry of Human Capacities also builds on this functional endeavor, conditioning education and health, not as isolated but as complex muscle groups. The realization of sovereignty is its bodyweight workout—"street workout"—because the country must be able to endure, and it must be able to pull itself up to the top of the bar and the world. Thrust that stops migration, traction that strengthens the economy, and controlled get up that restores self-esteem. Doping agents such as economic or military dominance are available to the United States. Hungarians have other options. We do not necessarily want to squat with maximum weight. We need real, well-functioning fitness, a country with a straight national spine, well-moving joints, low body fat percentage. We have limited resources, so we have few tools to work with. Instead of a candy-colored gym, we have the well-known *Russian* kettlebell, *Turkish* get-up, and core training remain.

Core training, strengthening the abdominal muscles that stabilize the trunk and deep back muscles are the foundation of any functional workout program. The core means 'essence, best of something.' The core is the central—most important—component of something. The core message of a book is what the main message of the book is. If something is very hard and very intense, then the educated Englishman calls it hard-core. (Note that core muscle is the most important!)

If you think about it, Orbán started with this, strengthening the national backbone, increasing financial strength, and reducing public debt, which serves as a stabilizing muscle, and establishing a constitution for long-term stable governance. The basis of all weight training and your bodyweight exercise is to keep the spine straight. Why would national politics be the exception? The core function of core training is stability. Viktor Orbán has always focused on this first. The Fundamental Law favors a stable worldview. The electoral law favors a politically stable government.

A significant proportion of sports injuries are attributable to the weakness of the stabilizing muscles, and the maintenance of stability is also the basis of policy for a government. If someone has weak stabilizing muscles, they may overload certain joints, which is the cause of sports injuries. When the Socialists ruled without a worldview-based foundation, a "core strength," they sought to maintain political stability through the distributive politics of social policy, overloading the country's financial capacity, and almost ended in a bankruptcy. In contrast, Orbán builds on the people's worldview; national stability does not require overloading the country's financial "joints," and the government enjoys people's support without it. If bodyweight exercises illustrate sovereignty, it is better to understand why Orbán starts politics with a national "core training." The omega and alpha of your bodyweight exercises are core strength, from the handstands to the more strenuous planche.

György Matolcsy's unorthodox policy can be interpreted as a kind of financial handstand because he put everything economists had thought about public debt management upside down. This book is not a dissertation in political science but is intended to achieve understanding. Fitness, design, and Viktor Orbán's system can be considered as analogs of each other and can be understood in terms of functionality.

FEEDBACK IS REQUIRED TO COMPLETE EACH PROCESS. ONE OF THE essential principles of personal training planning is that the result should be measurable. It is necessary to record the baseline, assess the condition with fitness and mobility tests, then select the exercises, adapt the diet, and integrate it into the daily routine. Top athletes think this way too. The training plan shall be subdivided into cycles so that the highest level of standby of the athlete is scheduled for the race day. During the workout, a workout log is maintained and results from workout to workout are documented to determine where the athlete is progressing, whether everything is going according to plan, or whether changes need to be made.

This is how the design process works, manufacturing and testing different prototypes, endurance tests, and market research surveys.

Orbán's power technology relies heavily on poll data. From this, you can measure the effectiveness of the 'training' and the success of the story. This is what connects sport, design, and even business to politics: it is about the future.

Popularity and the social support of a politician are crucial for a politician, so the purpose of the measurements is to test the "country design" he designed in practice. Andy Grove, the Hungarian-born founder of Intel, developed the so-called OKRs—Objectives and Key Results. In the life of a company, goals set long-term goals, and key results translate into measurable results. Starting from Google, half of the world has adopted this approach through the Bono AIDS Foundation.

The long-term goals of the Orbán management are heard at Tusnádfürdő and the key results in the country evaluation speech. One part of the Prime Minister's speech at the private meetings in Kötcse sets out the two- to three-year long-term goals of the government term, while the other part outlines the results achieved so far. The institutionalized form of feedback is national consultation or community forums, to name two examples.

The elusive flow of the spirit of the age permeates every aspect of life. One of the phenomena is the appearance of applied sciences and the practical realization of dogmatic high culture. Mass production and mechanization have made it possible to replicate the quality and to make processes affordable, and accessible. The second half of the twentieth century developed design, fitness, positive psychology. Although a member of a particular profession lives in his or her world, the patterns they are familiar with appear elsewhere. What technology has produced, politics has reaped: companies first competed with each other, more recently countries. Disruptive technology also disrupts politics. A functional approach serves not only design and well-being but also politics.

# 55

# Orbán = Trump?

Two self-made man. Trump knocks on the door, Orbán finds the loophole. Donald Trump relies on his instincts; Orbán is analytical. Trump is more of an *Art of the Deal* businessman, a strongman of bilateral agreements, while Orbán is a strongman of politics. Trump plays golf, Orbán thinks in football's team play. They are both familiar with *The Art of War*. In others, they have nothing in common.

President Trump, according to the American neoliberal press, is a notorious liar who is unfit for the post he holds. Harmful to America and ignorant compared to European politicians. Scandal after scandal, they say, the party cannot stand him, he split the country with demagogic slogans and hypnotized the lower-educated nationalist masses. It is an illusion of money rather than actual growth that causes its governance success. He is sometimes rude, and his promises will remain unkept promises. The Hungarian media tried to attract this political character to Ferenc Gyurcsány.

The author of the scandal book, *Fire and Fury*, paints a picture of the President of the United States in stark contrast to Orbán, beginning with the fact that an inside staff member was leaking the government's embarrassing affairs. According to the author of the book, in the Trump team, everyone hoped that Mr. Trump would not become president, they wished to use the presidential election campaign to raise awareness of the

Trump brand, not thinking for a minute that they could win. Yet, they were wrong.

Trump and Orbán are difficult to compare because the United States Constitution limits one man's presidency to eight years. A game is finite if it is up to eight years and not infinite to think over thirty years. If we were to put Viktor Orbán on par with an American president, Ronald Reagan it would be. Reagan, a Republican president in line with the Hungarian middle-class values, brought economic prosperity to America and dismantled communism in Europe. Or Barack Obama, who, like Orbán, climbed from the bottom, became president due to the love of people and his charismatic rhetorical qualities, and after his second term, he remained popular. He was a polished and loyal husband. Or Abraham Lincoln, who became President of the United States at the age of 52 after a series of congressional and senatorial elections and is revered as one of the greatest presidents.

The mainstream press used to mention Orbán's name on the front page with Donald Trump. In itself, it is a tremendous achievement, even if the editorial maliciousness is behind it. They see Viktor Orbán's rule as a milestone in the rise of populism and try to connect the narrative of the downgrading of (Hungarian) democracy with Trump, to keep him away from power. Still, the story of Orbán's political image was built up in the minds of the liberal press, too, putting him on the front page. Editors saw in his politics the same universality that is generally regarded as an exceptional leadership trait of the great powers.

The underground narrative is Trump, and Orbán found the same thing, both realizing that the world is starting to disbelieve in America. China is beginning to upset the world's view that America is first. This insight is what binds them together, not the narrative invented by biased journalism.

Let's divide the United States into three parts.

The first pillar is democracy. Gatekeepers and checking mechanisms limit the right of the American people to have a say. Competition in the classic sense of the word cannot be called democratic due to the influence of the public, mostly by the private press, and the individual supporters of presidential campaigns. As a result, whoever gets into the presidential office, his worldview about American patriotism is the same as his rivals.

The second element is the presidential institution. Checks and balances constrain the president-elect. The foreign-military weight of the president is more relevant than his power over domestic politics.

The third pillar is the US economy. The economic environment has the fewest checks and balances. A consumer-friendly climate in a single market with more than three hundred million people and free-market competition. Companies grow strong in the national market and, therefore, could expand their influence through their capital strength. The US state seeks to promote and possibly enforce a liberal democratic system everywhere in the world, limiting the power of local state power by checks and balances, and securing the free market that allows American companies to thrive. The democratic model of the liberal state can also work because society is labor-intensive, and the state does not provide everyone with the same level of health care, education, and pensions. These must be earned by everyone in the form of savings (e.g., by investing in stocks of American companies).

China has solved the problem differently. The political organization is a one-party system without checks and balances, while checks and balances constrain the elections and the economy. Thanks to its freedom of movement, the political power could build an economy that favors Chinese businesses and prevents foreign corporations from exerting influence. Chinese companies grew strong by the *Made in China* principle, with factories that are majority Chinese-owned to produce goods for the world. By introducing know-how manufacturing processes in China, the Western world taught China how to make things, and after a few years, the Chinese, with their Western know-how, manufactured the same products independently of the originals. Copying is part of Chinese culture. Plagiarism is not necessarily considered immoral.

While foreign companies cannot enter the Chinese market on their own, Chinese companies are not restricted from expanding their influence abroad, where the market is open to competition. The Chinese state provides the financial means necessary for the expansion. China not only manufactures but also exports. Since it supplies almost everything to the world, it has copied virtually everything and is present in practically every market, including the largest, the single American market. America, as the world's leading economic power, is starting to lose weight. In addition to its economic power, China's military power is significant, too, but it is not involved in world peacekeeping. There is no need for it because America does this work instead of China.

Viktor Orbán's "illiberal state" is the inverse of the American model. The competition among political parties is democratic due to the abolition of gatekeepers and electoral mechanisms that once restricted elections. Orbán shifted the checks and balances from the political system to the economy, which is hurting the interests of Western powers. The bigger players demand the establishment of a democratic system of institutions because the more the government's hands are tied and the freer the market, the easier it is for capital-intensive Western corporations to gain market power. The mission of the economic policy measures of the Orbán government is to protect and keep the Hungarian economy strong, despite foreign overpowering. This is accomplished with the introduction of sector-specific taxes (banks, retail-chains, telecom), the abolition of private pension funds, the reduction of overheads, tobacco shops, and, at the same time, the strengthening of domestic small and medium-sized enterprises.

With pure business logic, Trump realized that while America could not break through the Great Wall of the Chinese economy, the Chinese were taking over the American market without restrictions. Since he, as president, has no opportunity to restrict the free market, his only instrument is to impose special duties on China in the form of protective tariffs. The genuine function of Orbán's system of checks and balances is to protect the national economy.

President Trump's other instinct is that not only is there a problem with America's external narrative, but that Americans no longer believe in America as they once did. The principle of an open society forged the American nation, but all immigrants were Europeans and shared the same worldview. Black people in the United States did not have the right to vote, only with the Civil Rights Movements of the 1960s did they achieve full equality, and when they did, black people shared the same views as white people. This shared worldview is loosened by illegal immigration. It was along this line that the Trump Presidency divided the country. Between Americans who believed in America, and who forged a nation, and between those who immigrated to America and built a parallel society. The majority of left-liberals are on the side of immigrants for the same reasons as in Hungary or other European countries.

The commonality between Trump and Orbán is that they have seen a change in their country's internal and external narratives. For Orbán, the political program was to unite the Hungarian nation along a united worldview, as opposed to Trump, who can only detect this phenomenon. Orbán realized that the shared national creed was making America great, and Trump only felt that this was what was beginning to fall apart.

"If the only thing you know about Viktor Orban is from Western media accounts, you would think that he was nothing but some kind of mafia thug. The Viktor Orban you encounter in person is very, very different from the Viktor Orban shown to Americans by our media. In Orban—who speaks good English—was energetic, fiercely intelligent, funny, self-deprecating, realistic, and at times almost pugilistic in talking about defending Hungary and her interests. Orban is what Trump's biggest fans wish he was (but isn't), and what Trump's enemies think him to be (but isn't)." Wrote Rod Dreher in an article in The American Conservative. "If Donald Trump had the smarts and skills of Viktor Orban, the political situation in the US would be much, much different—for better or for worse, depending on your point of view."

Orbán also learned from mistakes. He did adopt the pillars for his system from America—the labor-based economy, Christian values, sovereignty, power-giving narrative—but not by copying it. He was looking at the interests of the country, not of the great foreign powers. The rest of the world does not have a problem with what democracy is like in Hungary because if anyone were interested, there would not have been Trianon, there would have been no iron curtain, and we would not be left behind in 1956.

Everybody is motivated by money—money becomes power, and this is what Viktor Orbán wants to limit. By giving his government freedom of movement and reorganizing the national economy with checks and balances. And to keep it that way, he designed the competition among political parties on the analogy of the free market, where consumers decide. Foreign interests should no longer interfere with Hungarian politics by removing a government with its financial and media influence. And to make sure loyal politicians could not assist foreign interests by eliminating the checks and balances from the market and putting them back on the government.

The national side conceived a strong worldview, and integrity built the capital of trust. This form of state can only be interpreted independently. Not *this* and *that*, nor a hybrid of dysfunctional structures. But a system.

This is the System of National Cooperation—the Orbán system.

**THERE IS ONE IN THE WORLD.**

# 56

# System

By convention, we maintain that the communist system was a *system*, and the change of regime *changed the system*. Paper can handle anything, so let me argue with that statement. The communist system was not a system, and the change of regime was not a change of system either.

In 1990, the Constitution was only amended, although the form of state changed, and democratic transformation took place. But the result, the republic, was not a real system. Because the main criterion of a system is it should work. But the 'system' did not work. Neither in communism nor after the transition called the change of regime. Until 2010, neither Hungary nor the current government could stand on its own feet. Politics meant formal institutions, establishing parties, forming governments, redistribution, but *hasta la vista* to that.

In communism, socialism was not working, and neither were the market economy or its ideology, because nobody believed in it. At most, it was because of the pressure that they lied that everything was beautiful. As soon as people had the opportunity to vote freely, the government was overturned at the first opportunity, and people elected a new one. József Antall's, Gyula Horn's, the first government of Viktor Orbán, and the Medgyessy-Gyurcsány-Bajnai era did not have a system either. Here, too, the system did not work, the country could not be flown straight without a pilot: there was no unified worldview and no vision spanning government cycles. As the 'system' based on the previous legal structure did not work, it had to be changed—to a real system.

The underground narrative is that the first political system that functions as a system predictably and well, is the System of National Cooperation. The Orbán system is not a dictatorship because it operates in a non-violent and democratic way: when a voter enters the polling booth, he pulls the curtain and re-elects Viktor Orbán in his solitude—by free will.

American democracy is also a system. It has a purpose, is structured and believed by the Americans. A dictatorial regime has an end in itself; it has no purpose, it is not systematically built, but poorly constructed, and no one except the fanatic beneficiaries believe in it. Intellectuals especially do not accept it.

Today's opposition intellectuals are deceiving themselves with many things. 'Sooner or later, the Orbán system will suddenly fall like communism.' Because Orbán's course is supposed to be a dictatorship, and that's how dictatorships collapse. If there is one thing I wanted to refute with this book, it was this misconception.

Gábor Bojár co-founded Graphisoft, a Hungarian software company with his two employees in 1982, which has since grown into a multinational company with 500 employees. During one of our conversations, I naively asked how he could protect his idea of not being knocked off. "Because it is hard to do." A software company, he explained, is not a single idea, but a thousand small details that very few people know. He went on to say, "Think about it, if it is difficult for you, who are the best at it, how hard it must be for someone else!"

The opposition deceived themselves with self-fulfilling misconceptions. They did not notice or did not want to notice how difficult it was to do—thirty years of relentless effort hard. And of course, you need talent and a lot of luck and companions.

Most of all, they deceived themselves by interpreting the Kádár system and the change of regime as a working system. What Orbán has built is a stable system: it stands on its own, is built on worldview and works. It is not anti-democratic, only the entry threshold is extremely low, and once you gain power, you are relatively free to maneuver. Here checks and balances are less restrictive on governance and more of an economy.

As the Hungarians did not have a unified worldview about the love of homeland, Orbán began to work towards it. For the time being, only his voters accept all three conditions, national unity, sovereignty, and the protection of Christian values. In earlier systems, the country had no purpose. Orbán changed everything and gave Hungarians a vision of the future. With a strong Hungary program, he wants to achieve a more significant share of the world in terms of size and weight and get more from scarce resources.

> So, you may not like the current government and the current economic policy, but to say that we have not advanced, we have not made progress, that every year we have not taken at least a little step forward, to say this is such a lie that no thought can build on it. [...] That is why all political debates in Hungary today are about power issues and have lost the intellectual outlook. We stand for something, I strive to represent a national self-interest, freedom, and esteem, but on the other hand, I do not see anything that can stand for anything valuable. That is why Hungarian political debates are so meaningless, there is nothing in them that raises the soul or the heart or the future and opens up a bit of perspective for political debates. Everything is down in the mud.

## WHY CAN'T HIS OPPONENTS BEAT VIKTOR ORBÁN?

On account of the same thing that made Michael Jordan, Muhammad Ali, and Michael Phelps the greatest athletes of all time, because they were willing to sacrifice everything for victory, were above average and fought as *infinite* players. Because as a celebrated champion, they practiced more and fought harder than the others. Regularity, a logically structured training plan, a predictable relationship between input and output. As Arnold Schwarzenegger said, "There are no shortcuts—everything is reps, reps, reps."

For the same reason that the thirteen Grammy winner, Oscar winner, and Nobel Laureate of Literature Bob Dylan's style is unmatched. Because identity, talent, and spirit of the age, all three met professional skills.

For the same reason that George Soros became one of the most influential people in the world, because he was able to recognize opportunities, took risks, and was a master of his profession. For the same reason that Apple has become one of the most valuable companies in the world. The closed system of hardware and software, innovative solutions, and symbolism touching the depths of the human psyche, Steve Jobs' visionary vision and the corporate culture, brand loyalty, and continuous innovation built around it. For the same reason that IKEA is so popular: because its design is simple, family-friendly, and smart— witty, understandable, and functional.

For the same reason that Alex Ferguson's Manchester United became the world's invincible football team. An indestructible unit of a large format manager and leading players, with a solid background, nurturing talent and a loyal fan base.

For the same reason that the United States is the most powerful country in the world. Because we humans think so. We believe the story that was built on our worldview. That folks have drawn on the blank slate something original, call it art, because after all, that's the philosophy of the thing.

*Footballers are, after all, artists in the philosophy of the things.*

What else can be added to this? Perhaps the millions of prayers were not in vain. My father's motto is a Ben-Gurion quote: "in order to be a realist, you must believe in miracles."

# Epilogue

At the beginning of 2019, a friend of mine recommended me to a Finnish radio station that wanted to interview a "Fidesz-supporting young man." I contacted Risto Majaniemi by email. He asked me to pick a place somewhere in downtown Budapest where we could meet for the interview. I suggested what it would be like to have an interview at the Central European University, I thought we would find a quiet point at the university, and the university leadership would not mind. "At the CEU?" He asked, surprised. "Yes, because I do not agree with shutting down the CEU." He started the interview right away with this topic, which became newsworthy, although I made it clear at the outset, I'm a loyal supporter of Viktor Orbán; however, CEU and Orbán are not a matter of or/or. I am not a party droid, but a free-thinking intellectual, I can argue against the closure of a university, but I still support Viktor Orbán, and I look up at him as a role model.

When considered the most significant contemporary architect in the world, Frank O. Gehry was in Budapest his hosts guided him by a car around the city to show him the capital's architectural highlights. During the first two days of his three-day visit, Gehry repeatedly inquired about where Makovecz's buildings were in Budapest. His hosts told him there were not any in Budapest. So they had to redesign the program, on the last day they went to Piliscsaba (approx. 30 km from Budapest) after Gehry visited Makovecz at his Kecske Street studio and left for the airport. From then on, their shared photo was always behind Uncle Imre's desk on the bookshelf.

In 1997, Imre Makovecz received the Gold Medallion of the Académie Royale d'Architecture, and some of his drawings were purchased by the Pompidou Center. Although the world saw the genius in him, he could not be commissioned in the Hungarian capital, because the cultural liberal *mafia state* of Budapest prevented it. The wounds are endless.

Both my grandmother and my grandfather are art historians. I was raised as the grandson of Katalin Dávid and Pál Miklós. My grandparents set an example for me. They lived most of their lives, not in a free world, but they were free because they never limited their thinking on an ideological basis. They knew about quality, and they taught me that. "Value, even if different from mine, is value." When it comes to values in politics, it is Viktor Orbán. Imre Makovecz in architecture, Péter Korniss in photography, Judit Reigl and Dezső Váli in painting, Dezső Ránki and Edit Klukon in classical music, Péter Esterházy and Gáspár Nagy in literature, László Levendel and András Csókay in friendship, and the list goes on.

Art or politics? Two simple rules should be noted. All art should be judged on quality. If one creates art as a means of politicization, not as a politician, then the rules of the political game apply to him. The right to express political views, and the right to get involved in politics actively is not the same. All intellectuals can have opinions, artists can freely express their views on the world, but if this art becomes political activism, then you have to take the risk of a knockout, as this is the nature of the political combat. A university can—and should—have a worldview and may employ former politicians as educators. If these professors use the cathedral of the university to agitate as party politicians, it is neither ethical nor compatible with the spirit of the *universitas*.

Viktor Orbán is the least understood by his generation. Perhaps it is because they belong to the same generation, they were young together, once they rebelled together, they became grandparents together, and it is difficult to accept that Orbán became a historical figure. Paper-based intellects have increasingly become losers in the digital world, and their physical and mental health is weakened and difficult to find their place. On the left-liberal side, they were well aware that there was less and less need for cultured intellectuals. The only thing they are wrong about—but very much—is that it was Viktor Orbán's fault.

It is the world that transformed, and for those who want to succeed time is money, the world is full of useful knowledge, you need to learn languages, know how to communicate and sell, and the leisure time for reading, if any, must be profitable. To get ahead does not require what we once called literacy, so the latter has no monetary value, and educated intellectuals will continue to exert less influence. Viktor Orbán may have sensed the foreboding of this, which means not only that the world does not need philosophers, and neither do Hungarians. Whoever wants to stay alive needs a relentless effort. Self-discipline and a focused workout program are necessary, because if you do not train, the stronger will overcome you. They will defeat you not necessarily physically, but more on the spiritual plane. An open society overthrows nation-states without identity, and a drained, soulless superficiality finally replaces culture.

### WHAT'S NEXT?

One thing is sure: fear is a wicked counselor. Left-liberal intellectuals are not only afraid of Viktor Orbán, but they are equally scared of Ferenc Gyurcsány. They feel they have to hate Orbán and have a good face to Gyurcsány, and more recently, the far-right, because they have no choice—they say. So, they fell to the floor between two chairs because they knocked themselves out from the right, and the ground was pulled from under them from the left.

For the record, Orbán is not governing poorly, but the left is in the midst of the same moral crisis as in 2006. I am not inclined toward left-wing liberal narratives, and I am somewhat annoyed at being blamed for Orbán rather than them blaming themselves. They promised Hungarians an easy, *jobless* life. They promised a dream and could not fulfill it. They became losers in their own right— 'self-made' losers. New-generation politicians express more disappointment than hope, lack much respect, lack of humility, style, and altruism. Rather than liberals they are marxists: 'How can we take away from one another for what you have worked for?' rather than 'we work for it.'

IF VIKTOR ORBÁN WERE TO BE LABELED WITH A TOKEN, THAT WOULD be aptness. This is lacking in the opposition, and it may have been the real reason, the original emotion, which on the national side laid the foundation of the common belief in Viktor Orbán to be elected leader. Paternity is also about aptitude but on a smaller scale. Those who chose Viktor Orbán who did not need liberal intellectuals, but a good father. Who accepts you as you are. He says, "Go, Hungarians!" You are the most talented, the most viable, and you can do it. He is the one who trusts you and encourages you not to give up. Whoever tells you how to make a difficult decision will take care of your family, the one who you can look up to and respect. And whoever keeps his word promises and it will be so.

In addition to being talented, a sense of responsibility for the future (generation) links paternity to statesman ethos.

If Viktor Orbán plays the role of 'father' in the reconstruction of the Hungarian nation, then this role was played by Tivadar

Herzl in the life of the Jewish people after the scattering. The vision of the Hungarian-born dreamer of the State of Israel corresponds in many ways with Orbán's vision.

I would like to end my book with a prophecy from Herzl's book *The Old-New-Land*:

*But we, we had the power that was needed. Whence did we have it? From the terrible pressure to which we were subjected on all sides, from poverty and persecution. That was the centripetal force that drew all our scattered forces to a focus and strengthened a union that included not only the downtrodden, but the powerful; not only the young, but the wise; not only thoughtless enthusiasts, but cultured men and women. Not only hands but heads... all together. A people, a whole people, found itself together - nay, found itself again. We made the new society not because we were better than others, but simply because we were ordinary men with the ordinary human needs for air and light, health and honor, for the right to acquire property and security of possession. [...] We did only that which, under the given circumstances and at the given moment, was a historical necessity.*

# Notes

## PART ONE: BIASES

[2 ] **"Success = talent +...a lot of luck.":** Daniel Kahneman, Thinking, Fast and Slow (London: Penguin Books, 2011), p. 177.

[4 ] **This Chapter is based on the following articles from Wikipedia:** 'Rendszerváltás Magyarországon' (Change of regime in Hungary), and 'Magyar történelem' (History of Hungary).

[4 ] **"On a particular intellectual...healthy marriage.":** Viktor Orbán's speech at the XXVIII. Fidesz Congress (29 Sept. 2019).

[7] **"I am talking about...that ridiculous?":** Kéri László, Orbán Viktor (Politician portraits, Politikusportrék, Budapest: Századvég, 1994), p. 32.

[7] **"You don't have to...leaves behind.":** Kéri 1994, p. 33.

[8] **"the person and the situation":** Lee Ross, and Richard E. Nisbett, The Person and the Situation: Perspectives of Social Psychology (London: Printer & Martin, 2011).

[9] **"What Happened to Hungary?":** Ágnes Heller, What Happened to Hungary? (The New York Times, 16. Sept. 2018).

[9] **"factfulness":** Hans Rosling, Factfulness (London: Hodder and Stoughton, 2018).

[9] **"Harari, also on the digital revolution":** as an example, see Yuval Noah Harari, 21 Lessons for the 21st Century (London: Jonathan Cape, 2018).

[9] **"Steven Pinker's books contain hundreds of state-of-the-art references":** as an example, see Steven Pinker, Enlightenment Now: The Case for Reason, Science, Humanism, and Progress (New York: Viking, 2018).

[10] **"It is deucedly...the truth.":** Péter Esterházy, Celestial Harmonies (New York: Ecco - HarperCollins, 2004). Translation by Judith Sollosy.

[12] **"the aforementioned book on that topic":** George Soros, The Alchemy of Finance (New Jersey: John Wiley & Sons, 2003).

[12] **"It is okay to...hasty retreat.":** Mark Tier, The Winning Investment Habits of Warren Buffett and George Soros (New York: Truman Talley Books, 2005), p. 47.

[13] **"The speech given by...their place.":** Interview with Péter Nádas from 2016: https://mandiner.hu/cikk/20160917_nadas_peter_nagyszeru_az_oszodi_beszed_2006.

[13] **"The result of the...of Gyurcsánys.":** Viktor Orbán's keynote speech at the annual 'Civic Picnic' in Kötcse (17 Sept. 2019).

[13] **"Gyurcsány once told the...no scandal.":** philosopher and public intellectual Tamás Gáspár Miklós authored his column as TGM, titled Undorodom tőletek (I'm sick of you guys, Index.hu, 14 Jun. 2019).

[14] **I've quoted from two articles from The Economist.** The corrupting of democracy was published in the print edition under the section Leaders under the headline Democracy's enemy within (29. Aug. 2019). How Viktor Orban hollowed out Hungary's democracy was published in the print edition under the section Briefing under the headline The entanglement of powers (29 Aug. 2019).

[14] **"Newspapers and periodicals should...distorted material.":** British National Union of Journalists Code of Conduct as of June 1994, 1.i.

[14] **"Newspapers, whilst free...and fact.":** BNUJ Code of Conduct as of June 1994, 3.

[14] **"How to report this...work for.":** George Mikes, How to be an Alien (London: Penguin Books, 1966), p. 82.

## PART TWO: SELF-MADE

[16] **"I have to admit...space, too.":** An anonymous source interviewed by Kósa András in his book Orbán Viktor, a káosz embere. (Viktor Orbán, the Man of Chaos, Budapest: Noran Libro, 2018), p. 230.

[16] **Three books by Malcolm Gladwell.** The Tipping Point: How Little Things Can Make a Big Difference (New York: Little Brown & Company, 2011), David and Goliath: Underdogs, Misfits and the Art of Battling Giants (New York: Little Brown and Company, 2013), Outliers: The Story of Success (London: Penguin, 2008).

[17] **"quiet":** Susan Cain, Quiet: The Power of Introverts in A World That Can't Stop Talking (New York: Crown Publishing, 2012).

[17] **"Practically, not just theoretically...own sources," and "If we stop the...from within.":** Szájer József, A globalista utópizmus áfiuma és az ellene való orvosság (The Opium of Globalist Utopism and Its Antidote, Lecture, 5 Mar. 2019, published by the blog 'Látószög').

[18] **"The popular caricature of...craves power.":** Alex Ferguson with Michael Moritz, Leading (London: Hodder & Stoughton, 2015), pp. 235–236.

[18] **"Everyone gets up in...it's politics.":** Kósa 2018, p. 123.

[18] **"I was to help...and management.":** Ferguson 2015, p. 239.

[20] **"We listened to the...seventh place.":** Kéri 1994, p. 9.

[20] **"All football depends on...the winner.":** Zsolt Róbert, Puskás Öcsi (Budapest: Szabad Tér Kiadó, 1989) p. 124.

[20] **"We believed in liberalism...a rebellion.":** Igor Janke, Hajrá, magyarok! (Rézbong Kiadó, 2012), p. 70.

[20] **"So for us Hungarians...the match.":** Interview with Viktor Orbán, Echo TV (7 Dec. 2017).

[22] **"Fidesz is a true...it happen.":** Interview with Viktor Orbán, 888.hu (15 Dec. 2016).

[22] **"Character is something you...from education.":** Interview with Viktor Orbán, 888. hu (15 Dec. 2016).

[23] **"The young man has...into a myth.":** Ungvári Tamás, A rock mesterei (Masters of Rock, Budapest: Zeneműkiadó, 1974), pp. 179–180.

[23] **"a combination of extraordinary...extraordinary talent.":** Debreczeni József, Orbán Viktor (Budapest: Osiris Kiadó, 2002), p. 98.

[23] **"Transylvania's peculiar genre is...and shocking,":** Hamvas Béla, Öt géniusz (Five Geniuses, Szombathely: Életünk Szerkesztősége, 1988), p. 37.

[24] **"For example, while I...earn esteem.":** Kéri 1994, p. 15.

[24] **The research on parenting** was published by Steven D. Levitt, and Stephen J. Dubner in their book Freakonomics: A Rouge Economist Explores the Hidden Side of Everything (New York: Harper, 2009), pp. 147–179.

[24] **"Did you have many...bought books.":** Kéri 1994, p. 10.

[24] **"I want to say something...to school.":** Kéri 1994, p. 13.

[24] **"The best four years...changed cultures.":** Kéri 1994, p. 17.

[24] **"The technical background of...and unionized.":** Janke 2012, p. 64.

[25] **"Hungarians do not think...real memories":** An essay by Babits Mihály, A magyar jellemről (On the Hungarian Character) published in Babits Mihály művei: esszék, tanulmányok (Essays, Writings, Budapest: Szépirodalmi Könyvkiadó, 1978) p. 651.

[25] **"Outstanding humor, as one...the player.":** Babits 1978, p. 661.

[25] **The outline is based on the screenplay structure by Blake Snyder's book,** Save the Cat! The Last Book on Screenwriting You'll Ever Need (Studio City CA., 2005, Michael Wiese Productions), pp. 67–96.

## PART THREE: IDENTITY

[26] **"Where I come from...such an uncultivated place.":** Transcript from the documentary "Mi leszel, ha nagy leszel?" (What are you gonna be when you grow up?, Fekete Doboz Alapítvány, 1988).

[28] **"Today, Hungary is more like a ship...are held secure.":** Viktor Orbán's annual evaluation speech of the country (1 Feb. 2011).

[28] **"Hungary also needs to know...east wind.":** Viktor Orbán's annual evaluation speech of the country (5 Feb. 2010).

[28] **"We've been through it...than ours...":** Viktor Orbán's speech at Kossuth Square (6 Oct. 2006).

[28] **"The spring wind is...flood of immigrants.":** Viktor Orbán's annual evaluation speech of the country (28 Feb. 2016).

[28] "a symbol always denotes...the symbol is alive...": Dávid Katalin, Bibliai jelképek kézikönyve: A teremtett világ misztériuma (The Handbook of Biblical Symbols, Budapest: Szent István Társulat, 2002), p. 7.

[28] "I reveal the historical...freedom approaches.": Viktor Orbán's speech on the 5th anniversary of adopting the Fundamental Law (25 Apr. 2016).

[28] "Think of death!...the art of the master!": Kiszely Gábor, A szabadkőművesség (Freemasonry, Budapest, Korona Kiadó, 1999), p. 52.

[29] "I'd rather say...I didn't belong to anyone.": Kéri 1994, p. 11.

[30] Babits's essay can be found in the book already cited, Babits 1978, pp. 628–665.

[30] "We were among...System of National Cooperation.": Annual evaluation speech of the country (10 Feb. 2017).

[30] "So, this meaningful statement...is what's characteristic.": Babits 1978.

[30] "... who is the most uniquely Hungarian...calm and sincerity.": Babits 1978.

[30] "The insane dream of...instead of Hungarians.": Viktor Orbán's speech in front of the House of Terror Museum (23 Oct. 2017).

[30] "Thinking about timeframes...Go for it!": Viktor Orbán's speech at Tusnádfürdő (28 Jul. 2018).

[30] "The flag of Hungary...respectively.": The Fundamental Law.

[31] "We believe in the power of love and togetherness.": Viktor Orbán's most famous line from his historic speech at Kossuth Square (13 Apr. 2002).

[31] "I am sending you out...innocent as doves.": Matthew 10:16,

[31] "Ortberg, a gifted storyteller...I rest my case.'": Ken Blanchard, and Phil Hodges, Lead Like Jesus: Lessons from the Greatest Leadership Role Model of All Time (Nashville: W Publishing Group, 2016), p. 9–10.

[31] "Who would have thought...and their bosses.": Annual evaluation speech of the country (10 Feb. 2017).

[31] "I think there is...from the pain.": Janke 2012, p. 192.

[31] "square, sincere, and meaningful life." and "nations are free...and undesirable.": Viktor Orbán's speech at the XII. Congress of the Alliance of Christian Intellectuals – Keresztény Értelmiségiek Szövetségének XII. kongresszusán – (14 Sept. 2019).

[32] "Genius of the West...loyalty.": Hamvas 1988, p. 65.

[32] "Genius of Transylvania...refinement.": Hamvas 1988, p. 66.

[32] Quotes on Gábor Bethlen are from Gyula Szekfű's monograph Bethlen Gábor (Biography of Gábor Bethlen, Budapest: Helikon, 1983) pp. 143–189.

[32] "between Europe and Byzantium": Hamvas 1998, p. 34.

[32] "The Transylvanians have...intricate contradictions.": Hamvas 1998, p. 37.

[33] Bayer Zsolt, 1100 év Európa közepén – 1100 Years in the Heart of Europe – Nemzeti Könyvtár, National Library series Vol. 76. (Budapest: Magyar Közlöny Lap- és Könyvkiadó, 2017).

[33] **József Szájer's book**, Ne bántsd a magyart! (Don't Hurt the Hungarians!, Budapest: KKETTK Közalapítvány, 2019), **and his lecture on the topic**, A globalista utópizmus áfiuma és az ellene való orvosság (The Opium of Globalist Utopism and Its Antidote, Lecture, 5. Mar. 2019, published by the blog 'Látószög').

[33] **"The fact that we like to think...intellectual resources."**: Szájer Lecture, 2019.

[33] **The article about Harari inspiring Viktor Orbán:** Kósa András, Melegházasságban élő izraeli sztártudós inspirálja mostanában Orbán Viktort (Magyar Nemzet, 23 Nov. 2017).

[33] **"In a word,...Liberty is the word."**: Illyés Gyula, Ki a magyar (Who is a Hungarian, Budapest: MEFHOSZ Könyvkiadó, 1939), p. 45.

[33] **"On the one hand...and the Church."**: Kéri 1994, p. 118.

[33] **"The years around 1848...we can be proud of."**: Kéri 1994, p. 85.

[33] **"Liberal philosophy...an ethnic group."**: Kéri 1994, p. 87.

[33] **"Fidesz is an opportunity...I'm balanced."**: Kéri 1994, p. 33.

[33] **"With his sharp eyes...the conquering enemy."**: Szájer Lecture, 2019.

[33] **"The main antidote...for the willing!)"**: Szájer Lecture, 2019.

[33] **Dezső Kosztolányi quoted from** his essay Ábécé a nyelvről és lélekről (Alphabet of Language and Soul).

[33] **Gyula Illyés quoted from** his essay Ki a magyar (Who is a Hungarian).

[33] **Mihály Babits quoted from** his essay A magyar jellemről (On Hungarian Character).

[33] **Péter Esterházy quoted from** his book A Little Hungarian Pornography (Evanston, IL: Northwestern University Press, 1997). Translation by Judith Sollosy.

[34] **On 18 April 2011, the Hungarian Parliament adopted the Fundamental Law of Hungary** by 262 votes to 44 with 1 abstention. The text of the Fundamental Law was drafted by a committee headed by József Szájer (Fidesz). (source: Wikipédia)

## PART FOUR: TRAINING

[35] **Steven Pinker's original joke** can be found in his book, The Sense of Style (London, Penguin, 2015), p. 154.

[35] **"there's nothing wrong...has ever been."**: Christopher Clarey, Cavic Finds a Personal Triumph in the Narrowest of Defeats, The New York Times (16 Aug. 2008).

[35] **"He is the most focused person I have ever met"**: Bob Bowman, The Golden Rules: Finding World-Class Excellence in Your Life and Work (London, Piatkus, 2016), p. 217.

[35] **"The most interesting...with excellence."**: Bowman 2016, p. 259.

[35] **"We will ask for more...hallmarks of champions,"**: Bowman 2016, p. 42.

[35] **"There were gifted people...left behind at once."**: Kéri 1994, p. 19.

[35] **"Some tasks had...a good idea?"**: Kéri 1994, p. 16.

[35] **"deliberate practice":** Anders Ericsson, and Robert Pool, Peak: How All of Us Can Achieve Extraordinary Things (London, Vintage, 2016).

[35] **"drive":** Daniel H. Pink, Drive: The Surprising Truth About What Motivates Us (London, Canon Gate Books, 2009).

[37] **"The situation is that...the media they operate.":** Viktor Orbán's speech at Tusnádfürdő (22 Jul. 2017).

[37] **"Physical strength...take a person seriously.":** Kéri 1994, p. 12.

[37] **"A campaign is the event...run a successful campaign.":** Kéri 1994, p. 59.

[38] **"Grit":** Angela Duckworth, Grit. (London: Vermilion, 2017).

[38] **"After 1956, some...Fidesz and the college.":** Kéri 1994, p. 86.

[38] **Quotes from the 2018 opposition student demonstrations** from Márk Herczeg's article Több ezren tüntettek a Kossuth téren a modernebb közoktatásért, 444.hu (23 Feb. 2018).

[40] **"I went to school...disciplined life.":** Kéri 1994, p. 16.

[40] **"The fight ahead of you...":** from János Arany's poem, Domokos napra (For Domonkos Name Day).

[40] **"Taking an image of...from the others.":** Kéri 1994, p. 119.

[40] **"But we held together...bonds of camaraderie.":** Viktor Orbán's speech at the XXVIII. Fidesz Congress (29 Sept. 2019).

[40] **"relentless":** Tim S. Grover, Relentless: From Good to Great to Unstoppable (New York: Scribner, 2014).

## PART FIVE: STARTUP

[42] **"He [Orbán] can be very suggestive in debates.":** Kósa 2018, p. 199.

[42] **"You take the initiative when others get scared.":** Kósa 2018, p. 25.

[42] **Steve Jobs's Stanford Speech** https://www.youtube.com/watch?v=UF8uR6Z6KLc.

[42] **"listen to your heart" narrative:** Cal Newport: So Good They Can't Ignore You: Why Skills Trump Passion in the Quest for Work You Love (London: Piatkus, 2016).

[44] **"disruptive":** C. M. Christensen, The Innovator's Dilemma: When New Technologies Cause Great Firms to Fail (Boston: Harvard Business Review Press, 2016).

[44] **"I think the MSZMP...We didn't go.":** Kéri 1994, p. 47.

[46] **"Nobody liked the word...own ideas.":** Kéri 1994, p. 52.

[46] **"Voters could feel...their grandchildren.":** Kéri 1994, p. 56.

[46] **"I was a Fidesz sympathizer too,":** Mandiner.hu https://mandiner.hu/cikk/20190813_fekete_gyor_andras_en_is_voltam_fidesz_szimpatizans

[47] **"chasm":** Geoffrey Moore, Crossing the Chasm: Marketing and Selling Disruptive Products to Mainstream Customers (New York: HarperCollins, 2014).

[47] **"We have struggled...the Socialist Party.":** Kéri 1994, p. 56.

[47] "Initially, our primary...be beaten.": Kéri 1994, p. 55.

[47] "Art is long...to being a master.": J. W. Goethe, Wilhelm Meister's Apprenticeship. Translated by Thomay Carlyle. (New York: P.F. Collier & Son, 1917).

## PART SIX: ART

[48] "Hungarian genius...": Esterházy Péter, Így gondozd a magyarodat! (How to groom your Hungarian). Translation by Judith Sollosy.

[48] "Very confident, very prepared.": Kósa 2018, p. 21.

[52] "Unfortunately, for many...all congresses.": Kéri 1994, p. 105.

[52] "Politics also means...and so on.": Kéri 1994, p. 74.

[52] "In 2010, we gave...strong jaws.": Viktor Orbán's speech at Szigetszentmiklós (3 Mar. 2017).

[52] "The Classics of Chinese Military Science series": Szun-ce, A háború művészete (Budapest: Helikon Kiadó, 2015).

[52] Sun Tzu, The Art of War (Translated by Ralph D. Sawyer, Running Press, 2003).

[53] Harold Evans, Do I Make Myself Clear? (London: Little Brown, 2017), p. 139.

[53] "The conclusion is clear...by 100!": Peter Kreilgaard, Daniel Soren, and Henrik Sorensen, Management by Football (Management Books, 2010), p. 30.

[53] "You must deliver outstanding results every time!": Kreilgaard 2010, p. 23.

[53] "Match is a battle...at the top.": Interview with Viktor Orbán for the hompage of the Puskás Academy (24 Jul. 2015).

[53] "Let us say that...with strength.": J. P. Carse, Finite and Infinite Games: A Vision of Life as Play and Possibility (New York: Free Press, 1986), p. 31.

[53] "Infinite players look...constant reinterpretation.": Carse 1986, pp. 30–31.

[53] "After the first week...we had to avoid.": Kéri 1994, pp. 56–57.

[53] "Uncle Guszti was one...built on the people,": Zsolt 1989, p. 71.

[53] "the rule of thumb...not the power.": Viktor Orbán's speech at the XXVIII. Fidesz Congress (29 Sept. 2019).

[53] "In his analysis of...good old friends.": Lendvai 2016, pp. 18–19.

[53] "over-government": Sárközy Tamás, Kétharmados túlzáskormányzás: Avagy gólerős csatár a mély talajú pályán (Two-Thirds Over-Government, Budapest, Park Kiadó, 2014).

[53] "we were alone in a situation where we had nothing,": Kéri 1994, p. 67.

[53] "Chess and Poker": Wiedermann Helga, Sakk és póker: Krónika a magyar gazdasági szabadságharc győztes csatáiról (Budapest: Kairosz, 2014).

[53] "Whoever is in debt...creditors dictate.": György Matolcsy's speech at Parliament (16 Nov. 2012).

[53] "If you ask me...in the future.": Janke 2012, p. 205.

[53] "We never went out...desire to win.": Zsolt 1989, p. 50.

[53] **"For the fan...with his game.":** Zsolt 1989, p. 108.

[53] **"I'm Catholic...in any other language.":** Zsolt 1989, p. 178.

[53] **"When there is no harmony, there is no victory.":** Zsolt 1989, p. 69.

[54] **"illiberal":** Fareed Zakaria, The Rise of Illiberal Democracy (Foreign Affairs, 1997. Nov-Dec, Vol. 76. No. 6. pp. 22–43.)

[54] **"Four Turns":** Lakner Zoltán, Négy fordulat: Baloldali útkeresés (Pécs: Jelenkor Kiadó, 2014), 238. p.

[54] **"OKR-s":** Doerr 2018.

[55] **"If the only thing...point of view.":** Dreher's article in The American Conservative: https://www.theamericanconservative.com/dreher/viktor-orban-among-the-christians/.

[56] **"So, you may not like...in the mud.":** Interview with Viktor Orbán, Echo TV (7 Dec. 2017).

[56] **"Footballers are, after all, artists in the philosophy of the things.":** Interview with Viktor Orbán for the Puskás Academy (4 Aug. 2013).

[Epilogue] **The story of Frank O. Gehry in Budapest** written by Sólymos Sándor, Frank O. Gehry Budapesten II. Építészfórum.hu (5 Jul. 2006).

[Epilogue] **"But we, we had... historical necessity.":** Theodor Herzl, Altneuland: The Old-New-Land (public domain).

# Bibliography

*The Second Helvetic Confession – A Második Helvét Hitvallás*. Budapest: A Magyarországi Református Egyház Kálvin János Kiadója, 2017.

*Towards a Middle-Class Hungary (A pamphlet by Fidesz) – A polgári Magyarországért: a Fidesz–Magyar Polgári Párt vitairata*. Budapest: Fidesz Központi Hivatal, 1996.

Abrahams, Dan. *Soccer Brain*. Birmingham: Bennion Keary, 2013.

Afremov, Jim. *The Champion's Mind: How Great Athletes Think, Train, and Thrive*. New York: Rodale, 2013.

Albright, Madeleine. *Fascism: A Warning*. London: HarperCollins, 2018.

Ariely, Dan. *Predictably Irrational: The Hidden Forces That Shape Our Decisions*. New York: HarperCollins, 2008.

Aronson, Elliot. *The Social Animal – A társas lény*. Budapest: Közgazdasági és Jogi Könyvkiadó, 1987.

Babits, Mihály. *On the Hungarian Character – A magyar jellemről*. In: Belia György (editor): Babits Mihály művei. Esszék, tanulmányok. Budapest: Szépirodalmi Könyvkiadó, 1978.

Bandler, Richard; Grinder, John. *Frogs Into Princes – Neuro Linguistic Programming*. Moab, UT: Real People Press, 1979.

Barna, Imre. *Bob Dylan: A Novel – Regény*. Budapest: Zeneműkiadó, 1986.

Bayer, Zsolt. *1100 Years in the Heart of Europe – 1100 év Európa közepén*. Nemzeti Könyvtár 76. Budapest: Magyar Közlöny Lap- és Könyvkiadó, 2017.

Bayer, Zsolt. *The Fidesz Bible I. – A nagy Fideszkönyv. I. (H)őskorszak*. Budapest: Magyar Egyetemi Kiadó, 2006.

*The Holy Bible – Biblia: Ószövetségi és újszövetségi szentírás*. Budapest: Szent István Társulat, 2016. English translation from: https://biblehub.com

Black, Jonathan. *Making the American Body*. Lincoln: University of Nebraska Press, 2013.

Blanchard, Ken; Phil Hodges. *Lead Like Jesus: Lessons from the Greatest Leadership Role Model of All Time*. Nashville: W Publishing Group, 2016.

Bowman, Bob. *The Golden Rules: Finding World-Class Excellence in Your Life and Work*. London: Piatkus, 2016.

Boyle, Michael. *Functional Training for Sports – Funkcionális edzés mesterfokon: Edzéstechnikák edzők, személyi edzők és sportolók számára*. Translated by Végh Gabriella. Budapest: Jaffa Kiadó, 2014.

Branden, Nathaniel. *The Six Pillars of Self-Esteem*. New York: Bantam, 1995.

Cain, Susan. *Quiet: The Power of Introverts in A World That Can't Stop Talking.* New York: Crown Publishing, 2012.

Carnegie, Dale. *How to Win Friends and Influence People.* New York: Simon & Schuster, 2011.

Carse, James P. *Finite and Infinite Games: A Vision of Life as Play and Possibility.* New York: Free Press, 1986.

Christensen, Clayton M. *The Innovator's Dilemma: When New Technologies Cause Great Firms to Fail.* Boston: Harvard Business Review Press, 2016.

Covey, Stephen R. *The 7 Habits of Highly Effective People: Powerful Lessons in Personal Life.* London: Simon & Schuster, 2004.

Csíkszentmihályi, Mihály. *Flow. Az áramlat: A tökéletes élmény pszichológiája.* Translated by Legéndyné Szabó Edit. Budapest: Akadémiai Kiadó, 1997.

Dávid, Katalin. *Handbook of Biblical Symbols – Bibliai jelképek kézikönyve: A teremtett világ misztériuma.* Budapest: Szent István Társulat, 2002.

Debreczeni, József. *The Prime Minister (József Antall's biography) – A miniszterelnök.* Budapest: Osiris, 1998.

Debreczeni, József. *Orbán Viktor.* Budapest: Osiris Kiadó, 2002.

Deutschman, Alan. *Change or Die: The Three Keys to Change at Work and in Life.* New York: Regan, 2007.

Doerr, John. *Measure What Matters: The Revolutionary Movement Behind the Explosive Growth of Intel, Google, Amazon and Uber.* London: Penguin, 2018.

Duckworth, Angela. *Grit: Why passion and resilience are the secrets to success.* London: Vermilion, 2017.

Duhigg, Charles. *The Power of Habit: Why We Do What We Do in Life and Business.* New York: Random House Trade, 2014.

Dweck, Carol S. *Mindset: Changing the Way You Think to Fulfil Your Potential.* London: Robinson, 2017.

Eco, Umberto. *Ur-Fascism.* The New York Review of Books, June 22, 1995.

Ellenberg, Jonah. *How Not to be Wrong: The Power of Mathematical Thinking.* London: Penguin Books, 2015.

Ericsson, Anders; Pool, Robert. *Peak: How All of Us Can Achieve Extraordinary Things.* London, Vintage, 2016.

Evans, Harold. *Do I Make Myself Clear?* London: Little Brown, 2017.

Ferguson, Alex; Moritz, Michael. *Leading.* London: Hodder & Stoughton, 2015.

Field, Syd. *Screenplay: The Foundations of Screenwriting.* New York: Bantam Dell, 2005.

Frankl, Viktor E. *Man's Search for Meaning.* Boston: Beacon Press, 2006.

Gladwell, Malcolm. *Blink: The Power of Thinking Without Thinking.* New York: Back Bay Books, 2005.

Gladwell, Malcolm. *David and Goliath: Underdogs, Misfits and the Art of Battling Giants.* New York: Little Brown and Company, 2013.

Gladwell, Malcolm. *Outliers: The Story of Success.* London: Penguin Books, 2008.

Gladwell, Malcolm. *Talking to Strangers: What We Should Know about the People We Don't Know.* London: Allen Lane, 2019.

Gladwell, Malcolm. *The Tipping Point: How Little Things Can Make a Big Difference.* New York: Little Brown & Company, 2011.

Godin, Seth. *All Marketers are Liars.* London: Penguin Books, 2009.

Godin, Seth. *The Icarus Deception.* London: Portfolio Penguin, 2012.

Godin, Seth. *Tribes.* London: Piatkus, 2008.

Goethe, J. W. *Wilhelm Meister's Apprenticeship.* Translated by Thomas Carlyle. New York: P.F. Collier & Son, 1917.

Goldberg, Jonah. *Liberal Fascism – Liberálfasizmus: A baloldal rejtett története Mussolinitől napjainkig.* Translated by Berényi Gábor. Budapest: XX. Század Intézet, 2012.

Goleman, Daniel. *Emotional Intelligence – Érzelmi intelligencia.* Translated by N. Kiss Zsuzsa. Budapest: Háttér Kiadó, 2008.

Grant, Adam. *Give and Take: A Revolutionary Approach to Success.* London: Weidenfeld and Nicolson, 2014.

Greene, Robert. *The 48 Laws of Power.* London: Profile Books, 2000.

Grove, Andrew S. *One-on-One With Andy Grove.* London: Penguin Books, 1988.

Grover, Tim S. *Relentless: From Good to Great to Unstoppable.* New York: Scribner, 2014.

Gyurgyák, János (editor). *What is Politics? – Mi a politika?* Budapest: Osiris, 1996.

Hamvas, Béla. *Five Geniuses – Öt géniusz: A bor filozófiája.* Életünk Könyvek sorozat. Szombathely: Életünk Szerkesztősége, 1988.

Harari, Yuval Noah. *21 Lessons for the 21st Century.* London: Jonathan Cape, 2018.

Harari, Yuval Noah. *Sapiens: A Brief History of Humankind.* London: Vintage, 2011.

Harding, Luke. *Mafia State.* London: Guardian Books, 2011.

Harsányi, László. *Training Science – Edzéstudomány.* Budapest–Pécs: Dialóg Campus Kiadó, 2016.

Herzl, Theodor. *Altneuland: The Old-New-Land* (public domain). (In Hungarian: Herzl, Tivadar. *Ősújország.* Az 1938-as magyar változat reprint kiadása. Translated by Márkus Aladár. Budapest: Bethlen Gábor Könyvkiadó, 1993.)

*Hét évszázad magyar versei – Seven Centuries of Hungarian Poetry.* Budapest: Szépirodalmi Könyvkiadó, 1966.

Hidvégi, Áron Arnold. *The Whys and Hows of the Self-Made Workout – Önerőből: A self-made edzés miértje és hogyanja.* Budapest: Aron Store, 2019.

Hill, Napoleon. *Think & Grow Rich.* New York: Ballantine Books, 1983.

Hoobyar, Tom; Dotz, Tom; Sanders, Susan. *NLP: The Essential Guide to Neuro-Linguistic Programming.* New York: HarperCollins, 2013.

Illyés, Gyula. *Who is a Hungarian – Ki a magyar.* Budapest: MEFHOSZ Könyvkiadó, 1939.

Isaacson, Walter. *Steve Jobs.* London, 2011, Abacus.

Isaacson, Walter. *The Innovators.* New York: Simon & Schuster, 2014.

Janke, Igor. *Forward! – Hajrá, magyarok! Az Orbán Viktor-sztori egy lengyel újságíró szemével.* Translated by Szalai Attila, and Szenyán Erzsébet. Rézbong Kiadó, 2012.

Jung, Carl Gustav. *Psychological Types – A lélektani típusok.* Budapest: Európa Könyvkiadó, 1988.

Kahneman, Daniel. *Thinking, Fast and Slow.* London: Penguin Books, 2011.

Kamprad, Ingvar. *The Testament of a Furniture Dealer.* IKEA, 1976–2007.

Kéri, László. *Orbán Viktor.* Politikusportrék. Budapest: Századvég, 1994.

Kiszely, Gábor. *Freemasonry – A szabadkőművesség.* Budapest: Korona Kiadó, 1999.

Kleon, Austin. *Steal Like an Artist.* New York: Workman, 2012.

Kósa, András. *Viktor Orbán, The Man of Chaos – Orbán Viktor, a káosz embere.* Budapest: Noran Libro, 2018.

Kreilgaard, Peter; Daniel Soren, and Henrik Sorensen. *Management by Football.* Management Books, 2010.

Lábady, Tamás. *The General Principles of Hungarian Civil Law – A magyar magánjog (polgári jog) általános része.* Budapest-Pécs: Dialóg Campus Kiadó, 1998.

Lakner, Zoltán. *Four Turns – Négy fordulat: Baloldali útkeresés.* Pécs: Jelenkor Kiadó, 2014.

Lendvai, Paul. *New Conquest – Új honfoglalás.* Budapest: Noran Libro, 2016. (In English: *Orbán: Europe's New Strongman*, Hurst and Co, 2017.)

Levitsky, Steven, and Daniel Ziblatt. *How Democracies Die.* New York: Crown Publishing, 2018.

Lewitt, D. Steven, and Stephen J. Dubner. *Freakonomics: A Rouge Economist Explores the Hidden Side of Everything.* New York: Harper, 2009.

Magyar, Bálint (editor). *Hungarian Octopus – Magyar polip.* 1–3. köt. Budapest: Noran Libro, 2013 (1.), 2014 (2.), 2015 (3.).

*The Fundamental Law of Hungary – Magyarország Alaptörvénye.* (2012. január 1.) Budapest: Magyar Közlöny Lap- és Könyvkiadó, 2012.

Mikes, George. *How to be an Alien.* London: Penguin Books, 1966.

Moore, Geoffrey A. *Crossing the Chasm: Marketing and Selling Disruptive Products to Mainstream Customers.* New York: HarperCollins, 2014.

Nádori, László. *Exercise Theory and Methodics – Edzéselmélet és módszertan.* Budapest: Testnevelési Főiskola Továbbképző Intézete, 1985.

Napóleon. *The Art of Rule – Az uralkodás művészete.* Translated by Takács, M. József. Budapest: Helikon Kiadó, 2016.

Newport, Cal. *So Good They Can't Ignore You: Why Skills Trump Passion in the Quest for Work You Love.* London: Piatkus, 2016.

Orbán, Viktor. *20 Years: Speeches, writings, interviews 1986-2006 – 20 év: Beszédek, írások, interjúk 1986–2006.* Budapest: Heti Válasz Kiadó, 2006.

Orbán, Viktor. *On the Main Street of History: 1998-2002 – A történelem főutcáján: Magyarország 1998–2002.* Budapest: Magyar Egyetemi Kiadó, 2003.

Orbán, Viktor. *The Country as One – Egy az ország.* Budapest: Helikon Kiadó, 2007.

Orbán, Viktor. *The Road to Victory – Út a győzelemhez: Minden hangszeren*. Budapest: Kairosz Kiadó, 2014.

Orwell, George. *Essays – Esszék*. Budapest: Független Kiadó, 1988.

Pink, Daniel H. *Drive: The Surprising Truth About What Motivates Us*. London: Canon Gate Books, 2009.

Pinker, Steven. *Enlightenment Now: The Case for Reason, Science, Humanism, and Progress*. New York: Viking, 2018.

Pinker, Steven. *The Sense of Style*. London: Penguin, 2015.

Reagan, Ronald. *An American Life – Egy amerikai élet*. Translated by Magyarics Tamás. Budapest: Antall József Tudásközpont, 2014.

Ries, Eric. *The Lean Startup: How Constant Innovation Creates Radically Successful Businesses*. London: Portfolio Penguin, 2011.

Ries, Al, and Jack Trout. *Marketing Warfare*. New York: McGraw-Hill, 2006.

Robbins, Anthony. *Unlimited Power*. New York: Fawcett Columbine, 1986.

Roberts, Kevin. *Lovemarks: The Future Beyond Brands*. New York: Power House Books, 2004.

Rosling, Hans: *Factfulness: Ten Reasons We're Wrong About the World – and Why Things Are Better Than You Think*. London: Hodder and Stoughton, 2018.

Ross, Lee, and Richard E. Nisbett. *The Person and the Situation: Perspectives of Social Psychology*. London: Printer & Martin, 2011.

Sárközy, Tamás. *Two-Thirds Over-Government – Kétharmados túlzáskormányzás: Avagy gólerős csatár a mély talajú pályán*. Budapest: Park Kiadó, 2014.

Schwartz, David. *The Magic of Thinking Big*. London: Vermilion, 2016.

Schwarzenegger, Arnold. *The Encyclopedia of Bodybuilding – A testépítés nagy enciklopédiája*. Translated by Cserna György. Budapest: Alexandra Kiadó, 1998.

Schwarzenegger, Arnold. *Total Recall: My Unbelievably True Life Story*. London: Simon & Schuster, 2012.

Seidman, Dov. *How: Why How We Do Anything Means Everything*. New Jersey: John Wiley & Sons, 2007.

Sinek, Simon. *Leaders Eat Last: Why Some Teams Pull Together and Others Don't*. London: Portfolio Penguin, 2017.

Sinek, Simon. *Start With Why: How Great Leaders Inspire Everyone to Take Action*. London: Portfolio Penguin, 2011.

Slywotzky, Adrian. *The Art of Profitability – A profit művészete*. Ford. Barabás, T. János. Budapest: HVG Kiadó, 2003.

Snow, Shane. *Smartcuts: The Breakthrough Power of Lateral Thinking*. New York: HarperCollins, 2014.

Snyder, Blake. *Save the Cat! The Last Book on Screenwriting You'll Ever Need*. Studio City CA: Michael Wiese Productions, 2005.

Soros, George. *The Alchemy of Finance*. New Jersey: John Wiley and Sons, 2003.

Stanier, M.B. *The Coaching Habit*. Toronto: Box of Crayons Press, 2016.

Szájer, József. *Don't Hurt the Hungarians! – Ne bántsd a magyart!* Budapest: KKETTK Közalapítvány, 2019.

Szekfű, Gyula. *Bethlen Gábor.* Budapest: Helikon Kiadó, 1983.

Sun Tzu. *The Art of War* (Translated by Ralph D. Sawyer, Running Press, 2003).

Tamási, Áron. *Ábel.* Bukarest: Kriterion Könyvkiadó, 1973.

Tamási, Áron. *My Motherland – Szülőföldem.* Budapest: Révai Kiadó, 1943.

Thaler, Richard H., and Cass R. Sunsten. *Nudge: Improving Decisions About Health, Wealth and Happiness.* London: Penguin Books, 2008.

Thaler, Richard. H. *Misbehaving: The Making of Behavioural Economics.* London: Penguin Books, 2015.

Thiel, Peter, and Blake Masters. *Zero to One: Notes on Startups, or How to Build the Future.* London: Virgin Books, 2014.

Tier, Mark. *The Winning Investment Habits of Warren Buffett and George Soros.* New York: Truman Talley Books, 2005.

Tocqueville, Alexis de. *Democracy in America.* Ware: Wordsworth, 1998.

Török, Gábor. *The Living Island: A Journey to the Realm of Politics – A lakott sziget: Utazás a politika világába.* Budapest: Athenaeum Kiadó, 2017.

Trump, Donald J. *The Art of the Deal.* London: Arrow Books, 1987.

Whybrow, Peter C. *American Mania: When More is Not Enough.* New York: Norton & Company, 2006.

Wiedermann, Helga. *Chess and Poker – Sakk és póker: Krónika a magyar gazdasági szabadságharc győztes csatáiról.* Budapest: Kairosz, 2014.

Wilson, Jonathan. *Inverting the Pyramid.* London: Orion, 2014.

Wolff, Michael. *Fire and Fury: Inside the Trump White House.* New York: Henry Holt & Co., 2018.

Zsolt, Róbert. *Puskás Öcsi.* Budapest: Szabad Tér Kiadó, 1989.

# Index